With love from
Anne.

# THE BORDER IN COLOUR

*By the same Author*

ALPINES IN COLOUR AND CULTIVATION
ROSES IN COLOUR AND CULTIVATION
SHRUBS IN COLOUR AND CULTIVATION

*In preparation*

ANNUALS IN COLOUR AND CULTIVATION
CARNATIONS IN COLOUR AND CULTIVATION

*

OF CABBAGES AND KINGS

*In preparation*

OF QUINCES AND QUEENS

# THE BORDER IN COLOUR

*By*

*T. C. MANSFIELD*

WITH

80 PLATES IN COLOUR

AND

22 ILLUSTRATIONS

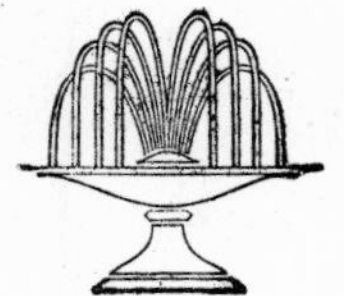

COLLINS 14 ST. JAMES'S PLACE LONDON

PRODUCED BY
ADPRINT LIMITED LONDON

*First published February* 1944
*Revised edition March* 1947
*Third edition* 1948

PRINTED IN GREAT BRITAIN BY
W. S. COWELL LTD IPSWICH AND LONDON

# CONTENTS

TO "SAPPER"

MOST FAITHFUL OF FRIENDS

AND BEST OF GARDENERS

# PREFACE

THE present book of the series follows the precedent set by the earlier books, and maintains the accuracy of colour reproduction. The pictures are again composite, and produced under studio conditions with simulated backgrounds.

The problems which confronted the photographer, John Hinde, were again considerable, and probably a little more varied than in the case of the earlier reproductions. It must, however, be agreed that whatever vagaries of behaviour were encountered the results are again exceptional, and I hasten to add my own personal thanks to my collaborator whose skill, patience, and persistence are in the greatest measure responsible for the illustration of this work.

For my own part, I can only thank the many hundreds of correspondents from all parts of the world who have expressed their appreciation of the earlier books of the series; who have sent me corrections, notes, and advice, and have done so much to encourage the production of further books of the series. In particular I value the letters of service men and women, whose love of the garden is by no means lessened by their present activities.

I tender my grateful thanks to:

Col. F. R. Durham, The Royal Horticultural Society;
Mr. R. L. Harrow, Director, Royal Horticultural Society's Gardens, Wisley;
The Director, Kew Gardens;
Mr. J. H. Wilson and Miss Durrant, of the British Colour Council;
Messrs. John Waterer, Sons, and Crisp, Ltd., Twyford;
Letchworth Plants, Ltd., Letchworth, Herts.;
Orchard Neville Nurseries, Ltd., Baltonsborough, Somerset;
Messrs. Blackmore and Langdon, Bath, Somerset;

all of whom have given exceptionally valuable assistance.

Glastonbury *June*, 1943

# PREFACE TO THE SECOND EDITION

The present edition, in which a number of species and varieties have been added in various Glossary articles, also contains a Cross Index of Common Names of herbaceous plants. This new feature of the book should be particularly helpful to beginners in gardening who are not yet quite familiar with the scientific, or horticultural, names under which the plants appear in the Glossary.

In addition to the persons mentioned in the Preface to the first edition, the author would like to thank all those correspondents who have, by their stimulating letters, encouraged the amendment of the book to its present form.

While during the War the production of new varieties has been considerably limited, not a few have found their way into commerce, and have now been added to those already listed in the first edition. The author sincerely hopes that growers will keep him informed of their newer varieties in order that he may continue to keep the series up to date.

He would also like to express his personal appreciation to Mr. S. F. Winter, of Messrs. Adprint Ltd., for his most valuable help in reading the proofs.

Glastonbury *November*, 1946

*Note on the Use of the Visor*

To facilitate the quick identification of plants illustrated in the plates, a transparent visor is provided, divided into lettered squares.

The visor is placed over the plate with the top line coincident with the top of the plate, and the outer perpendicular lines coincident with the edges of the plate. The letters following the names at the foot of the plate then indicate into which squares each particular plant has fallen.

Anthemis tinctoria "Buxton's variety" ABCDEFGHJ
Phlox decussata "Mia Ruys" KLOPQRSU
Anthemis Sancti-Johannis MQT

2

Aquilegia. Modern long-spurred types

CHAPTER I

# INTRODUCTION

THE herbaceous plant is the medium from which the changing picture of the average garden gains its permanence. The herbaceous plant is essentially perennial, generally easy to propagate, and forms, in consequence, the means from which the inexpensive garden may be maintained without the sacrifice of beauty. From the earliest times the simple border has been one of the most beautiful expressions of gardening art, and its wide popularity even at the present time points to its intrinsic worth.

But before we delve into the mysteries of nomenclature and single out individual plants for especial mention, we must first of all consider the conditions under which these beauties are enabled to exert their charms upon us. More simply stated: we must consider cultivation. The herbaceous garden is essentially designed to be of some permanence, and it must, therefore, cater for the well-being of its occupants for a considerable period, even though their actual position within the structure may change from year to year.

Primarily, the plants may be divided into sections in the following manner: those which are of easy cultivation in normally well-cultivated soil; those which thrive better in slightly acid soil; and their complement of plants giving their best when grown in alkaline soil.

Then comes a second division into the plants which thrive best in positions affording them the maximum benefit of the available sun, and the ones that prefer to grow in conditions providing some shade.

Since the design of any border must, to some extent, depend upon the height of the plant at the time of its greatest development, we must consider the eventual height to which it will attain.

Moreover, as the gardener uses living colour precisely in the same way as the landscape painter, some accurate knowledge of the colour of flowers and foliage must be available to him. In addition to all these things, the normal gardener has extremely catholic tastes and refuses to be bound by the pedantry of the definition of a herbaceous plant, but uses with a glad indifference to the designation of the botanist such plants or bulbs as Gladioli,

Dahlias, Begonias, and the like. So it is that the range of plants selected for discussion will encroach to some extent upon the field of bulbous and half-hardy perennial plants, since by usage these have been adopted as occupants of the traditional herbaceous border.

Throughout the Glossary which follows, a number of indicating signs have been used to denote all this information, together with what is the most important fact from the gardener's aspect: the time of flowering of the plant.

The definition of "herbaceous plant" may loosely be stated to be a plant which flowers perennially but has soft stems, as opposed to the hard woody stems of the classes called trees or shrubs. More correctly, the herbaceous perennial is a plant which protects itself against a large measure of winter evaporation by casting off its overground growth, including the stem. It will be seen, therefore, that the occupant of the herbaceous border cannot always be said to be herbaceous by definition, and the only criterion which may safely be applied is that of fitness.

CHAPTER II

# THE SOIL

THE soil is the raw material from which the gardener derives his future satisfaction, if he handles it aright, and periods of dejection, should he deny it the attention it needs. It is therefore necessary to consider in some detail what is meant by the soil, which we may roughly divide into five parts:—the inorganic debris of mineral origin; the organic remains of decaying plants or vegetable matter; the living organisms, partly vegetable and partly animal; the soil moisture; and finally the air which permeates it. Between these five constituents it is necessary to preserve a balance.

Let us consider first of all the inorganic part. This consists in the main of the disintegrated crust of the earth's surface, and may vary in the size of its individual pieces in a very large degree—let us say, for example, from boulders to microscopic particles of clay. For garden purposes we may consider the largest particles as stones, from thence to grit or sand, from thence to silt, and lastly to the finest particles of all, which we will call clay. It must be obvious to the veriest novice that of all this material the only part which can be of use in providing the plant with its chemical necessities is that which is most finely divided, namely, the clay. And so it is. The clay constituent of all soils must be considered as its most important chemical ingredient. It is true that stones, silt, and sand also play an important part, but this part is merely mechanical, leading to such things as aeration and drainage. In the inorganic part of the soil it is necessary to keep a balance between the clay and the larger particles, and to use them to dilute the clay, as it were, to suit the tastes of the growing root.

Now let us turn for a while to the organic part of the soil, which is generally closely mixed with the mineral particles. The dead bodies of insects and animals, the dead leaves of trees and shrubs and herbs, all form part of its potential humus content, as we call it. In the soil itself, however, these are broken down by the action of microscopic fungi and bacteria, and are changed from leaves and the like to a dark-brown or black substance, the humus. While this is going on by means of an extremely complicated process, the bacteria produce nitrogen in the form of nitrates easily assimilated by the plant.

The plant cannot obtain its nitrogen directly from the air. Some of the bacteria, however, can, and they utilise it to form their own bodily structures. When they die, as die they must, the nitrogen they have absorbed from the air becomes available to the plants as food in the form of nitrates. As all plant food must be highly soluble in water—since if it were not, it could not be absorbed by the roots—these nitrates would be washed away and dissolved out of the soil by the action of rain, and the soil rendered devoid of them, were it not for the presence of the bacteria in the earth, which continue to extract nitrogen from the air and pass it on to the green plant, to ensure that there shall be no deficiency of nitrogen.

Organic matter in the soil is therefore the only natural source of nitrogen for most plants, and it is for this reason that the gardener must incorporate it in the soil if plants are to grow really well.

The third constituent of the soil, which we have already mentioned, consists of bacteria, or microscopic plants, as we might call them, and protozoa, which act in the same relation to them as the sheep to the grass—in other words, the protozoa consume the bacteria. When for some reason the relation between these two types of inhabitants of the soil becomes disturbed, and the number of bacteria falls off, while the protozoa increase in number, the soil is said to be "sick," and for obvious reasons plants will no longer thrive in it. Methods of curing this so-called sickness of the soil are discussed at a later stage, but enough has already been said to stress the importance of maintaining the well-being of the soil-bacteria.

The fourth constituent of the soil is the soil-water, which normally occupies about three-quarters of the pore space of the soil, the remaining one-quarter of the pore space being filled by air, the fifth constituent. As the soil becomes dry, so the proportion of the pore space occupied by air increases, and that filled with water decreases; conversely, as the soil becomes waterlogged, the amount of air decreases and the water increases. Since plants cannot thrive either in a soil which is unduly dry or in one unduly wet, it is essential that the balance between air and water in the soil is also kept. This can be illustrated by the arrest of decay in waterlogged peat. The bacteria which transform the peat into humus require for their well-being air and water in the correct proportion. As the peat becomes waterlogged, decay of the vegetable matter is stopped because the bacteria which normally perform this reducing process are unable to live.

From what has already been said, the gardener will be able to appreciate that the production of the flowering plant in the garden is not only an art, but also a science, and if he will approach the problem of cultivating the soil in a truly scientific spirit, he will be able to produce a maximum of beauty with a minimum of effort—and expense. That he will sometimes, as indeed he must, find problems which he cannot solve is inevitable, for has not man tilled the soil for tens of thousands of years; and can he not find in the space of the garden, of a few hundred square yards, problems in cultivation which defy not only him, but the savant?

We have stated earlier that it is the clay which is the sole source of the plant's requirements of mineral salts. It should not be assumed, however, that for this reason clay provides the perfect soil. At one end of the range the particles which make up the soil are very large, but as it approaches clay, the particles become extremely small. If a box is filled with large stones, it can be seen immediately that the air spaces between the stones are very large. If a box is filled with sand, however, the air spaces cannot be distinguished by the eye—and it must be remembered that the soil particles which make up the sand are infinitely larger than those which make up the clay. From this it can be deduced that a clay soil which is tightly packed can contain so little air space that it *can* be impervious to water. This, in fact, is exactly what the gardener does when he puddles clay. The gardener calls the ideal soil "loam," but some definition of loam appears to be necessary. Loam is really a natural mixture of sand, silt, clay, and humus, and can be extremely variable, since any one of these four constituents can be present to excess. As regards texture, the perfect soil is one which is half-way between coarse sand and clay, but composed of particles of varying size.

Because of the extreme smallness of the particles making up the clay, it becomes sticky when wet. If lime is added to it, the tiny particles flocculate and are held together in larger numbers, making the texture more coarse, and therefore more porous. By adding lime to a sticky soil, we can improve the texture of the soil without unduly altering its chemical properties.

To return to the consideration of large and small particles of soil. We know that a cubic foot has a surface area of 864 square inches. If we divide this cube into cubic inches, the surface area immediately becomes 10,368 square inches. Thus it can be seen that the greater the number of tiny pieces into which the cubic foot of soil is divided, the greater its surface area becomes. It has been estimated that the total surface area of the clay particles making up one cubic foot of soil is greater than three acres. This is not only interesting as a piece of information; it is of prime importance to the gardener. The soil retains water only as a thin film over each of its particles, and it is in this form that the soil-water is most readily absorbed by the growing plant. Water which is exhausted in one part of the soil cannot easily be replenished from another part, since this can only take place by evaporation and recondensation, unless the water-film permeating the soil is continuous, when water will be drawn from one surface to another by the elasticity of its own surface tension. This can be demonstrated by taking a clean polished plate and dipping it into a bowl of water. The surface of the plate will be covered in parts with a thin film of water. If a piece of soap is used to touch some part of the film, the water around will be seen to draw rapidly away, demonstrating the power exerted by the water-film.

It would appear from this information that the more finely divided the inorganic soil, the more water it is able to retain. It is not always an inorganic soil, which retains the most water, which is the most effective base from the point of view of producing good crops, since in the finest of clay the plant can obtain the water from the soil only with great difficulty. In spite of the highly retentive qualities of clay, organic matter in the soil possesses an even greater degree of retentiveness. It is said that some forms of peat, which is almost entirely organic soil, contain as much as 95 per cent of water. When it is pointed out that a good loam does not hold more than half this figure as a maximum, the advantage of incorporating organic matter in the soil can be readily seen, for by incorporating such material in a light, sandy soil it is possible completely to transform its power to retain water in such a fashion that the water retained as a film round the soil-particles is completely overborne.

Thus the addition of organic matter to clay soil serves the purpose of opening its texture, and providing humus; but if too large a quantity is added it can so increase its power to retain moisture that it becomes too damp.

The addition of organic matter to a light soil improves its texture, increases its power to retain moisture and provides humus, and it is obvious that the quantity of organic manure to be incorporated in a sandy soil must be greater than that required in a heavy one.

But the incorporation of organic matter in the soil is attended by other difficulties. Frequently, nay, continually, the gardener is told to use well-rotted manure, but seldom is he given the reason. In the early stages of decay, the process of decomposition gives rise to the production of acid substances and carbon dioxide, which is harmful to the roots of the plants. The acidity can be corrected by the addition of lime, but this increases for a time the output of a harmful gas. The ideal soil is neutral in its reaction and should be neither violently acid nor alkaline.

Thus in the garden all materials which are intended to add organic content to the soil should be well rotted before use, and should be regulated by principles of moderation, and not by the principle that twice as much is twice as good. The gardener must in fact aim at a neutral, balanced soil of good texture.

What, then, is the answer to the prayer of the gardener whose garden consists mainly of chalk?

The physical properties of chalky soils are marked; they are generally light in character, but apt to become sticky when wet and to cake on the surface when drying. They consume their added organic content rapidly by decay, but are generally deficient in potash, whereas they have a good supply of phosphoric acid. They should be well and continuously fed with farmyard manure and the potassic fertilisers, and the incorporation of humus in the soil should continue until the depth of the fertile soil has been increased to at least twelve inches.

But many calcareous soils consist of a quite large percentage of chalk and border on the more beneficial loams; in fact, some of the finely textured heavy marls have a high content of chalk and, in spite of this, a good supply of potash. These soils require much less organic matter to be added, though with far nicer care.

To summarise the theoretical discussions in a few words: The aim of the gardener must be, in the first instance, to produce a soil of balanced texture, and with no overwhelming predominance in its inorganic or organic balance.

Some mention has already been made of the living organisms which people the soil, and some indication has been given of the deleterious effects of an unbalanced soil population, soil "sickness" being one of the troubles mentioned. It would be wise at this juncture also to consider the nature of the micro-organisms themselves, with especial reference to those which are of particular importance to the gardener.

The bacterial population consists of a large number of types which produce ammonia and nitrates from the humus content of the soil, and the nitrogen-fixing bacteria which utilise the atmospheric nitrogen to produce the nitrates so essential to plant life.

These bacteria, which may be regarded in the light of tiny plants, obviously require to live under conditions suitable to their well-being, if they are to be of full use to the garden population at large. These conditions are: that there shall be in the soil a supply of organic matter, a small amount of calcium carbonate, sufficient moisture and air, and that the soil should not be acid.

From these stated requirements it can be seen that these bacteria must be infinitely more at home in that part of the soil which comprises the "top spit" than they are in the lower spits, since it is here that the balance of their requirements is most accurately met. This is one of the reasons why it is so necessary, when digging, to retain the top spit at the top, and not to bring up the subsoil to replace it.

Mention has also been made of the protozoa which prey upon the bacteria. When these become too numerous and the soil becomes sick, such sickness can be cured by partial sterilisation by means of steam or chemicals. The most effective sterilisation is that accomplished by steam, and if the soil is raised to a temperature of 180° F. and kept at that temperature for a period of ten minutes, all insects and weed seeds are killed together with the protozoa, as are many of the moulds. The bacteria are also killed, but some persist in the form of spores, which are resistant to this degree of heat, and resume their very rapid process of division immediately the soil has regained its normal temperature. The result is a very speedy increase in the rate of production of ammonia and nitrates, since the protozoa are no longer present to prevent this.

Certain nitrogen-fixing bacteria also live in the nodules found upon the roots of certain leguminous plants—beans, peas, lupins, and others. These bacteria exist in the soil but do not fix nitrogen until they enter the roots of the host plant. They are able to do this through the agency of the root hairs at a time when they can move in the water-film, a condition which is encouraged by the presence of phosphates in the soil.

These bacteria are very useful to the gardener, since they will propagate more freely in acid conditions than the other bacteria inhabiting the soil, and they are therefore of greater importance in soils which are acid or lack lime.

Enough has been said to show that a completely sterile soil is far from desirable, and would be useless as a medium in which to grow plants until it had become re-peopled with beneficial bacteria; for this reason freshly burnt earth is an undesirable component of garden soil.

But the problem of the gardener is still further complicated by the requirements of individual plants. Some plants grow well in acid soils, others better in neutral or alkaline soils. Some are subject to disease in acid soils; the cabbage is apt to contract club root in such soils, while potatoes grown in acid soils are seldom troubled with scab. Thus to the complexity of the prob-

Aster Amellus "King George" ABCDEF

Aster Frikartii JKNOPQRSTU

Aster Amellus "Sonia" GHLM

Aster Novi-belgii "Belgian Queen" ABCDEFGH
Aster Novi-belgii "Celestial" JKMNOPQU
Aster Novi-belgii "Red Rover" RST

lem of the soil is added the diversity of the demands of individual plants, and no cut-and-dried solution of any one of his problems exists.

Certain help is available, however. The known requirements of plants are stated in the Glossary. It is possible to lay down a set of general rules for most types of soil, but in the main the gardener is driven back upon his own mother-wit and his notebook.

He should regard the soil as an object for experiments, but not haphazard experiments. He should do in some measure exactly what is done in the laboratory: alter one condition only at a time. One planting may be made in the sun, another, in identical soil, in the shade. Results should be noted in the notebook.

Let us state an example. One group of plants should be grown with peat mould added to the soil in a measured quantity, another identical group in an identical situation with no peat mould added. The comparison of results should be made with regard to all features—vigour of growth, freedom of flowering and fruitfulness, and ability to persist, as well as the degree of variation from the normal condition noted.

Under these circumstances much knowledge will be garnered of the appropriate treatment required to ensure success.

CHAPTER III

# THE SITE AND ITS PREPARATION

IN many gardens the site of the herbaceous border, or borders, chooses itself, because only one possible site exists, and here it must be accepted on the principle that half a loaf is better than no bread. The ideal site is, of course, one which is unshaded by overhanging trees and is in fact situated well away from trees, since these will impoverish the soil, and render it dry and inhospitable.

If sites running from north to south are chosen, it must be remembered that in the main such borders will get sunshine on each side for an average of only half a day in summer. If they are flanked by close fences or hedges, this effect will be even more marked.

Borders running from east to west will get the benefit of a whole day's sun in summer upon one face, and if the border faces two ways, the other side will have the bulk of its plants with root shade in the summer.

Under such conditions there will, therefore, be a great variation in the amount and time of incidence of the summer sun: that is, when the plants of the border will have assumed their maximum growth.

In a border facing east, the morning sun will be most effective; in one facing west, the afternoon sun alone will be incident; and while the border facing north will have little or no sun upon its northern face, that which faces south will have the benefit of a maximum of summer sunshine.

Formal borders with straight or symmetrical edges present no problem. Where borders of irregular shape are chosen as most suitable to the site, due regard must be paid to the eventual heights of the occupants which will be planted in the bays, since this will have a great influence upon their effectiveness in summer, and on the whole in small borders similar results can be obtained as expertly with regular edges. In certain cases, however, large borders benefit by being of irregular shape, as in this way large sweeps of grass can be brought into artistic conjunction with masses of colour impossible to obtain in the straight-edged types.

The preparation of the border, after its shape has been decided, consists first of marking out its actual position. Thereafter, the site should be efficiently dug. If the site is covered with turf, this

Linaria purpurea AE
Linaria purpurea "Canon Went" BCDGH
Astilbe congesta BEFJKHLMNOQT
Astilbe hybrida "Granat" JKLNOPQRSTU

Aster ericoides "White Heather" GJKLO

Aster cordifolius "Silver Spray" ABCDFH
Polygonum Bistorta JKLMNP

should be lifted off in strips as the work progresses, and the soil dug two spits deep, the surface turf being chopped into pieces as big as a fist and incorporated in the top spit, to which should also be added, if the soil is a heavy loam, basic slag at the rate of six ounces per square yard. As an alternative, a dressing of four ounces of superphosphate of lime per square yard may be made fourteen days after the original surface has been well limed.

Sandy soil benefits to a marked degree by the incorporation of organic manures, and farmyard manure at the rate of half a bushel per square yard may well be used in the spring before planting. Sandy soil is generally deficient in lime, and if after testing this is confirmed, a dressing of half a pound per square yard will not be excessive. Soil from the compost heap should also be added at as heavy a rate as the quantity available will allow. Dressings of superphosphate of lime will help still further to increase the fertility of the soil if used at the rate of four ounces per square yard, and bone meal may be applied at half this rate.

Where the surface soil is so slight that the gardener has literally to create the soil from which the garden is eventually to develop, nothing could be better than that the borders should be confined to growing lupins for several years. All the top growth of the plants should be dug in annually.

Where soils are both excessively light and dry, the yearly compost heap should, among its other constituents, take all the waste paper available, and the homogenised results should be well dug into the soil.

Sewage is probably the most effective application upon ground bordering on pure sand, for it is here that it shows few of the bad characteristics which follow its use upon heavier soils. Indeed, in many of the prepared forms in which it is obtainable to-day it shows no objectionable reactions, and resembles in texture a good dry, odourless, crumbling humus.

The value of such material produced in Great Britain and thrown away annually exceeds £20,000,000. Thus the most valuable basis of phosphatic manure, in a world which is rapidly using up its supplies of guano and rock phosphates, is dissipated.

The use of sewage is probably hindered by prejudice, but this will steadily be overcome by more adequate realisation of the fact that the plant incorporates nothing in its composition which it does not manufacture itself in the course of its growth.

Chalky soils resemble sand in some respects and present a somewhat similar problem. Here again the point is usually to create surface tillage. The addition of organic manures such as farmyard manure and sewage is imperative, and where these are not available, the material from the compost heap, well-rotted turf, in fact any organic compounds available, will help in the creation of a surface soil. Where the top soil is so shallow as to be almost non-existent, the problem becomes enormous, but is still capable of solution. Such soils, even when created, are usually deficient in phosphoric acid; the addition of superphosphate of lime at the rate of eight ounces per square yard will help to remedy the deficiency.

Of the loams little has so far been said, since these provide the ideal base for the perfect border, if it is to be cultivated correctly.

They must be well and efficiently dug two spits deep with organic manure incorporated at the rate of half a bushel per square yard in the lower spit; the surface turf should be chopped, and placed between the lower spit and the top one, and the whole surface be left rough to become weathered with frost. The loams benefit by moderate liming, and a superphosphate dressing should generally be used.

The marls are similarly treated but require no addition of lime, since they are already rich in that substance.

For quick reference a list of manures and fertilisers has been appended, together with their rate of application for appropriate soils. The gardener will find this the quickest way to determine his requirements.

| RATE PER SQUARE YARD | CHALK | CLAY | LOAM | PEAT | MARL | SAND |
|---|---|---|---|---|---|---|
| *Organic Manures:* | | | | | | |
| Farmyard Manure | 10 lb. | 5 lb. | 7 lb. | 5 lb. | 7 lb. | 12 lb. |
| Sewage | 8 " | — | 4 " | — | 4 " | 8 " |
| Composts | 8 " | 8 " | 4 " | — | 4 " | 8 " |
| Leaf mould | 6 " | 3 " | 3 " | — | 3 " | 6 " |
| Peat | 14 " | 7 " | 3 " | — | 3 " | 14 " |
| Dried blood | 8 oz. | — | 4 oz. | 4 oz. | 4 oz. | 8 oz. |
| Seaweed | 12 lb. | — | 7 lb. | 7 lb. | 7 lb. | 14 lb. |
| *Nitrogenous Manures:* | | | | | | |
| Nitrate of potash | 1 oz. | — | 1 oz. | 1 oz. | 1 oz. | 1 oz. |
| Nitrate of soda | 1 " | — | — | 1 " | — | 1 " |
| Sulphate of ammonia | 1 " | 1 oz. | 1 oz. | 1 " | 1 oz. | 1 " |
| Nitrolim | — | 1½ " | 1½ " | 1½ " | — | 1½ " |
| Nitrate of lime | — | 1 " | 1 " | 1 " | — | 1 " |
| Nitrochalk | — | 1 " | 1 " | 1 " | — | 1 " |
| *Phosphatic Manures:* | | | | | | |
| Superphosphate of lime | 8 oz. | 4 oz. | 4 oz. | 4 oz. | 4 oz. | 8 oz. |
| Bone meal | 4 " | 2 " | 2 " | 2 " | 2 " | 4 " |
| Steamed bone flour | 4 " | 4 " | 4 " | 4 " | 4 " | 4 " |
| Hoof and horn meal | 16 " | 8 " | 8 " | 8 " | 8 " | 16 " |
| Basic slag | 8 " | 4 " | 4 " | — | 4 " | 8 " |

| RATE PER SQUARE YARD | CHALK | CLAY | LOAM | PEAT | MARL | SAND |
|---|---|---|---|---|---|---|
| *Potassic Manures:* | | | | | | |
| Sulphate of potash . . | ½ oz. | — | — | ½ oz. | ½ oz. | ½ oz. |
| Muriate of potash . . | 1 ,, | — | — | 1 ,, | — | 1 ,, |
| Kainit . . . . | 2 ,, | — | — | 2 ,, | 2 ,, | 2 ,, |
| Wood ash . . . | 6 ,, | 8 oz. | 8 oz. | 8 ,, | 8 ,, | 14 ,, |

The appended diagram shows those artificial fertilisers which may be mixed together before being applied. These are connected in the diagram by unbroken lines. Those which should not be mixed are found in the diagram indicated by crosses. The fertilisers which may be mixed immediately before application are joined with dotted lines.

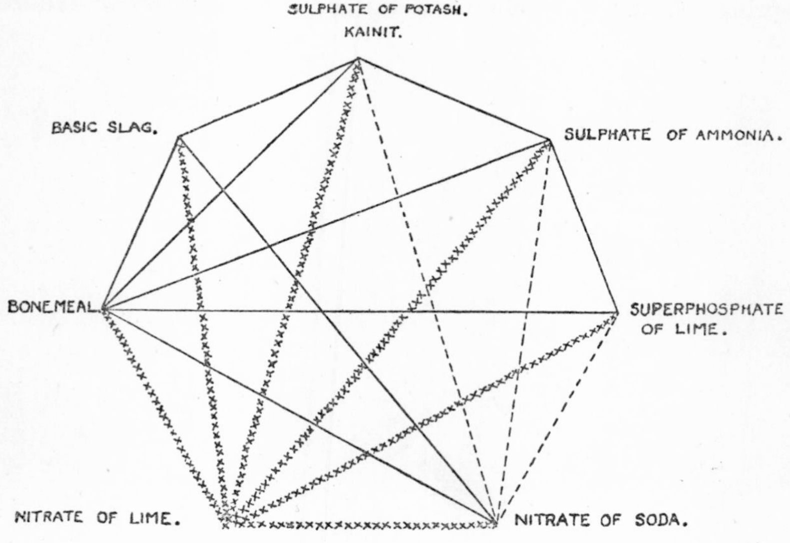


*Figure* 1

Before leaving the consideration of the soil, to delight in visions more entrancing, the gardener must be reminded of the value of the compost heap.

The herbaceous garden produces year by year a wealth of organic material, which must in the course of natural sequences die and give way to the growth of a new year. The process of tidying up in the autumn should, in addition—and, in fact, throughout the year—consist also of a collection of all the leaves and tops of the plants, together with all weeds and waste vegetable material, which should form the basis of the compost heap.

This garden refuse should be spread over the ground in the form of a heap six to eight inches deep, with all the thick, fleshy stems well crushed. It should then be trampled well down and thoroughly wetted. Over the surface the gardener dusts ¾ ounce of sulphate of ammonia, ½ ounce of superphosphate of lime, and 1 ounce of powdered chalk to each square yard of surface.

The whole should then be covered with two or three inches of soil before a similar layer of vegetable matter is added, to be treated exactly in the same way, and the process of building continued until the heap has reached a height of three or four feet.

The material in the heap will quickly heat up, and if it can be turned the resultant compound will be made more homogeneous.

The compost which can be obtained from the heap in the spring will be just as valuable to the garden as well-rotted manure.

Begonia. Group of flowers produced from seedlings

Begonia "Percy Symons"

CHAPTER IV

# DESIGNING AND MAINTAINING THE HERBACEOUS BORDER

THE design of the herbaceous border, if one starts from the beginning, may just as well take place upon paper, in the comfort of an armchair, before a good fire upon a winter's evening, as in the discomfort of the wet and windy garden upon a short and dull day at the same period of the year.

The shape of the border has of course been determined. The beds themselves have been prepared and nothing remains but to select the plants from which the pattern is to be built. These may be obtained from friends, from the nurseryman, or they may be propagated from seed. In the last case some time must elapse before adequate results can be obtained. Certain cases of acquisition of individual plants by stealth are recorded, but no herbaceous border was ever entirely acquired by this method.

The herbaceous border presents a problem in design to the beginner quite unlike any other form of gardening, since, in order that it shall be successful, plants have to be placed in position when they have no developed top growth, and some knowledge of their eventual height and some estimate of colour must be gauged.

In the pages which follow, certain basic designs are suggested, and considerable help will be afforded the garden constructor in the Glossary, where heights and colours, flowering periods and estimates of the space occupied are noted.

The border may face one way or two ways. If it is approachable from two sides, the taller plants will have to be located toward the middle of the bed, and slope down toward the edges. On the other hand, if the border faces one way only, the taller plants will be located at the back. In either case variation in height among the taller plants is necessary and possible, and they provide a good point at which to start. But before the actual pattern is commenced, the gardener should decide whether he desires this particular border to be composed of flowers exhibiting a wide range or a small range of colours: that is, whether he wants what may be called—for want of a better definition—a one-colour border, or one which features many colours. He must also decide whether he would like the colour patches which build up the design to be large or small. As a rule simplicity is the quality to be aimed at, and most certainly by the employment of colour in large masses. The objection to one-colour borders generally is that they have only a limited period of beauty, as it restricts the gardener's selection when it is necessary to find early- and late-flowering varieties.

These points having been decided, it is wise primarily to group in three sections the plants for which the gardener treasures a measure of affection, having due regard to the situation of the border—whether sunny, or partly in sun and partly in shade, or shaded.

The chosen plants should be arranged in groups roughly indicative of their height. The first group should comprise plants of from four to six feet, the second group plants of from two to four feet, and the third group plants less than two feet in height. If the border is very narrow, it may not be possible to use more than two of these groups, and then the gardener will have to decide whether he desires a taller or dwarfer border.

Let us suppose that these lists read in the following way:

*Four feet to six feet*

| | | |
|---|---|---|
| 1. | Delphinium | 6–7 |
| 2. | Tree Lupin | 7–8 |
| 3. | Rudbeckia lacinata | 8–9 |
| 4. | Verbena bonariensis | 7–9 |
| 5. | Hollyhock (Althaea rosea) | 7–9 |
| 6. | Salvia uliginosa | 7–9 |
| 7. | Thalictrum dipterocarpum | 5–7 |
| 8. | Campanula pyramidalis | 7 |

*Two feet to four feet*

| | | |
|---|---|---|
| 9. | Lupin | 6–7 |
| 10. | Phlox decussata | 8–9 |
| 11. | Eryngium amethystinum | 7–8 |
| 12. | Echinops Ritro | 7–8 |
| 13. | Verbascum phoeniceum | 7–8 |
| 14. | Anthemis tinctoria | 6 |
| 15. | Gypsophila paniculata | 9 |
| 16. | Linum narbonnense | 5–7 |

*Up to two feet*

| | | |
|---|---|---|
| 17. | Dianthus barbatus | 7 |
| 18. | Aster Amellus | 8–9 |
| 19. | Veronica longifolia | 7–9 |
| 20. | Alyssum saxatile | 6 |
| 21. | Campanula carpatica | 7–8 |
| 22. | Polemonium humile | 8 |
| 23. | Nepeta Mussini | 7–9 |
| 24. | Origanum pulchrum | 6–7 |

Begonia. Group of seedlings

Begonia "Florence Bush" EFJK

Begonia "Golden Queen" CDGH

Begonia "Mildred Butler" LMPQ

Let us assume our border to be twenty-four feet in length by six feet in width. Let us place our taller-growing varieties first; following this distribution with the medium varieties, and finally the dwarfs.

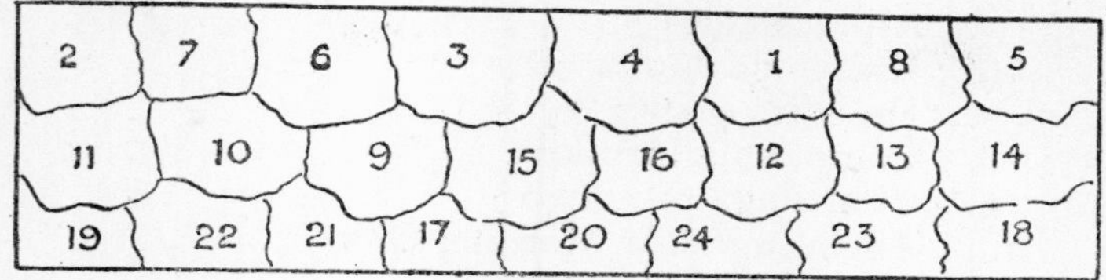


*Figure* 2

It will be seen that our selection of plants with red or pink flowers is very weak, and we shall therefore choose Lupins of deep pink, and a Phlox of bright red, if we care for these colours, and as our Lupins and Phloxes will not be in flower at the same time we need not worry to separate them too much. Nevertheless, the colour balance of our original selection is weak and could be much improved in its length of attractiveness if we substituted bright plants with longer flowering periods for some of those selected.

Let us try again. Let us incorporate in the original plan:—

| | | |
|---|---|---|
| 2 Potentilla Miss Willmott | . . replacing No. | 17 |
| 2 Potentilla Gibson's Scarlet | . . ,, ,, | 24 |
| 2 Geum Mrs. Bradshaw | . . . ,, ,, | 22 |
| 2 Heuchera sanguinea | . . . ,, ,, | 19 |
| 2 Physostegia virginiana | . . ,, ,, | 20 |
| 2–4 Sidalcea Rose Queen | . . ,, ,, | 15 |

We have in no way interfered with our back rank, but we have almost entirely replaced the front of the border, and consequently some rearrangement of the centre may be necessary.

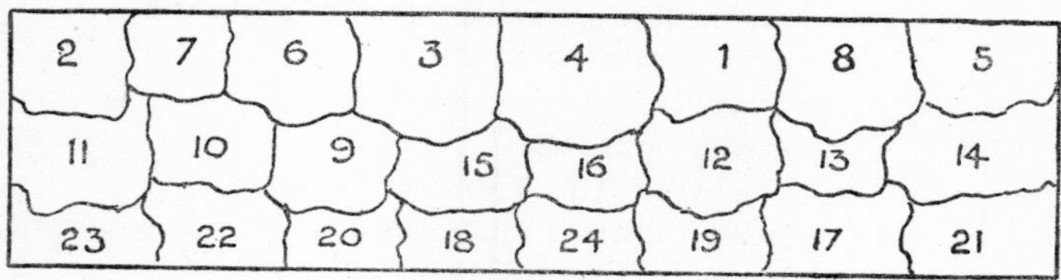


*Figure* 3

We have now corrected the lack of reds, but have not over-balanced in that direction.

We can now proceed to a scheme somewhat more ambitious and employ as our basic tall plants:—

*From four feet upwards*

1. Bocconia cordata
2. Eremurus robustus
3. Malva Alcea
4. Delphinium
5. Althaea rosea
6. Kniphofia caulescens
7. Heliopsis scabra
8. Campanula lactiflora
9. Cimicifuga racemosa
10. Anchusa italica Morning Glory
11. Cephalaria tatarica
12. Verbascum Cotswold Beauty

*Two feet to four feet*

13. Verbena corymbosa
14. Helenium Moerheim Beauty
15. Echinops bannaticus
16. Liatris pycnostachya
17. Lupinus polyphyllus Weber
18. Lupinus polyphyllus Downer's Delight
19. Lupinus polyphyllus Brenda Prichard
20. Papaver orientale Mrs. Stobart
21. Phlox Caroline Vandenberg
22. Phlox Daily Sketch
23. Phytolacca decandra
24. Polygonum Bistorta
25. Pyrethrum Eileen May Robinson
26. Pyrethrum Madeleine

*Two feet to one foot*

27. Aster Amellus King George
28. Aster Amellus W. Robinson
29. Sidalcea malvaeflora Kathleen Bunyard
30. Anemone japonica Profusion
31. Aster Amellus Perry's Favourite
32. Catananche caerulea
33. Erigeron hybridus Merstham Glory
34. Eryngium planum var. Violetta
35. Geum coccineum Lady Stratheden
36. Helenium autumnale pumilum Crimson Beauty
37. Heuchera sanguinea Oxfordii
38. Paeonia corallina
39. Phlox decussata Mia Ruys
40. Platycodon grandiflorus

*One foot or less*

(Where the border is required to slope down to nothing at the front, the employment of the following plants, not shown on the plan, is advised. They should be used in this order:—41, 45, 47, 42, 46, 48, 43, 49, 51, 44, 50, 54, 53, 52.)

41. Aster acris nanus
42. Aster pygmaeus Niobe
43. Aster pygmaeus Ronald
44. Aster pygmaeus Victor
45. Campanula carpatica
46. Ceratostigma plumbaginoides
47. Dracocephalum Forrestii
48. Erigeron hybridus Elsie
49. Gaillardia aristata Tangerine
50. Geum Borisii
51. Lychnis Haageana
52. Nepeta Mussini
53. Oxalis floribunda
54. Viola cornuta purpurea

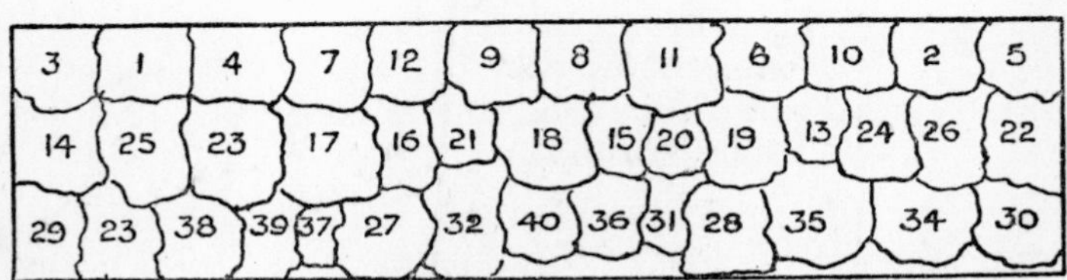


*Figure* 4

When a selection of PLANTS SUITABLE TO A SHADED OR SEMI-SHADED BORDER is required, more difficulty arises, but a good basis upon which to build up can be found among the following:

*Tall*

Astilbe Davidii
Astilbe Peach Blossom
Boltonia asteroides
Digitalis ferruginea
Meconopsis Wallichii
Senecio Veitchianus
Verbascum phoeniceum
Hemerocallis fulva
Lobelia cardinalis Huntsman
Spiraea Aruncus
Spiraea Filipendula

*Medium*

Aconitum Napellus
Anemone japonica
Asphodeline lutea
Astilbe Granat
Astilbe Gertrude Brix
Dicentra spectabilis
Iris sibirica
Kirengeshoma palmata
Lychnis chalcedonica
Meconopsis betonicaefolia
Mimulus ringens
Phlomis Samia

*Dwarf*

Cardamine pratensis fl. pl.
Chrysogonum virginianum
Dicentra eximia
Geum rivale Leonard's variety
Helleborus niger
Helleborus colchicus
Meconopsis cambrica fl. pl.
Primula Auricula
Epimedium sulphureum rubrum
Trollius europaeus

One of the difficulties which beset the gardener in the construction of borders is that of obtaining a good display of autumn flowers. For that reason it seems politic to list in some detail a number of AUTUMN-FLOWERING PLANTS suitable for use in the herbaceous border.

Achillea filipendulina
Anemone japonica varieties
Anthemis tinctoria
Aster Novae-Angliae varieties
Aster Novi-Belgii varieties
Bocconia cordata
Boltonia asteroides
Centaurea dealbata
Chrysanthemum uliginosum
Cimicifuga simplex
Echinops Ritro
Gaillardia aristata
Gentiana sino-ornata
Geum Borisii
Geum Heldreichii

Helianthus Miss Mellish
Kirengeshoma palmata
Kniphofia caulescens
Kniphofia Macowanii
Kniphofia Mt. Etna
Kniphofia multiflora
Lobelia cardinalis Huntsman
Lobelia syphilitica
Malva moschata
Nerine Bowdeni
Oxalis floribunda
Rudbeckia lacinata
Rudbeckia speciosa
Salvia uliginosa
Sedum spectabile
Viola cornuta
Zauschneria mexicana

The condition of the soil should be good at the time when planting is undertaken, especially when the soil is heavy. A good test is to trample the soil heavily. If it will readily fall apart afterwards, and does not cake into a homogeneous mass, it can be safely said to be in good condition to plant.

The process of planting should be undertaken systematically; the plants should be placed in position on the prepared bed as planned and the work begun at one end, with the gardener continually working towards the other end so that he does not have to tread over the finished work.

Long tap roots should be removed with a sharp knife, and, similarly, all damaged or broken roots should be cut away. Holes should be prepared to such a depth that all the blanched stems of the plant are below the surface of the ground, and should be of sufficient width that the roots may be well spread. The plant should then be thoroughly trodden in so that the soil around it appears to be of the same firmness as the rest of the bed.

Plants liable to be attacked by slugs—as an example we quote the Delphinium—should be covered with heaped-up coarse ashes, which will help to protect the crowns both from damage by frost and bad drainage, and from the depredations of itinerant slugs. Where beds are known to be infested with insect pests, planting should be preceded by a dressing of commercial naphthaline at the rate of two ounces per square yard, and as a further preventive soot may be dusted round the crowns of the plants before filling in.

Planting should generally be done in the autumn, but the date should depend mainly upon circumstances; it can be delayed until

March if conditions so dictate. Whenever the planting is done, however, the border should be lightly forked over on the surface in March, and as soon as the plants have started into new growth the more vigorous types should be thinned. Particular care should be taken in this respect of the Asters, Delphiniums, Heleniums, Lupins, and Phlox, which should have all weakly shoots removed together with those which exert any cramping influence on the development of the plant.

When taller plants have reached a height exceeding one foot, they should be securely staked. This should as a rule be done in early May, as the most rapid growth of the plant takes place then, and the symmetrical beauty of the individual plant must be preserved if the border is to provide its most attractive picture.

Much argument has been bandied about with regard to watering. With a plant not firmly established it may be necessary to water copiously for a prolonged period so that it may become established. The walls of the cells in the roots of the plant can be compared with valves, or perhaps even more simply with one-way streets: that is, they will pass material from the outside to the inside only. The force with which they attract moisture from the outside is dependent entirely upon the strength of the concentration of the liquid within. Thus, as prolonged evaporation reduces the quantity of water in this solution, the strength increases, and thereby the attraction for the moisture without is also increased. If, however, the plant is most copiously watered, the concentration of the solution within is consequently reduced and the power of suction of its roots diminished. In addition, the cell walls become distended as they take in water, and therefore reduce the ability of the cell to assimilate further. If the water provided for the plant drains or dries out quickly, as it normally would in periods of prolonged and widespread drought, watering will merely have reduced the ability of the plant to take in water at a time when it is necessary that this ability should be increased.

If, however, watering is done in order to decrease evaporation from the plant, that is to say, if the leaves are heavily sprayed with water to prevent prolonged evaporation, then no rapid change takes place within the root cells, and the plant retains its ability to fend efficiently for itself.

Thus the gardener's contention that once he begins to water he must continue to do so is scientifically vindicated.

The plant exists to ensure that its kind continues to exist, and completes its life cycle upon the production of its ripe seed. The gardener, who is not in the main concerned with the collection of ripe seeds, but more with the beauty brought into his world by the process of fulfilment, can prolong the flowering period of his plants by cutting away the flower-heads as they fade, since thereby the plant will be encouraged to produce still more flowers.

In this way many plants may be enabled to flower for a long period. In the case of Delphiniums or Lupins, the whole of the overground growth of the plant may be removed, and they will produce a second crop of flowers which, though seldom equal in quality to the first ones, come when they will be most appreciated.

This is a procedure which throws considerable strain upon the plant and requires that it should have the very best of cultivation and attention.

No mention has been made of hoeing. Hoeing, as a discouragement to weeds, is undoubtedly useful and should take place throughout the year. Fortunately, the well-designed and well-planted border needs hoeing for this purpose only at an early stage in the year, and if performed efficiently twice, this should be enough to keep the border completely clear of weeds.

Subsequent care of the herbaceous border from year to year consists generally of lifting the plants, dividing them where necessary, ensuring the continued fertility of the soil by incorporating further additions of well-rotted manures, and replanting. Generally speaking, it is better that the herbaceous border should be replanted yearly than that it should be left for a period of years. On the whole, it is better that this should be done towards the end of October, while the plants still remain visible, and while there is plenty of time for their re-establishment.

During this replanting stage, changes which have become necessary should be made. It is a very good plan to keep a notebook in which the gardener can jot down during the year all the pleasing associations of plants which have impressed themselves upon his eye and mind. For this purpose one-half of the book should be set aside, while in the other half he should compile a similar list of unfortunate associations of plants which have proved either displeasing or failures. By consulting his notebook he will be able to increase the colour value of the border in a way which he could not do were he merely to trust to memory.

He should also note, during the course of the year, the names of plants he has seen elsewhere and which he would like to incorporate in his own border. Before replanting is actually tackled, these should be procured, and the position planned out for their accommodation.

## CHAPTER V

# PROPAGATION OF HERBACEOUS AND OTHER PLANTS

IT is essential that the gardener or garden lover should have a practical knowledge of the best ways in which he shall be able to maintain or increase his stock of plants. Since all plants, like animals and individuals, lose their virility as they age, the time inevitably comes when they must be replaced by younger and more active stock.

The main methods which may be used for producing additional stock are:—

(*a*) from seed; (*b*) from cuttings; (*c*) from division—(*b*) and (*c*) being variations of what is known as vegetative reproduction. As examples we may quote Salvias, which we raise from seed; Pinks, which we raise from cuttings; and Michaelmas Daisies, which we obtain by division.

If we raise our plants from seed it is possible to have considerable variation in the plants when they are produced and flower. In the case of cuttings the plant is really a small independent part of the original plant from which we took it, and any other part of the same plant, duly furnished with roots, will have the same characteristics.

This is important when we wish to produce a number of plants, for example, all of exactly the same shade of colour, or of the same height. For this reason vegetative reproduction is important, since it can help us to raise standardised plants of hybrids which do not normally come true from seed.

The number of plants which can be obtained from cuttings is much greater than the average gardener realises, though unfortunately this method has been used by the amateur to a much smaller degree in the case of herbaceous plants than in the case of the hard-wooded shrubs.

We will deal first of all, however, with production from seed.

Where the degree of accuracy in colour or height or size of the flower is immaterial, the bulk of herbaceous plants can be raised from seed. In fact, where large numbers of plants are required, propagation from seed is undoubtedly the quickest way. For this purpose it is necessary that the seed should be fresh, for

Campanula rhomboidalis fl. pl. BCDGH
Pentstemon campanulatus roseus BEFJKNO
Campanula mirabilis KLMOPQ

Campanula lactiflora BCDFGH
Echinops Ritro EJFKLPHM
Catananche caerulea major EFGMNOPQSU

while many seeds retain their power of germination over a long period, this is not invariably so, and the gardener will get much better results by using fresh seed than seed which is dried up.

On the whole, however, seeds are remarkably tough, the standard example of their hardihood being the proved case of the successful germination of the pip taken from raspberry jam that had been boiled! At the other end of the range, almost every gardener knows that tender plants killed off by severe frosts are often replaced by seedlings which spring from the soil round about them.

This will convey a clear indication that the plant in its embryo form, that is the seed, has a much higher degree of resistance to extremes than its parent, the full-grown plant. This is possibly due to the fact that its water content is much lower.

Even greater extremes have been weathered by seeds, and a textbook example quotes seed which has been known to germinate after having been kept for two months in liquid air. On the whole, however, it is a safe rule that seeds should be sown as soon as ripe. This we will regard as our first essential. The second essential is cleanliness. All vessels should be kept scrupulously clean, and the soil should be free from pests and weed seeds, which can be achieved by sterilising both the soil and the boxes or pans which are to contain it.

In cases of delayed germination the use of unclean or unsterilised material will result in the rapid growth of weeds and mosses and fungi, which will have the effect of discouraging germination, if not completely preventing it.

Where the pans or boxes remain open to the air, as they will on many occasions, windborne seeds will provide a sufficient measure of contamination without the additional difficulty arising from the soil itself.

The seeds may be sown in pans or boxes. If boxes are used, they should be treated a day or two before with a solution of Cuprinol, which is a good fungicide and helps to preserve the boxes in good condition for a considerable period. The base of the box or pan should be covered with a layer of pot crocks about an inch deep. These, too, should have been sterilised.

Seed composts (prepared as described at the end of this chapter) should be placed in the pots or boxes, pressed firmly down, and consolidated until the soil is half an inch below the level of the rim of the box or pot. This should then be placed in a bath of water reaching nearly to the rim, and when well soaked, should be taken out and placed on one side to drain.

When this has been satisfactorily accomplished, the seed should be sown finely and evenly on the surface. This sounds simple, but if the seed is very small it is not easy to effect, and the seed should then be mixed with six or seven times its own bulk of fine sand, then placed in the V formed by a folded piece of card about the size of an ordinary visiting card, and gently shaken to and fro as it is drawn from one end of the box or pan to the other.

In the case of large seeds, these may be evenly spaced over the whole surface by just placing them into position. When the sowing is completed, dust a little soil over the surface, using a fine sieve for the purpose, and thinly cover with a layer of from one-sixteenth to one-eighth of an inch of coarse sand or grit.

This method of covering the surface has been found by experience to discourage the growth of things like moss and liverwort, and to help to maintain an even humidity, so necessary to the germination of the seed. The pans of ungerminated seed should be allowed to undergo all extremes of weather for a period of at least fourteen days, after which they may be brought in to either a cold frame or greenhouse, where the temperature is less variable. Should germination take place while they are still outside, they should be placed in the cold frame, where they are not subject to draughts or great changes in temperature.

As a rule, most seeds germinate better in the dark than in the light, and unless seeds are definitely known to be light-sensitive, the boxes or pans should be covered with asbestos sheets or slates and examined from day to day to see whether germination has yet begun.

After germination, the seed pans are best placed in the frame or greenhouse, and brought as near to the glass as possible, but not exposed to the scorching rays of the sun. They should be examined at close intervals and, if found to be dry, they should be soaked by being placed in a bath of water coloured by the addition of potassium permanganate, and then lifted out and allowed to dry, whereafter they are returned to their original locations.

In most cases growth is quite rapid after germination, but in a few it can be somewhat protracted. Care should be taken to avoid all excesses of both temperature and humidity after the seeds have begun to grow, as they are the most likely causes of damping-off and the like. When the seedlings have reached a stage when it becomes obvious that they will need more space in which to develop, they may be pricked out into boxes of similarly prepared soil, which should previously have been thoroughly soaked by plunging them into water coloured with potassium permanganate, and then lifted out to drain. Care should be taken when lifting the seedlings from the original pan that the roots are not damaged. For a few days after transplanting they should be

Chrysanthemum koreanum "Ceres"

Chrysanthemum "May Wallace"

kept in a shaded frame, which ought to be opened daily after about a week has elapsed.

Propagation by means of cuttings, as previously indicated, is one of the most useful ways of procuring stocks of specific varieties. Cuttings may be taken in three different ways: they may either be shoots of the soft shoot of wood, or they may be cuttings of the soft wood with a heel of hard wood—that is, taken at the point where the soft shoot joins the harder stem—or they may be cuttings roughly composed of one-half ripened wood and one-half partly ripened wood. In order to root them, a propagating case, or cutting frame, should be prepared in a position of the garden shaded from the hottest sun. A frame roughly a yard square will accommodate anything from 500 to 1,000 cuttings and can be increased on the unit principle. The base should be well drained with cinders or clinkers which have been weathered for some time before being used, and which should cover the bottom to a depth of two or three inches. Above this, there should be two inches of good soil, preferably sterilised; and, finally, there should follow a layer of at least four inches of sharp—that is, coarse—sand, which should be pressed down firmly with a six- or nine-inch board, and be well watered before any cuttings are inserted. The space above the sand and below the glass should be between four and six inches; the frame should thus be roughly fifteen inches deep.

Cuttings should be divided into two groups, the large and leafy ones and those which are small and carry fewer leaves. The small ones should be placed in rows one inch apart, with one inch between the cuttings. The larger ones may be similarly disposed with two inches between them. Cuttings should be prepared with a sharp razor blade and should be taken either before the parent plant has flowered, or after; generally, as soon as suitable stems have made their appearance. In most cases cuttings are taken just below the leaf joint, and the leaves are removed for about one-third of the length of the cutting.

Cuttings of Lupins, for example, are taken in the spring and comprise the shoots which develop in the leaf axils on the main stems. Cuttings of Campanulas are taken in precisely the same way, but are certainly not available until after the plant has flowered in July or August. Sometimes it is necessary to take cuttings with a heel of the old wood, generally a piece of the plant in which the old wood forms the so-called heel, but however the cutting is taken, the cut should be as clean and as small as possible. Approximately one-third of the length of the cutting is placed in the sand, and the best method of inserting is to prepare a sharply-pointed round stick which will make round holes into which they can be lowered in straight and evenly spaced lines, before actually putting them in.

In the case of all soft-wooded cuttings of herbaceous plants, rooting is considerably facilitated if the cuttings are not watered for three or four hours after they are put in; they should be allowed to flag until the leaves become limp, after which they may be watered in such a way that the sand about them is consolidated and made firm. Some plants respond better if they are put into ordinary soil in a shady site out of doors. Examples of this are the Wallflowers and Erysimums.

As a rule the beginner finds it very difficult to judge which part of the plant will make the most suitable cutting. It is a good plan never to choose one which is large and straggling, nor should shoots which are in any way damaged be chosen. Where the cutting is one with a heel, it should be cut at a point where the soft wood joins the hard stem, and it is, generally speaking, improved by cutting upwards and then severing it from the main stem rather than by a straight downward cut.

After the first flagging, it is necessary to water the frame every day, and it will be found that all flagging ceases at the end of the third or fourth day. At the end of a fortnight many of the plants will be found to have roots, but the length of time required for different varieties to become self-supporting varies very considerably. Though, in most cases, the somewhat experienced gardener can tell at a glance whether the plants now have roots or not, the beginner should lift one or another occasionally to examine whether it is rooted. When necessary, it can be replaced and watered back without undue inconvenience to it.

Certain small cuttings, notably those of the smaller Dianthus, may be better treated in pans which have been furnished with drainage material and an inch or so of soil, and filled to the brim with sand, after which the cuttings are inserted. They are then placed in a glass frame and kept there until rooting actually takes place, when they may be transplanted into boxes of good soil, or potted.

Leaf cuttings are generally made about the month of June, and examples are Haberleas, Begonias, and Lewisias. The leaves are pulled off complete with stalk where they are attached to the plant. No preparation should be made; they are simply inserted into pans containing a mixture of half leaf mould and half sand which has been finely sifted. It will be found that most leaves of this kind provide themselves quite quickly with roots, though considerable time may elapse before the leaves develop a new rosette.

Root cuttings provide a means whereby the gardener may quickly establish a large stock of much-wanted plants. The principle is that the thick roots of the plants are cut into pieces half an inch to an inch long in such a way that the top portion of the root is uppermost. They are inserted to half their depth into pans prepared similarly to those used for leaf cuttings, and are then completely covered with coarse sand so that one inch at the top of the pan remains free. After the pan has been carefully watered, a sheet of glass is placed over it and the pan treated exactly as if it contained germinated seed. Lupins, Delphiniums, Primulas, Erodiums, and Anemones may be treated in this way, as may also Trollius. This particular method of propagation, when used skilfully, will quickly supply the grower with a large number of plants perfectly true in colour and form from varieties producing very little in the way of top growth. When new surface growth has been formed, pieces of root may be removed from the pan and potted on as required.

But the easiest method of all of producing fresh material for the garden is by division. This can only be practised when the original plant is not tap-rooted. The plant is usually dug up in the late autumn or early spring, the soil is shaken away, and the root washed clear of soil in a bucket of water. Inspection will then show how the root may be best divided so that each separate plant may have a complete root system. A very sharp knife or razor blade is used to sever any stems which prevent easy division. In some cases the gardener will just divide his plants into four parts by cutting through with a spade; on the whole, however, this is a bad method because it does not relieve the root of the congestion which undoubtedly occurs in roots which lend themselves to division in this way. Michaelmas Daisies, Phloxes, Heleniums can all be so treated, and the new pieces will often provide plants even more virile than the parent from which they sprang.

Bulbous-rooted plants are also divided, but here the division is called scaling. In the case of plants like Lilies, Fritillaries, and the like, the parent bulbs have their outer scales shaken loose, which then are put into a box or pan of sandy soil, and covered with still more soil. In the course of time they will send up a leaf or two and may then be potted separately. They are generally slow to develop, but if they are potted on for a while and thereafter planted out in good soil they will eventually reach flowering size.

The cool, unheated greenhouse is a great help to the gardener in the maintenance of herbaceous borders. In fact, a greenhouse or cold frame is an absolute necessity. Propagation of border plants to fill the gaps necessitates a house and a cold frame, or a deep box similarly furnished, on the stage of the greenhouse. The purist may look askance at the idea of raising tender perennials in the greenhouse to supplement colour to the border, closing his eyes to the fact that it most frequently comprises perennials, tender perennials, bedding plants, annuals, shrubs, and is primarily an expression of personal taste.

Practically all the plants the gardener will need, other than varietal plants, can be obtained by vegetative reproduction or from seed. By the use of the cold greenhouse, plants from which it is desired to propagate can be brought into growth earlier than they would be if they remained out of doors, and so facilitate the preparation of cuttings.

If a deep box is well furnished with drainage material and then covered with a layer of good loam, finally finished off with four inches or so of sharp sand, cuttings from plants thus brought on into early growth may be treated exactly as described on p. 36, and a considerable lengthening of their period of growth is thus achieved. The seeds of tender perennials may be sown in boxes which at first may be protected on frosty nights with a sheet of newspaper. At a later stage seedlings may be put out and kept in growth in the house before the weather becomes sufficiently mild to allow them to be planted out.

Bulbous- or tuberous-rooted plants may be potted and brought into growth ready for planting out. In fact, there are a hundred and one ways in which the house may be used for the benefit of the garden. It is, however, important that the atmosphere during the colder months should be kept as dry as possible. Watering at such a time should be done so carefully that neither the floor nor the staging is moistened. If plants or seedlings have to be watered at this season, watering should preferably take place in the morning of a mild day, and the house may be well ventilated, so that the leaves are not allowed to remain wet for any length of time.

During the summer, when the house will be little used for supplementing plants to make up the borders, it may be used to obtain a certain measure of brightness of its own. Begonias, Zinnias, Pelargoniums, and similar plants may replace the younger stocks in the house during the spring and autumn, which by then should have been planted out in the nursery bed to gain strength and vigour for the following season.

A selection of plants which may be raised from seed sown in the spring is appended.

Chrysanthemum morifolium "Calypso"

Chrysanthemum koreanum "The Moor"

## A Selection of Plants which may be raised from Seed

Adenophora
Agapanthus
Alyssum
Anagallis
Anchusa
Aquilegia
Astrantia
Bocconia
Borago
Campanula
Carduus
Centaurea
Cheiranthus
Commelina
Cyclamen
Cynoglossum
Delphinium
Dianthus
Digitalis
Dracocephalum
Epimedium
Eryngium
Gazania
Gentiana
Geranium
Geum
Incarvillea
Iris
Kirengeshoma
Lewisia
Lilium
Linum
Lupinus
Lythrum
Melittis
Mimulus
Nomocharis
Pentstemon
Polemonium
Potentilla
Primula
Roscoea
Salvia
Scutellaria
Sisyrinchium
Thalictrum
Trollius
Verbascum
Viola

## John Innes' Compost for Seeds

| | |
|---|---|
| Two parts sterilised loam<br>One part peat<br>One part coarse sand | to which should be added: superphosphate of lime $1\frac{1}{2}$ oz., and powdered chalk $\frac{3}{4}$ oz. for each bushel. |

## The John Innes' Potting Compost

| | |
|---|---|
| Seven parts sterilised loam<br>Three parts peat<br>Two parts sand | to which add: 4 oz. of the John Innes' base, which may be obtained from any sundriesman, and $\frac{3}{4}$ oz. of powdered chalk for each cubic yard. |

Readers who require additional information should obtain *Seeds and Potting Composts*, by W. J. C. Lawrence and J. Newell, published by George Allen & Unwin Ltd. This deals exhaustively with the gardener's greatest need, a standard compost.

CHAPTER VI

# CONTROL OF INSECT AND OTHER PESTS

THE gardener must be ever on the watch for the depredations of insects and those other pests which adversely affect plants in the garden. In the main, plants of the herbaceous border are particularly free from disease, and the long list of aches and pains which will follow should be regarded in the same way that one peruses the contents of a medical dictionary.

The activities of ANTS are not generally regarded as being particularly harmful in the garden. Their presence is, however, usually a sign of the visitation of one or the other kind of aphides, and they should therefore be rendered as uncomfortable as possible, should they take up residence anywhere in the garden.

Where the roots of plants are affected by root aphis, the ants, drawn by the sweetness of their secretion, almost invariably build a nest to watch over them with all the care that a nursemaid will devote to her charges, and between the ants and the aphides the plant will pass away. There follows a treatment which is of benefit to the plant, and a misfortune to the ant: Six ounces of sugar should be dissolved in one pint of hot water; to this should be added ten grams of sodium arsenate. (This, by the way, is a deadly poison and should be placed out of harm's way.) A piece of cotton-wool is soaked in the poisonous mixture and placed in a tin. After the lid has been punched full of holes it should be replaced, and the tin put in proximity to the ants' nest. This will both attract and poison them, while the lid will prevent the access of birds to the poison.

In greenhouses, finely powdered sodium fluoride, dusted over the floor when it is dry, proves very effective; but it must be remembered that this, too, is a deadly poison, and children and animals should be kept away after its use.

Where the roots are known to be infested with both ants and aphides, a small hole should be made down into the nest. A few crystals of paradichlorbenzine will prove fatal to both, and provided that such treatment takes place in the open air, and not in enclosed spaces, no danger will result to near-by plants. Paradichlorbenzine is quite volatile, but is not particularly poisonous, though of course it should neither be eaten nor inhaled. Provided that the most appropriate remedy is chosen for the plant or

Chrysanthemum morifolium "Bronze Early Buttercup" AEFK
Chrysanthemum morifolium "September Yellow" BCDGH
Chrysanthemum morifolium "Freda" JLMNOPQ

Chrysanthemum koreanum "Janté Wells" CDHKLMNOPQ

Chrysanthemum koreanum "Bubble" ABCEFGJK

plants affected, having due regard for their position, ants can be eradicated from the garden.

APHIDES will sometimes be found to infest either the roots or the stems of plants growing in the garden. Many proprietary brands of sprays are sold for dealing with them, and most of these are extremely effective. One very suitable, because it will not damage even the most delicate plant, is known as Molluscide, and can be effectively used as a general spray. Root aphis has already been mentioned under Ants, and in the garden no better remedy can be suggested for them than paradichlorbenzine. (See also under Root Aphides, p. 42.)

CUT-WORMS are soil-inhabiting caterpillars which are the grubs of the Owlet Moths, very destructive insects in many ways, the most widespread of which give them their name, for they cut off the plants at soil level by eating through the main stem. The first sign of their activity becomes apparent on the following day, when the plants suffer a sudden collapse. Since cut-worms work mainly at night, they can be controlled comparatively easily by broadcasting poison-bait at dusk on a quiet but warm evening, after a shower of rain. The bait is made of one ounce of Paris green with two pounds of coarse bran. The Paris green should be sprinkled with a fine sprinkler or sifter over the dry bran. While the mixture is in this state it may be stored. To make it ready for use it should be moistened with warm water, to which two tablespoonfuls of treacle have been added, until the bran is damp, but does not stick or adhere. The quantity suggested is enough to treat 400 square yards, and is sufficiently well diluted not to be dangerous to birds or animals.

EARTH-WORMS can be particularly annoying, especially in pans and boxes, where they interfere considerably with efficient drainage. If crystals of paradichlorbenzine are scattered over the surface of the soil while pans or boxes are still in the open, they will be killed, but the chemical should be removed before the boxes are returned to frames or greenhouses. An alternative method uses mowrah meal in a similar fashion. Before this is used the boxes should be well watered, and the meal applied lightly dusted over the whole surface.

The EARWIG, most curiously, gets its name from the queer shape of its wings. It is particularly fond of the Dahlia, Chrysanthemum, and Dianthus families, and its predilection for these causes much damage to the objects of its affection. It normally feeds at night, and the old method of trapping in pots into which paper or hay had been stuffed, and immersing the catch in boiling water, depended entirely upon providing shelter for them during the hours of light. They can be controlled by the same method as that suggested for cut-worms, but a still more effective method is that of punching a number of quarter-inch holes in the lids of tins which contain an inch or so of the following mixture: To three-quarters of a pint of warm water and a quarter-pound of treacle, which should be well mixed, add one ounce of sodium fluoride; stir one pound of coarse bran into the solution until a paste has been formed. The paste is poisonous and, if handled, care should be taken that the hands are washed afterwards. When the paste has been placed in tins, the lids should be replaced and the tins disposed in the shade of plants to act as traps. Additional attention consists of emptying them of the accumulated corpses occasionally.

Field Mice can be particularly noxious to the freshly planted bulbs of the Crocus species and of Tulips, and the only preventative one can suggest at this time of the year is to bait a number of traps with cut-off pieces of Crocus bulbs, placing them in parts of the garden where damage is known to have been perpetrated. To protect birds from the danger of the traps, these should be placed inside flower-pots which have been laid upon their sides, or in short lengths of drainpipe.

The Frog Hopper is easily recognised by the curious spittle-like mass with which it surrounds and protects itself. The insect contained therein is an active, yellowish-green oval creature which can be easily removed. But in the case of heavy onslaughts the best method of control is to syringe freely with a nicotine wash.

The Red Spider can be exceptionally damaging to the foliage of plants, particularly those which have become dry at the root. It causes the leaves of plants first to become mottled, then yellow, and finally to fall off. The treatment is to spray with Volck wash, which is perfectly harmless to plant life and easy to use.

The Rose Beetle is a very handsome, metallic-green insect often very injurious to the flowers of Paeonies and allied plants in the herbaceous garden, but its grubs are even more destructive to the roots of many plants. They resemble those of the cockchafer and are about an inch and a half in length and dirty-white in colour. The best deterrent is to dig in naphthaline at the rate of two ounces per square yard.

Root Aphides are most frequently met in the garden upon light soils, and methods for their discomfiture have been described under Aphis. Some indication, however, must be made, since they are not easily discernible except by the symptoms exhibited in the leaves of the plants. The first sign that the plant is affected by root aphis is the yellowing of one or another of the leaves of an otherwise healthy plant. Later malformation of the leaves develops, they become attenuated, and defaced by streaks or marbling; the plant becomes incapable of flowering, and examination of the collar of the plant—that is, the point where the stem reaches the ground—will show a peculiar, white, woolly appearance, due to the substance with which the aphides protect themselves from attack. This is a waxy material and has to be dissolved before any spraying can reach the insect.

Plants which are contaminated can be saved by lifting, washing free of all soil, and spraying with "Flit." All the soil should be completely sterilised and the plants transferred to an area known to be free. After replanting, they should be watered with a solution of ten grains of potassium permanganate to one gallon of water, at weekly intervals.

Snails and Slugs are some of the worst pests, especially where young seedlings are concerned, since they seem to concentrate on the young, tender growth of one's most valued plants. Fortunately, they can be controlled and prevented from damaging young plants. Coarse bran or oatmeal mixed with powdered metaldehyde provides one method. Half a tablet of Meta fuel is crushed to powder and mixed with a double handful of bran or oatmeal; this is placed in small heaps about the garden on a dry day and prevented from becoming wet by having a sheet of glass propped above it to keep off rain. It proves a source of attraction to slugs and snails, and where a garden is badly infested will often catch many hundreds in a single night. A further method is to employ Molluscide, which has the additional advantage of not being damaged by moisture. It can be obtained in two forms, one of which is dissolved in water to form a spray which will not be injurious even to the most tender of seedlings or plants, and the other a powder, which may be spread about. Moreover, the mixture earlier recommended for cut-worms is also effective in the case of slugs. Snails are gregarious and will often be found in large colonies in the shelter of large stones or low hedges. Such colonies should be collected and exterminated.

Lilies, Anemones, and Pansies, together with a whole host of other herbaceous plants, are destroyed by the activity of the Snake Millipedes, which move slowly and have a brown, hard, horny skin usually unaffected by insecticides. They can be destroyed by the use of naphthaline, but are more easily killed by using a strong solution of nitrate of soda, which also has the effect of encouraging the growth of the plant.

Thrips are only dangerous in pans or boxes of young seedlings which have been allowed to become too dry. Their advent can be prevented by efficient watering; but should they have arrived, the most effective cure is a light dusting with pyrethrum or insect powder.

WOODLICE can also be exceptionally destructive. They accumulate in colonies under stones and can be trapped in numbers by laying down slates or boards, under which they will form colonies. The paste suggested for the destruction of earwigs is also effective and should be broadcast where they are likely to be found.

Insects, however, are not the only enemies of plants. Frequently plants in the garden are attacked by MILDEW. A good spray, and a simple one to make, is bicarbonate of soda in the proportion of one ounce to ten gallons of water. This is probably the cleanest and the least likely to cause harmful effects to tender plants. Other mixtures are potassium sulphide, or liver of sulphur, one ounce to two gallons of water (but this mixture should be used while still fresh), and Bouisol, a proprietary colloidal compound, which is also exceptionally effective.

Seedlings are often attacked by diseases which the gardener calls DAMPING-OFF and attributes to the wet or sour condition of the soil, which is a contributing factor though not the prime cause. Actually, the disease is caused by microscopic fungi, which can be discouraged by the use of cheshunt compound. This is made by mixing two ounces of very finely powdered copper sulphate with eleven ounces of finely powdered ammonium carbonate. The solution is prepared by adding one ounce of the dry mixture to two gallons of cold water, and should be used immediately. In boxes or pans the disease can be prevented by scrupulous cleanliness, very careful watering, and the avoidance of extremes of temperature, which will all help to forestall the onset.

RUSTS can be controlled by spraying with Bordeaux mixture or, better still, with a mixture of two ounces of Bouisol, three ounces of Sulsol, two ounces of soft soap, and five gallons of water. This is an exceptionally good spray for the garden, since it will both control mildew and rust and exterminate the green fly.

# NOTES ON THE USE OF THE GLOSSARY

| | |
|---|---|
| NOMENCLATURE | In all cases where the plant has been named as a compliment to its producer, or discoverer, the information has been indicated by the abbreviation "comm." |
| HEIGHT | The heights given at the end of each description are the approximate heights in feet to which the varieties will grow under *normal* conditions. |
| PERIOD OF FLOWERING | The months indicated are the months in which the plant gives its most effective display. In foliage plants, this may be taken to be the period in which the foliage exhibits the greatest range of colour. |
| HABIT | A further note indicates whether the plant is deciduous (D.) (leaf-losing), evergreen (E.), herbaceous (H.) (dying down to the root annually), or a bulbous-rooted plant (B.). |
| SPREAD | The next note indicates the scope of the plant, that is the approximate space to be allowed for its development. Thus 2-ft. Sq. indicates a space of two feet square (that is 4 square feet). |
| PROPAGATION | Another note indicates the best method of propagation. Sd. (from seed), Cg. (by cuttings of the green wood), Ch. (cuttings with a heel of old wood), Cr. (root cuttings), D. (division of the old root), bulblets (by aerial bulblets produced in leaf-axils), offsets (by means of offsets from the parent bulb), scales (outer scales removed from the parent bulb). The figures which follow these indicate the best month in which to do this. Thus Ch.6 means that the plant is best propagated from cuttings with a heel of the old wood during the month of June, and Cr.5 indicates root cuttings in May. |
| SOIL | Plants may be divided for the purpose into three classes:<br>(*a*) those needing acid soils—the final note A indicates this;<br>(*b*) those needing calcareous soils—the final note C indicates this; |

(*c*) those needing neutral soils—the final note N indicates this.

(*d*) The use of all three letters indicates that the plant is equally at home in any of the three classes of soil.

COLOUR

For some plants, there follows a note indicating the colour of the flower as matched by the Horticultural Colour Chart (Parts I and II) published by the Royal Horticultural Society in co-operation with the British Colour Council. In cases where the flowers have been definitely matched the sheet number is followed by a stroke and the shade number. It should be noted that colours are only true in daylight, preferably in a north light.

# GLOSSARY

**ABRONIA** (Nyctaginaceae), from G. abros—delicate, alluding to the bracts which enclose the buds.

This is a group of low-growing and trailing plants commonly called Sand Verbena, all of which are endemic in California. Generally treated as half-hardy annuals, the varieties which follow are perennial but unsuited to be grown as such in the more severe parts of the United Kingdom. The seed, from which they can be freely raised, should be soaked for twenty-four hours in water before it is sown. The plants should be grown in a sunny aspect in well-drained sandy loam. Varieties in cultivation are:—

A. CRUX-MALTAE (Flower shaped like a Maltese cross), California, which makes a tangled mat of green, rounded leaves, and bears heads of deep purple-pink flowers with greenish throats.
*½-ft. July–September. E. 1-ft. Sq. Sd8. N.*

A. LATIFOLIA (Broad-leaved), California, is of similar growth and has kidney-shaped leaves and clustered heads of honey-scented lemon-yellow flowers reminiscent of Verbena.
*½-ft. July–September. E. 1-ft. Sq. Sd3. N.*

A. UMBELLATA (Umbelled), California, is distinctive in its somewhat earlier appearance in flower, and its rather small flowers of pink, produced in clustered heads.
*½-ft. June–September. E. 1-ft. Sq. Sd3. N.*

**ACANTHUS** (Acanthaceae), from G. akantha—prickle, many of the species being spiny; a suggested alternative derivation is G. ake—point, anthos—flower.

A group of hardy perennial plants drawn mainly from southern Europe, which are hardy in this country. Generally known as Bear's Breeches. The varieties are also sometimes known as "the Architect's Plant," the leaves having inspired the design of the Corinthian capitals. They thrive in sunny or partially shaded sites and are well suited to growth in the larger herbaceous borders. Species in cultivation are:—

A. MOLLIS (Soft, downy), S. Europe, has the typical many-lobed leaves about two feet in length and about a foot in diameter, and bears its upstanding long spikes of white and blue or even rose flowers in July–August. *3-ft. July–August. E. 3-ft. Sq. D10 or 3. N.*

A. MOLLIS VAR. LATIFOLIUS (Wide-leaved), S. Europe, has broader leaves, is a little more hardy and slightly taller.
*3½-ft. July–August. E. 4-ft. Sq. D10 or 3. N.*

A. Perringii (comm.), Asia Minor, is also known as *A. Dioscoridis var. Perringii*, and in catalogues as *A. Caroli-Alexandri*, and is the smallest and most dainty of the species. The much-cut leaves rosette the ground and the short flower-spikes are tightly packed with rose-pink flowers, like a reduced and glamorised edition of its taller relatives. It is eminently suited to the front of the border or a special location in the rock garden.

*1-ft. July–August. E. 1½-ft. Sq. D*10 *or* 3. *N.*

A. spinosus (Spiny), S. Europe, resembles A. mollis but has spiny leaves and tall, erect and well-furnished spires of white flowers heavily flushed with purple.

*3-ft. July–August. E. 3-ft. Sq. D*10 *or* 3. *N.*

**ACHILLEA** (Compositae) comprises a very large group of plants named after the Greek hero Achilles, who was supposed to have used the plant medicinally.

The majority of the plants have large, umbelled, flat heads of flowers, are easy to grow, are not particular as to site, and can be propagated by tearing up the original root into small pieces. The better varieties in cultivation are:—

A. filipendulina (Hanging by threads), S.W. Europe, which is also called *A. Eupatorium*, and is known as the Fernleaf Yarrow. It forms a tall plant with green, ferny leaves and huge, flat heads of golden-yellow. *5-ft. July–August. D. 3-ft. Sq. D*10. *N.* 5/1. *Pl.* 35.

A. Millefolium (Many-leaved), Europe, is the Common Yarrow or Milfoil, with an attractive but compact garden relative in A. Millefolium var. roseum, which has pretty flat heads of pink flowers, and A. Millefolium Cerise Queen, which has crimson-cerise heads.

*2-ft. July–August. D. 3-ft. Sq. D*10. *N.*

A. Ptarmica (Sneeze-provoking), Europe and N. America, is the Sneezewort, and has in its double forms some exceedingly good garden varieties. A. sibirica (Siberian) is a neater and larger form. A. Ptarmica var. Boule de Neige, A. Ptarmica var. Pearl, and A. sibirica Perry's White all have double white flowers, with the latter the best of all. All form basal tufts of toothed green foliage.

*1½-ft. June–August. D. 3-ft. Sq. D*10. *N.*

**ACONITUM** (Ranunculaceae), from G. akon—dart; arrowheads were sometimes poisoned by dipping them into a preparation made from the juice of the plant.

The Monkshoods are all herbaceous perennials with tuberous or thickened roots, foliage resembling that of the Delphinium, and hooded flowers, generally of blue colour. All contain poisonous juices from

Chrysanthemum koreanum "Venus"

Cyclamen neapolitanum album

which aconite can be extracted. Propagation may be by division of the root or from seed. All prefer a rich soil, and are better grown in partially shaded sites—generally at the rear of the border.

A. ANTHORA (resembling Anthora), C. Europe, resembles the Common Monkshood in its habit of growth, but has shorter spikes of flowers of clear yellow, with the helmets brought to a peak at the front.
*2-ft. July–September. H. 2-ft. Sq. Sd2. D10 or 3. ANC.*

A. ANTHORA VAR. AUREUM (Golden), C. Europe, is similar but has flowers of deeper yellow.
*2-ft. July–September. H. 2-ft. Sq. Sd2. D10 or 3. ANC.*

A. CAMMARUM (old name), Hungary, has tall but loosely-built spikes of flowers with closed hoods of purplish-blue.
*4-ft. July–Sept. H. 2-ft. Sq. Sd2. D10 or 3. ANC.* 37 *and paler.*
[*Pl.* 34.

A. FISCHERI (comm.), N. America, is the progenitor of many garden varieties and is in itself very variable. The helmet is generally broader than it is high, and appears to be a pointed visor.
*6-ft. July–August. H. 2½-ft. Sq. Sd2. D10 or 3. ANC.*

A. FORTUNEI (comm.), China, once known as the *A. chinense* of gardens, is another tall-growing variety with its deep purple-blue flowers, produced very late into the year.
*6-ft. August–September. H. 2½-ft. Sq. Sd2. D10 or 3. ANC.*

A. JAPONICUM (Japanese) has leaves of a deep, shining green, and deep violet-blue flowers, rather large and wide, but in a loosely-constructed spike.
*3-ft. July–August. H. 2-ft. Sq. Sd2. D10 or 3. ANC.*

A. LYCOCTONUM (Wolf-killing), Siberia, is the Wolfsbane, and a strong-growing plant with deeply notched green leaves and spires of pale-yellow flowers with the hoods somewhat restricted at the mouth.
*3-ft. July–September. 2-ft. Sq. H. Sd2. D3 or 10. ANC.*

A. NAPELLUS (With root like that of the Turnip), Britain, is a variety suitable for a semi-shaded site, flowering very late in the year. The hooded, deep violet-blue and sombre flowers decorate in suitable fashion the most poisonous of the tribe. The individual helmets of the flowers are broad and peaked.
*3-ft. August–October. 2-ft. Sq. H. Sd2. D3 or 10. ANC.*

A. NAPELLUS ALBUM (White), Britain, is one of the few albino varieties which are more attractive than the parent.
*3-ft. August–October. H. 2-ft. Sq. Sd2. D3 or 10. ANC.*

A. NAPELLUS VAR. SPARKSII (comm.), garden origin, is the most attractive of the garden derivatives, and the tallest. The spikes, which are freely produced, have ample flowers of deep indigo-blue.
*6-ft. August–October. H. 3-ft. Sq. Sd2. D10 or 3. ANC.*

A. PANICULATUM (Bearing loose clusters), Europe, is appropriately named, the loose sprays of one-sided pale-blue flowers gaining in attractiveness by their diffusion.
*3-ft. August–October. H. 2-ft. Sq. Sd2. D3* or 10. *ANC.*

A. WILSONII (comm.), China, has flowers of variable colour shading from pale blue to deep violet-blue, borne in long, upstanding spires.
*5-ft. September–October. H. 3-ft. Sq. Sd2. D3* or 10. *ANC.*

**ACTAEA** (Ranunculaceae), from G. aktaia—the elder, the leaves of the plant resembling that tree.

A group of native plants useful to the gardener for the strong growing possibilities in shaded sites. Though generally more fitted for the wild garden, the varieties can be used in the back of the shady borders. Good, rich soil is the most suitable medium.

A. SPICATA (Spiked), Great Britain, the Baneberry, has small terminal clusters of rather insignificant white flowers, followed by purplish-black berries. *3-ft. May. H. 4-ft. Sq. D3. ANC.*

A. SPICATA ALBA (White) is similar except that the berries, which are freely produced in summer or autumn, are clear white.
*3-ft. May. H. 4-ft. Sq. D3. ANC.*

A. SPICATA RUBRA (Red) adds red berries to its other attractions.
*3-ft. May. H. 4-ft. Sq. D3. ANC.*

**ADENOPHORA** (Campanulaceae), from G. aden—gland, and phoreo—to bear.

A group of plants which bear a marked resemblance to Campanula but differ botanically in the disc surrounding the base of the pistil. All the varieties have thickened roots and resent division, preferring to be placed in rich, fertile soil in a sunny place.

A. BULLEYANA (comm.), China, has small, funnel-shaped, pale-blue flowers borne in loose clusters upon gracefully disposed, freely branching spires. Basal foliage is lance-shaped and toothed.
*4-ft. July–August. H. 2-ft. Sq. Sd3. ANC.*

A. FARRERI (comm.), China, is small in stature but has larger, bolder, deep-blue flowers of rather more bland appearance.
*2-ft. June–July. H. 1½-ft. Sq. Sd3. ANC.*

A. POTANINII (comm.), Turkestan, has toothed, pointed, oval leaves and bears large sprays of open-mouthed flowers of pale blue, rising on stems a yard or so in height.
*3-ft. June–July. H. 2-ft. Sq. Sd3. ANC.*

Cyclamen neapolitanum

Dahlia "Little Diamond"

A. VERTICILLATA (Whorled), Dahuria, produces its leaves, as its name indicates, in whorls, and its small, pinch-mouthed, pale blue flowers in well distributed array on fragile, wiry stems.

*3-ft. June–July. H. 1½-ft. Sq. Sd3. ANC.*

**ADONIS** (Ranunculaceae), from the name of the Greek god Adonis, whose blood is said to have stained the petals of one of the species.

As is fitting to that named after one of the gods, these plants thrive in a place in the sun. Delightful when they flower, they become gross and comfortable as the spring progresses, though in the mature leaves one discerns traces of their more youthful beauty.

A. AMURENSIS (From the Amur), Siberia. Capped golden goblets, enshrined in green, fern-like leaves, conspire to catch the nectar of the gods. *1-ft. March. H. 1-ft. Sq. Sd3. C.* 603.

A. AMURENSIS FL. PL. (Double-flowered) loses little of its fellow's charms in spite of its additional petals.

*1-ft. March. H. 1-ft. Sq. Sd2. C.* 603.

A. VERNALIS (Spring-flowering), Europe, adds size to the charm of its golden flowers, which persist only long enough to provide a memory and provoke an anticipated joy in all future springs.

*1-ft. March. H. 1-ft. Sq. Sd2. C.* 603.

**AETHIOPAPPUS** (Compositae) (probably derived from G. aitho—to burn, and L. pappus—down, from the bitter taste of the flights) is also CENTAUREA, which see.

**AGAPANTHUS** (Liliaceae) (from G. agape—love, and anthos—flower).

The African Lily, or Lily of the Nile, forms a tuberous root and brightly polished, bright-green, ribbon-like leaves, and bears umbels of blue lily flowers in late August and onwards. The larger varieties are undesirably tender, but the two varieties now mentioned, though smaller, are much hardier than their grander relations. Both varieties thrive in rich soil in sheltered sunny positions and are delightful planted lightly against a wall facing south, and in suitable soil.

A. UMBELLATUS VAR. MOOREANUS (Umbelled; comm.) grows to a height not exceeding eighteen inches and bears many clustered heads of rich, medium-blue flowers.

*1½-ft. August–September. H. 1-ft. Sq. Sd3. N.* 039/2. *Pl.* 34.

A. UMBELLATUS VAR. MOOREANUS ALBUS (White) is but a pale shadow of the glory which has, perhaps fortunately, preceded it.

*1½-ft. August–September. H. 1-ft. Sq. Sd3. N.*

**ALLIUM** (Liliaceae), from L. allium—garlic; or perhaps from Celtic all—pungent or burning; but withal a relative of the preceding, and of the Onion.

Nearly all the varieties possess the pungent smell of the culinary onion, and all except A. neapolitanum—the scent of which has appropriately taken flight—may be used with varying success as a substitute. Many of the varieties multiply with rapidity and may be relied upon quickly to produce progeny which in clustered communities add a touch of summer gratitude, though their breath be rude! Planted among low-growing, evergreen shrubs, the results can be astonishing.

A. ACUMINATUM (Long-pointed), British Columbia, has narrow green leaves and clustered heads of rose-purple to red flowers.
1-*ft.* *June.* *B.* 1-*ft. Sq.* *Sd*2. *N.*

A. CAERULEUM (Sky-blue), Siberia, has leaves of triangular cross-section and bears, upon long, slender stems, globular heads of sky-blue flowers. 3-*ft.* *May–June.* *B.* 1-*ft. Sq.* *Sd*2. *D*9. *N.*

A. GIGANTEUM (Giant), Himalayas, has wide, strap-shaped leaves and immense heads of pink flowers on four-foot stems.
4-*ft.* *May–June.* *B.* 1-*ft. Sq.* *Sd*2. *D*9. *N.*

A. MOLY (comm.), Europe, is the Golden Garlic, with wide, strap-shaped leaves and with large, bright-yellow flowers in rounded clusters. 1½-*ft.* *May–June.* *B.* 1-*ft. Sq.* *Sd*2. *D*9. *N.*

A. ROSENBACHIANUM (comm.), Turkestan, has wide, smoother, green leaves and a large round head of rose-purple.
1-*ft.* *June.* *B.* 1-*ft. Sq.* *Sd*2. *D*9. *N.*

**ALSTROEMERIA** (Amaryllidaceae) was named in honour of Baron Alstroemer, a Swedish botanist.

All the varieties selected thrive in light but rich soil in sunny aspects. The Peruvian Lily is perfectly hardy and should be planted at least twelve inches deep.

A. AURANTIACA (Golden-orange), Chile, bears umbelled flowers of bright yellow spotted with brown on long stems from clustered, lance-like leaves.
3-*ft.* *June–September.* *H.* 2-*ft. Sq.* *Sd*10. *D*3. *N.* 11 *marked with* 7 [*and speckled* 827. *Pl.* 47.

A. AURANTIACA SPLENDENS (Shining) is an improved form, a little brighter and larger, and a little more self-satisfied.
3-*ft.* *June–September.* *H.* 2-*ft. Sq.* *Sd*10. *D*3. *N.*

A. CHILIENSIS (Chilean), Chile, is similar in growth and has flowers which may be white or pink or red, and good, bad, or indifferent according to taste!
3-*ft.* *June–September.* *H.* 2-*ft. Sq.* *Sd*10. *D*3. *N.*

A. PELEGRINA (Exotic), Chile, is less obtrusive in growth, clearly more refined, and has larger flowers of lilac, decorated with rose-purple.

*2-ft. June–September. H. 1½-ft. Sq. Sd10. D3. N.*

A. PULCHELLA (Beautiful but small), Brazil, is also known as *A. psittacina*, the Parrot Lily, and has dark red flowers tipped with bright green, and powdered with brown beauty-patches. It thrives best in a position of maximum sun.

*2½-ft. June–September. H. 2-ft. Sq. Sd10. D3. N.*

**ALTHAEA** (Malvaceae), from G. althaia—a healing medium, having reference to its use in medicine.

Generally a race of biennials, a few perennials figure among the genus, the best-known of which is the Marshmallow.

A. ROSEA (Rose), China, is the forerunner of the garden Hollyhock, which has probably taken into its strain *A. ficifolia*, the Fig-leaved Hollyhock, to give rise to a strain of plants variable both in colour and growth. The general characteristics are that the plant rises to a length of from six to nine feet, with basal rough, green, five- or seven-angled leaves, produced also at intervals upon the flowering stem. Colours vary from white to yellow, pink to dark red, and include some parti-colours. There are also double-flowered varieties. Culture requires a moderately fertile soil, and a space of approximately one square yard per plant; in the herbaceous border a little less space may be left. Propagation is from seed, except where individual varieties are required, when both eyes and cuttings may be rooted, and careful and generally surgical division must be practised. Seed is sown in early autumn, plants are potted on as soon as large enough, to flower the same season.

*9-ft. August–September. H. 3-ft. Sq. Sd9. C5. D4. ANC.*

**ALYSSUM** (Cruciferae), from G. a—no, lyssa—madness, from its traditional use as a cure for the bite of a mad dog.

In reality very dwarf shrubs, the following figure by usage as border plants.

A. SAXATILE (Rock-loving), Europe, presents an intriguing picture, intermingling the conventional silver and gold, and its prevalence in all gardens fails to prevent its due appreciation by all except those who call it brazen.

*1-ft. May–June. E. 2-ft. Sq. Sd8. ANC.* 3.

A. SAXATILE CITRINUM (Lemon-yellow) is similar but has flowers of pale—nay, moonlight—yellow.

*1-ft. May–June. E. 2-ft. Sq. Sd8. ANC.* 602/1.

A. SAXATILE DUDLEY NEVILL (comm.) loses the so-called brassiness of its progenitor and gains instead the tone of old ivory.

*1-ft. May–June. E. 2-ft. Sq. Sd8. ANC.* 4/2.

A. SAXATILE FL. PL. (Double-flowered) adds to its larger, double flowers the charm of greater neatness of growth, which renders it a more tractable plant for the front of the border.
*½-ft. May–June. E. 1½-ft. Sq. Cg7. ANC.* 4/2.

**AMARYLLIS** (Amaryllidaceae), from the name of a classical shepherdess.

One can excuse the owner of such a name for being tender—indeed, one may probably expect it! Planted against a south wall in a good soil, the species selected delights the eye in late summer and early autumn.

A. BELLADONNA (Pretty Lady), Cape of Good Hope, has green, strap-like leaves and produces, in autumn, stout stems with clustered heads of rose-pink lily flowers, each about three inches in length.
*3-ft. September. B. 1-ft. Sq. Sd3. AN. Half-hardy.*

**ANAGALLIS** (Primulaceae), from G. anagallo—to decorate: undoubtedly as a decorative plant. Another derivation suggested is from G. anagelao—to laugh, possibly because of its beauty being conducive to contentment.

All the species which follow are doubtfully hardy in exposed places, but can be raised readily from seed and are charming at the front of the border.

A. LINIFOLIA (With flax-like leaves), from S. Europe, makes a tangled mat of intertwining stems and produces large, cobalt-blue flowers, each with a reddish-purple eye and yellow stamens, strikingly beautiful in the mass. It calls for cultivation in good but light soil.
*½-ft. May–October. E. 1-ft. Sq. Cg4. Sd3. N.* 43/1.

A. LINIFOLIA VAR. MONELLI (comm.), Spain, is neater, and the small leaves are of polished green. The flowers, which are very freely produced, are bright orange-scarlet. Cultivation similar.
*½-ft. May–October. E. 1-ft. Sq. Cg4. Sd3. N.* 14/1.

**ANCHUSA** (Boraginaceae), from G. anchusa—alkanet, the name given to an early aid to the complexion made from A. tinctoria. An alternative derivation is suggested in G. ancho—to choke, the neck of the corolla being congested with hairs.

The flowers of all varieties are edible, and at least add brightness to an otherwise dull salad! Culture is easy in good, fertile soil, and the plant thrives best in a sunny position.

A. BARRELIERII (comm.), Asia Minor, has the typical rough, green, pointed, oval foliage, and bears clustered heads of bright-blue flowers with white corolla tubes and yellow throats.
*2-ft. May–June. H. 2-ft. Sq. D3. Sd8. N.*

Dahlia "Tip" ABCEFG

Dahlia "Electros" JKNO

Dahlia "Blenheim" GHLM

Dahlia "Scarlet Queen" ABEFGK

Dahlia "Bishop of Llandaff" CDGH

Dahlia "Townley Welcome" KLMNOPQ

A. ITALICA (Italian), Mediterranean region, is best in its garden forms, of which A. ITALICA DROPMORE VARIETY is five feet in height and has large flowers of brilliant cobalt-blue; it is one of the brightest of all garden flowers.—A. ITALICA OPAL is similar in height but has flowers of opal-blue.—A. ITALICA PRIDE OF DOVER has less inches, only reaching three feet in height, and has large flowers of clear bright blue.—A. ITALICA MORNING GLORY reaches three feet and nas flowers of brilliant blue.

*Variable. May–June. H. 2-ft. Sq. Sd9. D3. ANC.*

ANCHUSA ITALICA

A. MYOSOTIDIFLORA (Forget-me-not-flowered), Siberia, is also known as *Brunnera macrophylla*, and is delightful in the spring when its branching sprays of bright flax-blue forget-me-not flowers are produced upon plants with small bright green leaves. Unfortunately, the plant becomes much more leafy with age and deserves then its new name. *2-ft. May–June. H. 2-ft. Sq. Sd9. D4. ANC.*

**ANEMONE** (Ranunculaceae), derived from L. anemone—daughter of the wind; hence Windflower.

Comprise a very large and beautiful genus from which a representative selection for the herbaceous border is somewhat difficult to achieve.

A. CANADENSIS (Canadian), N. America, is also known as *A. pennsylvanica* and *A. dichotoma*, and has green, palmately divided leaves and rather large, solitary flowers of clear white with golden stamens. It thrives best in a semi-shaded spot in light but leafy soil.

*1½-ft. May–August. H. 2-ft. Sq. D3. ANC.*

A. CORONARIA (Crown-like), Mediterranean region, is the specific name for the group comprising the St. Brigid Anemones, which produces poppy-like flowers of every shade of colour and combination of colours, except yellow. They are tuberous-rooted and grow well in any well-drained soil in a sunny site. To flower in the early spring the tubers should be planted in September, two inches deep and four inches apart, and in the severest of winters covered with a layer of bracken or straw.

*⅓-ft. March–May. B. ⅓-ft. Sq. Sd8. D8. ANC.*

A. FULGENS (Shining), Greece, is also known as *A. hortensis var. fulgens*, and is another tuberous-rooted anemone with green palmate leaves, and thrives in hot, dry surroundings, where the soil is fertile. It is particularly good planted in grass about the boles of deciduous trees. The brilliant scarlet flowers with their black anthers are borne on foot-long stems. Horticultural varieties are A. FULGENS FL. PL., a double-flowered form, and A. FULGENS ANNULATA, with a central ring of paler colour.

1-*ft. March–April. ⅓-ft. Sq. B. Sd8. D8. ANC.* 819/1.

A. HEPATICA (Liver-shaped—the leaves), Europe, is a very dwarf plant with three-cornered lobed leaves, and with small, deep-lavender flowers with pale yellow stamens. It is best planted in rich but moist, well-drained soil, preferably in semi-shade. It resents division. It has numerous colour forms ranging from white to rose and deep lavender, and is available also with many-petalled flowers.

*⅓-ft. March. 1-ft. Sq. H. D9. ANC.* 640.

A. HEPATICA ANGULOSA (Angled) differs in having rougher and more angular foliage, divided generally into three or five lobes, and possessing larger flowers which are correspondingly more beautiful.

*½-ft. March. H. 1-ft. Sq. D9. ANC.* 640.

A. JAPONICA (Japanese), Japan, China, produces green leaves made up of three-lobed or cut leaflets, and produced upon long, leafy stems rising to a length of about three feet. The colour varies from white and lavender to rose and deep red. A. Japonica has no idiosyncrasies about soil, and seems incredibly indifferent as to whether it will grow in sun or shade. It is, however, best planted and left alone. The recognised garden varieties are:—

*Single-flowered*

Alice, rose-carmine
elegans, pale-rose
Géant des Blondes, white
Honorine Joubert, white
Lorelei, silver-pink
Prince Henry, rose-red
rubra, red
Stuttgardia, deep pink

*Semi-double and double*

Autumn Queen, rose-pink
Beauté parfaite, white
Herbstrose, rose
Kriemhilde, lilac-purple
Louise Uhink, white
Magdalena Uhink, deep rose
Mignon, silver-pink
Mont Rose, pink
Profusion, rose
Whirlwind, double, white

3-*ft. September–October. H. 2-ft. Sq. D3. ANC.*

Dahlia "Furore"

Delphinium "Persimmon" CFGK

Delphinium Ruysii ABEFHGLM
Delphinium "Wendy" EJKLNOPQ

A. JAPONICA HUPEHENSIS (From Hupeh), China, is a dwarf variative which may have flowers of dirty lilac, dingy pink, or of bright rose-crimson, according to the strain from which it springs. A good plant is a treasured possession, a poor one should be speeded upon its path to the everlasting bonfire!

*2-ft. September–October. H. 2-ft. Sq. D3. ANC.*

A. NARCISSIFLORA (Narcissus-flowered), Europe, carries its clusters of apple blossoms with modesty upon stiff, foot-high stems above fan-like green foliage, and is always good.

*1-ft. May. H. 1-ft. Sq. D3. ANC.*

A. NEMOROSA (Of the glades), Europe, is the Wood Anemone, generally of pale lavender or of white, and suited to the front of the fully shaded border. It thrives best in light, leafy soil, and has as variatives: A. NEMOROSA ALBA FL. PL., with double white flowers, A. NEMOROSA ALLENII, with lavender-blue flowers, A. NEMOROSA BLUE BONNET, with deeper blue flowers, and A. NEMOROSA ROBINSONIANA, with blue flowers backed with white. A. NEMOROSA RUBRA is purplish.

*½-ft. May. H. 1-ft. Sq. D7. N.*

A. PULSATILLA (Shaking in the wind), Europe, is the Pasque-Flower, with finely-cut and youthfully pubescent foliage, and heavily tasselled, nodding flowers of deep lavender-blue containing the clustered golden anthers. There is considerable variation, some of the plants producing flowers with petals mean both in colour and size. A good form of A. Pulsatilla is worth prizing and can be propagated from cuttings of the root. The best forms are:—

| | |
|---|---|
| alba Snow Queen | white |
| Eva Constance | tawny scarlet |
| Farreri | deep violet |
| Mrs. van der Elst | glowing pink |
| rubra | red-purple |

All the varieties thrive best in hard, hot, limy soil, but A. Pulsatilla Mrs. van der Elst is somewhat capricious and needs the benefit of a rock garden, scree, or a choice spot in a special bed, preferably with a little shade. *1-ft. April–May. H. 1-ft. Sq. Sd7. Cr7. N.*

A. RANUNCULOIDES (Like a Buttercup), Europe, resembles a miniature A. nemorosa, but with daintier foliage of bronze-green, which forms a fitting foil for the cup-shaped golden-yellow flowers. Used with discretion at the front of a sunny border it can be very effective. There is a double-flowered form, A. RANUNCULOIDES FL. PL.

*¼-ft. April–May. H. 1-ft. Sq. D9. A. 3/1.*

A. SYLVESTRIS (Of the woods), Europe, is the Snowdrop Anemone, delightful in a shady border, and producing large, clear-white flowers, sometimes backed with pink, upon fifteen-inch stems.

*1½-ft. May–June. H. 1½-ft. Sq. D9. N. White.*

A. VITIFOLIA (With vine-leaves) is a tall plant with attractively shaped green foliage and loose heads of large, clear-white flowers produced in July–August.
*3-ft. July–August. H. 2-ft. Sq. D3. N. White.*

**ANEMONOPSIS** (Ranunculaceae), from Anemone, and G. opsis—resemblance.

A. MACROPHYLLA (Long-leaved), Japan, has flowers more reminiscent of the Jonquil, of waxy white overlaid with blue and violet, and is fitted to be an inhabitant of the shady border in carefully prepared light leafy soil. *1½-ft. May–June. H. 1-ft. Sq. D9. A.*

**ANOMATHECA** (Iridaceae), from G. anomos—irregular, and theka—capsule, referring to the seed pod.

A. CRUENTA (Blood-red), South Africa, is a pretty little irid very like a miniature Gladiolus in growth, bearing a spray of starlike salmon-pink flowers with the base of the petals stained with crimson. As an aid to retaining colour in the border it may be used in patches at the front, when it will provide a colourful area late into the year.
*⅓-ft. August–September. B. ¼-ft. Sq. Sd4. N.* 620/1.

**ANTHEMIS** (Compositae), from G. anthemon—flower.

An attractive group of plants with flowers like those of the Marguerite.

A. SANCTI-JOHANNIS (St. John's) makes a dwarf-growing, semi-shrubby plant with bright green, much-cut foliage, and many daisy flowers of bright orange on medium-length stems.
*1½-ft. May–October. H. 1½-ft. Sq. Cg6. N. Pl.* 1.

A. TINCTORIA (Used for dyeing), Europe, is generally a little taller and produces flowers a little larger, for a very long period. The basic colour is yellow and varies slightly in the following:—A. TINCTORIA BUXTON'S VARIETY, pale yellow; A. TINCTORIA KELWAYI, deep yellow; A. TINCTORIA KELWAYI ALBA, creamy-white; A. TINCTORIA PERRY'S VARIETY, bright golden-yellow; A. TINCTORIA SULPHUR QUEEN, pale yellow.
*2-ft.–3-ft. May–October. H. 2-ft. Sq. Cg6. N.* 1/2 *to* 1/3. *Pl.* 1.

**ANTHERICUM** (Liliaceae), from G. anthos—flower, and herkos—hedge, allusive to the growth of some of the species.

A. LILIAGO (the Silvery—St. Bernard's—Lily) has large green, grassy leaves with slender stems bearing silvery-white lily flowers in loose sprays. Requires a sunny position in light loam.
*1½-ft. June–July. H. 1½-ft. Sq. D3. Sd3. N. White.*

A. LILIAGO GIGANTEUM and A. LILIAGO MAJOR are varieties which grow considerably taller in height.

*3-ft. June–July. H. 2-ft. Sq. D3. Sd3. N. White.*

A. RAMOSUM (With many branches), Europe, is similar but has branching stems and smaller white flowers.

*2-ft. June–July. H. 1½-ft. Sq. D3. Sd3. N. White.*

**APHYLLANTHES** (Liliaceae), from G. a—not, without, and phyllon—leaf.

A. MONSPELIENSIS (Of Montpellier), North Africa, makes a mat of green rush leaves which will upon occasion emit small blue lily flowers from the tips, and which flowers a little better in a spot shaded from the hottest sun. *½-ft. June–July. E. 1-ft. Sq. D4. A.*

**AQUILEGIA** (Ranunculaceae), from L. aquila—eagle, the flower having some resemblance to an eagle's foot.

All varieties of the Columbine prefer a light but retentive soil which does not dry out in hot weather, and may be grown with equal success in either sunny or semi-shaded sites. *Pl. 2.*

A. ALPINA (Alpine), Europe, is a comparatively dwarf species suited to the herbaceous border, with pendent flowers of deep, clear blue with golden hearts. The form known as HENSOL HAREBELL, which breeds comparatively true from seed (a remarkable thing in a genus producing many captivating mongrels), is probably the best garden form of the type.

*1½-ft. May–June. H. 1-ft. Sq. Sd2. N.* 637.

A. CAERULEA (Heavenly blue), Colorado, is variable and can, at least in cultivation, be either dwarf or tall. The tall variety is especially suited to the border and bears large flowers of sky-blue with a white corolla. *2-ft. May–June. H. 1-ft. Sq. Sd7. N.* 642.

A. CANADENSIS (Canadian), Nova Scotia, is also variable, ranging from two feet in the maximum to eight inches in the case of the variety A. CANADENSIS NANA. The sepals and spurs are of bright red and the petal limbs of clear golden-yellow.

*2-ft. May–June. H. 1-ft. Sq. Sd7. N.* 17/1.

A. CHRYSANTHA (Golden-yellow-flowering), Rocky Mountains, is a still taller variety, with large flowers with straight spurs up to two inches in length. *3-ft. May–June. H. 1½-ft. Sq. Sd7. N.*

A. HYBRIDA (Hybrid), garden origin, consists in the main of hybrids obtained by crossing A. caerulea, A. chrysantha, and latterly A. canadensis, and in the modern types has long-spurred flowers with sepals and petals of contrasting colours. Of the named varieties Mrs. Nicholls, with large, long-spurred flowers of powder-blue with white petal limbs, and Crimson Star, with crimson sepals and white petals, are outstanding.

*2½-ft. May–June. H. 1½-ft. Sq. Sd7. N.*

A. longissima (The longest), Texas, is in its original form one of the quaintest of all the Columbines. Its pale-yellow flowers, slightly pink without, have long spurs exceeding five inches in length, which have peculiar beauty in their graceful distribution. Since its introduction it has given rise to many hybrids with exceptionally long spurs of all colours, and is worth being given a place in every garden.

*2-ft. July–August. H. 1½-ft. Sq. Sd9. N.*

A. Skinneri (comm.), Mexico, has yellowish-green sepals shading to deep pink in the spurs, with the petals of clear yellow.

*3-ft. June–July. H. 1½-ft. Sq. Sd8. N.*

A. vulgaris (Common), Europe, is the wild Columbine of the woods, with short, incurved spurs, and of variable colour. It can be found clad in white, pink, purple, and deep purple-blue, with single and with double flowers, but lacks the sophistication of the varieties with the large and more graceful spurs.

*2-ft. May–June. H. 1½-ft. Sq. Sd9. N.*

**ARABIS** (Cruciferae); the name is derived from the Arabic, but its meaning is obscure.

All are useful plants with comparatively long flowering periods, suitable for the front of the border, or for places where dwarf-flowering ground cover is required.

A. albida (White), Europe, is also known as *A. caucasica* and has rough, grey-green, notched leaves with sprays of four-petalled white flowers. Is so easily grown that it ranks in vigour with some of the other well-known weeds. Any piece torn off and planted will grow.

*¾-ft. March–June. E. 1½-ft. Sq. Ch7. N. White.*

A. albida fl. pl. (Double-flowered) is an attractive double-flowered variative with the individual flowers resembling double white Stocks, and is less invasive. A. albida "Taplow Rose" is similar but has pink flowers. *¾-ft. March–June. E. 1½-ft. Sq. Ch7. N. White.*

A. aubrietioides (Resembling Aubrieta), Europe, is a plant resembling A. albida but with flowers of clear soft rose. It is fortunately less rapacious than A. albida, and is sufficiently bright and easily grown to be among the best of the edging plants.

*¾-ft. March–June. E. 1-ft. Sq. Ch7. N.* 630/1.

A. blepharophylla (With fringed leaves), California, can be, in a good form, a very fine plant with rough, flat green rosettes and sprays of large deep-rose flowers on stout stems.

*¾-ft. April–June. E. ¾-ft. Sq. Sd8. N.*

A. LUCIDA (Shining), Europe, is a very brightly variegated plant with very clear white flowers. It grows, as a rule, much more sedately.

*¾-ft. April–May. E. ½-ft. Sq. Cg6. N.*

A. RUBELLA (Shining red), garden origin, is a hybrid with a multiplicity of names, *A. albida Rosabelle*, *A. Rosabella* and *A. albida coccinea* being among them. It is very similar in growth to A. albida, but has the largest and brightest pink flowers of all the pink-flowered types.

*¾-ft. April–June. E. 1-ft. Sq. Cg7. N.* 630.

**ARMERIA** (Plumbaginaceae), probably from the Celtic are-mor—by the sea.

The Sea Pinks are hardy evergreen plants, many of which are suitable for employment in the herbaceous border. All varieties are of easy cultivation, preferably in soil of reasonably light texture.

A. CEPHALOTES (Bearing large heads of flowers), S. Europe, is also known as *A. latifolia* and *A. pseudo-Armeria.* It grows to a height of sixteen to eighteen inches and has wide, grassy foliage and clustered flower-heads of rose-lilac, borne upon slender but wiry stems.

*1½-ft. April–June. E.* 1-ft. *Sq. D9. N.*

A. CEPHALOTES BEES' RUBY, garden origin, is one of the deepest-coloured of the varieties of A. cephalotes.

*1½-ft. April–June. E. 1-ft. Sq. D9. N.*

A. CEPHALOTES SPLENDENS (Shining) is similar but has flowers of bright rose. *1½-ft. April–June. E. 1-ft. Sq. D9. N.*

A. PLANTAGINEA (Plantain-like), Europe, has wide, grassy leaves and bears somewhat smaller flower-heads in the same range of colours.

*2-ft. April–June. E. 1-ft. Sq. D9. N.*

A. PLANTAGINEA GIGANTEA (Giant) is a still larger variation, sometimes reaching a height of three feet.

*3-ft. April–June. E. 1-ft. Sq. D9. N.*

**ARTEMISIA** (Compositae), from the G. Artemis, the Goddess of the Chase.

A group of plants many of which are more properly shrubs with hard, woody and persistent stems, but with a number which may be treated as herbaceous perennials, and be lifted and divided in October or March. All thrive in sunny sites in well-drained soil. The general characteristic is the gracefully cut foliage, invariably aromatic, and the contrasting value of its silver or grey tones.

A. BAUMGARTENI (comm.), S.E. Europe, is a many-stemmed plant with delicate wands of greenish-grey foliage, pendent at the tip of each shoot. Flowers are golden and of little value.

*1½-ft. June. H. 1-ft. Sq. Cg7. D9. N.*

A. LACTIFLORA (Milk—, i.e. white-flowered), China, is the White Mugwort, and makes a large plant with chrysanthemum-like foliage, green and smooth above, and mealy below. The flowers, borne in loose panicles, are small but are densely whitened.

*4-ft. June. H. 3-ft. Sq. D9. N.*

A. LUDOVICIANA (comm.), N.W. America, is the Cudweed Wormwood. It has almost uncut ovate leaves, white and woolly both above and below, and spiral heads of small white flowers.

*1½-ft. June. H. 2-ft. Sq. D9. N.*

A. NUTANS (Nodding), S.E. Europe, is somewhat similar in character but a little more dwarf, and of intense silvery-grey, and forms the perfect foil for plants with blue flowers.

*1¼-ft. June. H. 1-ft. Sq. Cg7. D9. N.*

A. STELLERIANA (comm.), N. America, has the attractive common names Beach Wormwood, Dusty Miller, Old Woman, and is variable according to the circumstances under which it is grown. It may be any height from one to three feet. The foliage, shaped like that of the Chrysanthemum, is silvery-white, and though the yellow flowers are inconspicuous, the plant presents an enchanting sight in the mixed border when carefully placed.

*1-ft.–3-ft. June. H. 3-ft. Sq. D9. N.*

A. VULGARIS (Common), Europe, is the Mugwort, and is very similar to A. lactiflora, dark green above, and very white and woolly beneath. The flowers, which again are tiny, are yellow, and borne in loose spires. *3-ft. June. H. 3-ft. Sq. D9. N.*

**ARTHROPODIUM** (Liliaceae), from G. arthron—joint, and pous, gen. podos—foot: from the appearance of the tuberous root.

A. CIRRHATUM (With tendril-like stems), New Zealand, sends up thin stems which bear long, thin, grass-like leaves and foot-wide sprays of small white lily flowers of appealing distribution. Light soil and full sunshine are the correct conditions for its adequate growth.

*3-ft. July. H. 2-ft. Sq. D3. A.*

**ASCLEPIAS** (Asclepiadaceae), from Aesculapius, the Graeco-Roman God of Medicine.

The common name is Milkweed or Silkweed. All are of comparatively easy cultivation in moderately rich soil in the herbaceous border, and the habit of growth of many of them makes them suitable also to the wild garden.

A. CURASSAVICA (probably from the island of Curaçao), Tropical America, is hardy only if well protected during the winter months. Stems and leaves bear some resemblance to those of the Lily, and the flower-heads are borne in terminal clusters or in clusters produced from the leaf axils. The corollas of its flowers are purplish-red and the centres of bright orange.

2-*ft.* *July–August.* *H.* 2-*ft. Sq.* *D*3. *N.*

A. INCARNATA (Flesh-coloured), N. America, is a plant for damp situations; is taller than the preceding, and has similar flowers of rose-purple. 3½-*ft.* *July–August.* *H.* 2-*ft. Sq.* *D*3. *N.*

A. SYRIACA (From Syria), N. America, is also known as A. Cornuti, and in a good garden form has clustered heads of purple to lilac flowers, produced with great freedom.

4-*ft.* *July–August.* *H.* 3-*ft. Sq.* *D*3. *N.*

A. TUBEROSA (Producing tubers) is alternatively known as the Butterfly Weed or Pleurisy Root and is probably the most attractive garden plant of the genus with its lightly clustered heads of bright-orange flowers.

2-*ft.* *July–August.* *H.* 2-*ft. Sq.* *D*3. *Sd*3. *N.* 15/1. 1/1. *Pl.* 46.

**ASPHODELINE** (Liliaceae), from G. a—not, and sphallo—to supplant, denoting that the plant would be difficult to surpass in beauty.

A. LUTEA (Yellow), Mediterranean region, is the Yellow Asphodel, the original Asphodel which will flourish in good garden soil in a sunny or partly sunny site. The basal leaves are long, flat, thin, and green, and the long flowering stem carries a spire of yellow starry flowers.

2½-*ft.* *June–July.* *H.* 2-*ft. Sq.* *D*3. *Sd*3. *N.*

A. LUTEA FL. PL. (Double-flowered), garden origin, has double flowers but is otherwise similar.

2½-*ft.* *June–July.* *H.* 2-*ft. Sq.* *D*3. *Sd*3. *N.*

**ASPHODELUS** (Liliaceae). The name is similarly derived as that of Asphodeline. Cultural conditions are identical.

A. ACAULIS (Stemless), Atlas Mountains, is a tiny gem with long, rounded, rush-like leaves formed into a sprawling rosette, bearing in the centre a cluster of deep pink buds which open into pale pink lily flowers about two inches in diameter. Owing to its early flowering it is best suited to growing in an unheated greenhouse, where its undoubted beauty will remain unspoiled.

½-*ft.* *January.* *H.* 1-*ft. Sq.* *D*7. *N.*

A. ALBUS (White), Mediterranean region, is similar in appearance to Asphodeline lutea, except for its leaves of triangular cross-section and its white flowers, and is of similar culture.

2-*ft.* *May–June.* *H.* 1½-*ft. Sq.* *D*3. *Sd*3. *N.* *White.*

A. FISTULOSUS (Holed, porous), S. Europe, is a little more dwarf and has the distinction of having a brown stripe on the centre of each petal.

1½-*ft.* *June–July.* *H.* 1-*ft. Sq.* *D*3. *Sd*3. *N.* *White.*

A. RAMOSUS (Many-branched), S. Europe, takes its name from the branching character of its inflorescence, which makes it the most striking variety. The flowering stems are taller and the flowers clear white with a purplish stripe.

*5-ft. May–June. H. 2-ft. Sq. D3. Sd3. N. White.*

**ASTER** (Compositae), from G. aster—star.

Aster comprises a large genus, abounding in good things for the garden, many of them considerably improved by cultivation and developed by hybridisation. All the varieties described are completely perennial, and do not include the so-called China Aster—whose botanical name is Callistephus. All perennial Asters flourish best if planted in moderately good garden soil, and benefit from periodic division. A vast range of variety exists in the genus which comprises plants both tall and short, early- and late-flowering, flowering in clusters or upon single stems, and useful from the front to the back of the border. The genus Aster may well be described as one of the maids-of-all-work of the herbaceous border.

A. ACRIS (Pungent), S. Europe, in spite of being the first variety to be mentioned, is one of the most fascinating. The leaves are very small, but of bright, almost vivid, green, and the clustered heads contain numberless pale-violet, orange-centred flowers whose petals are not so regular as those of the other types and present a picture of carelessly assumed beauty which is refreshing in a genus the only fault of which is, perhaps, that its flowers are too regular.

*2½-ft. June. H. 2-ft. Sq. D3. ANC.* 636. *Pl.* 49.

A. ACRIS VAR. NANUS (Small), S. Europe, is a diminutive variant which seldom exceeds fifteen inches in height and is a delightful occupant of the front of the border, where it can exert its charms to the full.

*1¼-ft. May–June. H. 2-ft. Sq. D3. ANC.*

A. AMELLUS (the name given by Virgil to an Aster-like plant), Europe, Asia, is the large-flowered type. The leaves are rough and hairy, almost spathulate; the flowers have the distinguishing large orange disc and, in the type, purple ray florets which make the individual flower about two inches in diameter and are borne in many-flowered clusters on plants that vary from eighteen inches to two feet high. The named varieties of great merit are:—

| | | | | |
|---|---|---|---|---|
| Beauté Parfaite | purple | *1½-ft.* | *July–August* | *1½-ft. Sq.* |
| Beauty of Ronsdorf | lilac-rose | *2-ft.* | *July–August* | *1½-ft. Sq.* |
| Friquet | pale-pink | *2-ft.* | *July–August* | *1½-ft. Sq.* |
| General Pershing | light pink | *2-ft.* | *July–September* | *2-ft. Sq.* |
| Heinrich Siebert | blue | *1½-ft.* | *July–August* | *2-ft. Sq.* |
| Hermann Lons | pale blue | *2-ft.* | *July–August* | *2-ft. Sq.* |
| King George | violet-blue | *1½-ft.* | *July–September* | *1½-ft. Sq.* |

[636. *Pl.* 3

Delphinium "Isla" ABEFJKNORS

Delphinium "Mrs. Townley Parker" CDGHLMPQTU

Delphinium "W. B. Cranfield" ABEFJKNORS Delphinium "Innocence" CDGHLMPQTU

| | | | | |
|---|---|---|---|---|
| La France | rosy-mauve | 2-*ft.* | *July–August* | 1½-*ft. Sq.* |
| Mignon | dark blue | 2-*ft.* | *July–August* | 2-*ft. Sq.* |
| Onward | blue | 1½-*ft.* | *July–August* | 1½-*ft. Sq.* |
| Perle Rose | rose-pink | 2-*ft.* | *July–August* | 2-*ft. Sq.* |
| Perry's Favourite | pale pink | 2-*ft.* | *July–August* | 2-*ft. Sq.* |
| Pink Pearl | pink | 1½-*ft.* | *July–August* | 1½-*ft. Sq.* |
| Preziosa | purple | 2-*ft.* | *July–August* | 2-*ft. Sq.* |
| Queen Mary | lavender-purple | 2-*ft.* | *July–August* | 2-*ft. Sq.* |
| Rotfeuer | red | 2-*ft.* | *July–August* | 2-*ft. Sq.* |
| Rudolf Goethe | lavender-blue | 2-*ft.* | *July–September* | 2-*ft. Sq.* |
| Sonia | bright rose | 2-*ft.* | *July–August* | 2-*ft. Sq.* [633/1. *Pl.* 3 |
| Ultramarine | mid violet-blue | 2-*ft.* | *July–August* | 2-*ft. Sq.* |
| Variety | violet-blue | 2-*ft.* | *July–September* | 2-*ft. Sq.* |
| Wells' Favourite | rose-pink | 2-*ft.* | *July–August* | 2-*ft. Sq.* |
| W. Robinson | rose-red | 1½-*ft.* | *July–August* | 1½-*ft. Sq.* |

A. CORDIFOLIUS (With heart-shaped leaves) is the blue Wood-Aster from N. America, which rises to a height of from one and a half to five feet and bears large and diffuse heads of flowers which are small individually, but are of such wide distribution that they are extremely impressive. In the type, the ray florets are pale violet-blue.
5-*ft.* *August–September.* *H.* 3-*ft. Sq.* *D*3. *ANC.*

A. CORDIFOLIUS IDEAL has pale blue flowers.
3-*ft.* *August–September.* *H.* 3-*ft. Sq.* *D*3. *ANC.*

A. CORDIFOLIUS NANCY has pale-purple flowers.
4-*ft.* *August–September.* *H.* 3-*ft. Sq.* *D*3. *ANC.*

A. CORDIFOLIUS PROFUSION has lavender flowers.
4-*ft.* *August–September.* *H.* 3-*ft. Sq.* *D*3. *ANC.*

A. CORDIFOLIUS SILVER SPRAY has white flowers.
4-*ft.* *August–September.* *H.* 3-*ft. Sq.* *D*3. *ANC.* *Pl.* 6.

A. ERICOIDES (Resembling Heath), E. N. America, is similar in appearance, the basal leaves being smaller and almost spathulate and the flowers smaller and generally white or very pale pink.
3-*ft.* *August–September.* *H.* 3-*ft. Sq.* *D*3. *ANC.* *Pl.* 6.

A. ERICOIDES BLUE STAR has lavender-blue flowers.
3-*ft.* *August–September.* *H.* 3-*ft. Sq.* *D*3. *ANC.*

A. ERICOIDES CHASTITY has white flowers.
3-*ft.* *August–September.* *H.* 3-*ft. Sq.* *D*3. *ANC.*

A. ERICOIDES HON. EDITH GIBBS has deep lavender flowers.
3-*ft.* *August–September.* *H.* 3-*ft. Sq.* *D*3. *ANC.*

A. ERICOIDES RINGDOVE has deep lavender flowers.
3-*ft.* *August–September.* *H.* 3-*ft. Sq.* *D*3. *ANC.*

A. ERICOIDES TWILIGHT also has lavender flowers.
3-*ft.* *August–September.* *H.* 3-*ft. Sq.* *D*3. *ANC.*

A. Farreri (comm.), Tibet, is a dwarf with ray florets of deep violet surrounding a disc of orange vermilion, each flower on a separate stem, and is a grand dwarf plant for the front of the border.
*1-ft. May–June. H. 1-ft. Sq. D9. ANC.*

A. foliaceus (Leafy), N.W. America, has large leaves almost spathulate, and bears somewhat small flowers of violet-blue.
*2-ft. July. H. 2-ft. Sq. D9. ANC.*

A. Forrestii (comm.), S.W. China, is of similar habit with deep purple-violet flowers and with orange-yellow centres.
*1-ft. June–July. H. 1-ft. Sq. D9. ANC.*

A. Frikartii (comm.) is one of the most free-flowering of all the Asters, with large flowers of sky-blue borne in immense profusion upon dwarf, neat plants.
*2-ft. July–September. H. 2-ft. Sq. D3. ANC.* 636/2. *Pl.* 3.

A. Frikartii Wonder of Staffa is similar except that its very large, attractive flowers are of deeper blue.
*2-ft. July–September. H. 2-ft. Sq. D3. ANC.*

A. himalaicus (Himalayan) has large leaves of rough, almost heavy texture and bears large lavender-blue flowers with buff backs.
*1-ft. May–June. E. 1-ft. Sq. D9. ANC.*

A. Linosyris (Flax-like), Europe, is a yellow-flowered Aster, sometimes known as *Linosyris vulgaris*, bearing rather small flowers of bright yellow with rather short ray florets.
*2-ft. July–August. H. 2-ft. Sq. D9. ANC.*

A. Novae-Angliae (Of New England), U.S.A., is a very tall-growing type with flowers made up of many rather thin ray florets of deep violet surrounding a deep-yellow disc. Named varieties are:—

| | |
|---|---|
| Barr's Pink | carmine-rose |
| Barr's Violet | deep violet. 2, 37/1. *Pl.* 56 |
| Dr. Eckener | bright carmine |
| Lil Fardell | rose |
| Mr. S. J. Wright | purple |
| Mrs. Rayner | violet-purple |

*5-ft. August–September. H. 3-ft. Sq. D3. ANC.*

A. Novi-Belgii (Of New York), Eastern U.S.A., is the parent of the best-known type of Michaelmas Daisies and grows to a height of about three feet, bearing many heads of bright violet-blue flowers.
*3-ft. August–September. H. 2-ft. Sq. D3. ANC. Pl.* 4.

The best-known varieties are:—

| | | | | | | | |
|---|---|---|---|---|---|---|---|
| A1 | blue | *4-ft.* | *September* | *H.* | *2-ft. Sq.* | *D3.* | *ANC.* |
| Anita Ballard | lavender (semi-double) | *4½-ft-* | *September* | *H.* | *2-ft. Sq.* | *D3.* | *ANC.* |
| Ballard's Crimson | rose-red | *4-ft.* | *September* | *H.* | *2-ft. Sq.* | *D3.* | *ANC.* |

Delphinium "Natalie" ABEFJKNORS

Delphinium "Blue Gown" CDGHLMPQTU

Delphinium "Duchess of Portland" ABEFJKNORS

Delphinium "Graham Seton" CDGHLMPQTU

| | | | | | | |
|---|---|---|---|---|---|---|
| Beauty of Colwall | lavender-blue | *4-ft.* | *September H.* | *2-ft. Sq.* | *D3.* | *ANC.* |
| Beechwood Challenge | crimson | *3-ft.* | *September H.* | *2-ft. Sq.* | *D3.* | *ANC.* |
| Blue Eyes | blue-lavender | *3-ft.* | *September H.* | *2-ft. Sq.* | *D3.* | *ANC.* |
| Blue Gem | clear blue | *3-ft.* | *September H.* | *2-ft. Sq.* | *D3.* | *ANC.* |
| Blue Gown | blue | *3-ft.* | *October H.* | *2-ft. Sq.* | *D3.* | *ANC.* |
| Blue Jacket | bright blue | *3-ft.* | *October H.* | *2-ft. Sq.* | *D3.* | *ANC.* |
| Blue Prince | dark blue | *3-ft.* | *October H.* | *2-ft. Sq.* | *D3.* | *ANC.* |
| Brightest and Best | deep pink | *4-ft.* | *Sept.–Oct.H.* | *2-ft. Sq.* | *D3.* | *ANC.* |
| Charles Wilson | crimson-cerise | *4-ft.* | *September H.* | *2-ft. Sq.* | *D3.* | *ANC.* |
| Climax | pale lavender-blue | *5-ft.* | *September H.* | *2-ft. Sq.* | *D3.* | *ANC.* |
| Dick Ballard | rose-pink | *3-ft.* | *September H.* | *2-ft. Sq.* | *D3.* | *ANC.* |
| Elta | rosy-lavender (semi-double) | *4-ft.* | *Sept.–Oct.H.* | *2-ft. Sq.* | *D3.* | *ANC.* |
| Ethel Ballard | pale pink | *4-ft.* | *Sept.–Oct.H.* | *2-ft. Sq.* | *D3.* | *ANC.* |
| Gayborder Supreme | violet-mauve (semi-double) | *3½-ft.* | *September H.* | *2-ft. Sq.* | *D3.* | *ANC.* |
| Glory of Colwall | lavender-mauve (double) | *4½-ft.* | *Sept.–Oct.H.* | *2-ft. Sq.* | *D3.* | *ANC.* |
| King of the Belgians | lavender-blue | *5-ft.* | *Sept.–Oct.H.* | *2-ft. Sq.* | *D3.* | *ANC.* |
| Little Boy Blue | violet-blue (semi-double) | *2½-ft.* | *Sept.–Oct.H.* | *2-ft. Sq.* | *D3.* | *ANC.* |
| Little Pink Lady | pink (semi-double) | *2½-ft.* | *Sept.–Oct.H.* | *2-ft. Sq.* | *D3.* | *ANC.* |
| Margaret Ballard | rose-lilac (semi-double) | *3-ft.* | *Sept.–Oct.H.* | *2-ft. Sq.* | *D3.* | *ANC.* |
| Mars | clear pink | *2-ft.* | *Sept.–Oct.H.* | *2-ft. Sq.* | *D3.* | *ANC.* |
| Molly | rose | *4-ft.* | *Sept.–Oct.H.* | *2-ft. Sq.* | *D3.* | *ANC.* |
| Mrs. G. Monro | white | *4-ft.* | *September H.* | *2-ft. Sq.* | *D3.* | *ANC.* |
| Nancy Ballard | lilac-rose | *3-ft.* | *October H.* | *2-ft. Sq.* | *D3.* | *ANC.* |
| Petunia | wine-purple (double) | *2-ft.* | *October H.* | *2-ft. Sq.* | *D3.* | *ANC.* |
| Red Rover | crimson | *3-ft.* | *Aug.–Sept.H.* | *2-ft. Sq.* | *D3.* | *ANC.* |
| Ring o' Roses | rose-pink | *3-ft.* | *September H.* | *2-ft. Sq.* | *D3.* | *ANC.* |
| Rose Bird | rose-pink | *4½-ft.* | *September H.* | *2-ft. Sq.* | *D3.* | *ANC.* |
| Royal Blue | violet-blue | *4-ft.* | *September H.* | *2-ft. Sq.* | *D3.* | *ANC.* |
| Ruby Tips | ruby-red | *3½-ft.* | *Sept.–Oct.H.* | *2-ft. Sq.* | *D3.* | *ANC.* |
| Snowdrift | white | *4-ft.* | *September H.* | *2-ft. Sq.* | *D3.* | *ANC.* |

A. PYGMAEUS is the name generally given to the A. dumosus × Novi-Belgii hybrids, which are similar in all respects save that of height to their larger brethren. All have heights of less than eighteen inches and are extremely good plants for late colour at the front of the border. They all flower very late in the year, and are generally at their best in October.

The named varieties are:—

| | | | | | | | |
|---|---|---|---|---|---|---|---|
| Bab Ballard | pink | ¼-*ft.* | *October* | *H.* | 1-*ft. Sq.* | *D*5. | *ANC.* |
| Baby Blue | bright blue | ¾-*ft.* | *October* | *H.* | 1-*ft. Sq.* | *D*5. | *ANC.* |
| Blue Bird | violet-blue | 1-*ft.* | *October* | *H.* | 1-*ft. Sq.* | *D*5. | *ANC.* |
| Countess of Dudley | bright pink | 1-*ft.* | *October* | *H.* | 1-*ft. Sq.* | *D*5. | *ANC.* |
| Daphne | clear pink | 1¼-*ft.* | *October* | *H.* | 1-*ft. Sq.* | *D*5. | *ANC.* |
| Dorothy Vokes | pink | 1¼-*ft.* | *October* | *H.* | 1-*ft. Sq.* | *D*5. | *ANC.* |
| Lady Henry Maddox | clear pink | ¾-*ft.* | *October* | *H.* | 1-*ft. Sq.* | *D*5. | *ANC.* |
| Lilac Time | lilac | ¾-*ft.* | *October* | *H.* | 1-*ft. Sq.* | *D*5. | *ANC.* |
| Marjorie | rose | ¾-*ft.* | *October* | *H.* | 1-*ft. Sq.* | *D*5. | *ANC.* |
| Nancy | pale pink | ¾-*ft.* | *October* | *H.* | 1-*ft. Sq.* | *D*5. | *ANC.* |
| Niobe | white | ⅓-*ft.* | *October* | *H.* | 1-*ft. Sq.* | *D*5. | *ANC.* |
| Peter Pan | pink | ½-*ft.* | *October* | *H.* | 1-*ft. Sq.* | *D*5. | *ANC.* |
| Remembrance | lilac (double) | 1⅓-*ft.* | *October* | *H.* | 1-*ft. Sq.* | *D*5. | *ANC.* |
| Ronald | lilac-pink | 1-*ft.* | *October* | *H.* | 1-*ft. Sq.* | *D*5. | *ANC.* |
| Venus | bright pink | 1-*ft.* | *October* | *H.* | 1-*ft. Sq.* | *D*5. | *ANC.* |
| Victor | lavender | ⅔-*ft.* | *October* | *H.* | 1-*ft. Sq.* | *D*5. | *ANC.* |

A. SUBCAERULEUS (slightly blue), Himalayas, forms a light mat of tough oval green leaves and bears its large, pale-blue flowers with large golden-yellow eyes each upon a single stem.
1¼-*ft.* *June.* *E.* 1-*ft. Sq.* *D*10. *N.*

A. SUBCAERULEUS APOLLO is similar in all other characteristics save only for its brighter orange eye and its intensely violet ray florets. A. SUBCAERULEUS HEAVENLY BLUE is bright blue, and A. SUBCAERULEUS VENUS is an entrancing shade of pale blue.
1¼-*ft.* *June.* *E.* 1-*ft. Sq.* *D*10. *N.*

A. THOMPSONII (comm.), Himalayas, differs in its wide, pointed and toothed, pale-green, rough foliage, and its wide heads of lilac-blue flowers with small yellow eyes.
2-*ft.* *August–September.* *H.* 1-*ft. Sq.* *D*3. *Cg*5. *N.* 636/1. *Pl.* 56.

A. THOMPSONII NANUS (Small), Himalayas, is a diminutive which flowers a little earlier and is a most "refined" plant for the front of the border. 1-*ft.* *July–August.* *H.* 1-*ft. Sq.* *D*3. *Cg*5. *N.*

A. YUNNANENSIS (From Yunnan), W. China, produces its large, ragged, purple daisy flowers singly on twelve-inch stems.
1-*ft.* *June.* *H.* 1-*ft. Sq.* *D*9. *N.*

**ASTILBE** (Saxifragaceae), from G. a—not, without, and stilbe—brilliance.

The flowers of many of the original varieties were both small and dingy. No one can now level the latter criticism at the modern varieties with any measure of justification. All the species are of moderately easy cultivation in moist soils in a sunny site or in leafy soil in a shady place, but should not be attempted in sunny sites in light sandy soil.

A. Arendsii (comm.) is the trade name for a series of hybrids of mixed parentage, which will be found under *A. hybrida*.

A. congesta (Crowded), Japan, produces handsome bright-green foliage having the lightness of the Male Fern, and bears tumbling sprays of creamy-white starry flowers which fade to buff with age and seem even more attractive as they pass.
1¼-*ft.* *August.* *H.* 1½-*ft.* *Sq.* *D*4. *A.* 403/3 *shading to* 016/14 and [00762/1. *Pl.* 5.

A. Davidii (comm.), China, is also known as *A. chinensis* (*sinensis*) *var. Davidii*, and is one of the tallest of the species. The feathered leaves are composed of leaflets resembling those of the Elm, and the flowers are produced in spires of two feet in length on stems about four feet long. The spikes, made up of tiny rose-pink flowers with blue anthers, give the effect of reddish-violet.
6-*ft.* *July–August.* *H.* 3-*ft.* *Sq.* *D*3. *A.*

A. grandis (Large), Central China, is a tall, creamy-white-flowering variety with noble branching, spreading spires.
6-*ft.* *August–September.* *H.* 3-*ft.* *Sq.* *D*3. *A.*

A. hybrida (Hybrid), garden origin, has already been mentioned under A. Arendsii. The feathery plumes are generally of brilliant colouring and have a toughness which their spired elegance seems to belie. As the hybrids vary very considerably in height they have been detailed:—

| | | | | | | | | |
|---|---|---|---|---|---|---|---|---|
| Amethyst | violet-purple | 4-*ft.* | *July–Aug.* | *H.* | 2-*ft.* *Sq.* | *D*3. | *A.* | |
| Avalanche | white | 3-*ft.* | *July–Aug.* | *H.* | 2-*ft.* *Sq.* | *D*3. | *A.* | |
| Betsy Cuperus | white, pink anthers | 5-*ft.* | *July–Aug.* | *H.* | 2-*ft.* *Sq.* | *D*3. | *A.* | |
| Ceres | rose-lilac | 3-*ft.* | *July–Aug.* | *H.* | 2-*ft.* *Sq.* | *D*3. | *A.* | |
| Deutschland | cream | 3-*ft.* | *July–Aug.* | *H.* | 2-*ft.* *Sq.* | *D*3. | *A.* | |
| Erica | carmine | 5-*ft.* | *July–Aug.* | *H.* | 2-*ft.* *Sq.* | *D*3. | *A.* | |
| Fanal | very deep crimson | 2½-*ft.* | *June–July* | *H.* | 2-*ft.* *Sq.* | *D*3. | *A.* | [*Pl.* 63 |
| Gertrude Brix | dark crimson | 2½-*ft.* | *June–July* | *H.* | 2-*ft.* *Sq.* | *D*3. | *A.* | |
| Gloria | ruby-rose | 2½-*ft.* | *June–July* | *H.* | 2-*ft.* *Sq.* | *D*3. | *A.* | |
| Granat | Cerise-crimson 25 *and paler* | 2½-*ft.* | *July–Aug.* | *H.* | 2-*ft.* *Sq.* | *D*3. | *A.* | [*Pl.* 5 |
| Grete Pungel | raspberry-red | 2½-*ft.* | *July–Aug.* | *H.* | 2-*ft.* *Sq.* | *D*3. | *A.* | |
| Hyacinth | lilac-pink | 2½-*ft.* | *July–Aug.* | *H.* | 2-*ft.* *Sq.* | *D*3. | *A.* | |
| King Albert | creamy white | 6-*ft.* | *July–Aug.* | *H.* | 2-*ft.* *Sq.* | *D*3. | *A.* | |
| Lachskoenigin | peach | 3½-*ft.* | *July–Aug.* | *H.* | 2-*ft.* *Sq.* | *D*3. | *A.* | |
| Moerheimii | creamy white | 5-*ft.* | *July–Aug.* | *H.* | 2-*ft.* *Sq.* | *D*3. | *A.* | |

| | | | | | | | |
|---|---|---|---|---|---|---|---|
| Moewe | deep pink | 4-*ft.* | *July–Aug.* | *H.* | 2-*ft. Sq.* | *D*3. | *A.* |
| Peach Blossom | satin pink | 4-*ft.* | *July–Aug.* | *H.* | 2-*ft. Sq.* | *D*3. | *A.* |
| Philadelphia | creamy white | 3-*ft.* | *July–Aug.* | *H.* | 2-*ft. Sq.* | *D*3. | *A.* |
| Pink Pearl | clear pink | 2½-*ft.* | *July–Aug.* | *H.* | 2-*ft. Sq.* | *D*3. | *A.* |
| Queen Alexandra | pale pink | 3-*ft.* | *July–Aug.* | *H.* | 2-*ft. Sq.* | *D*3. | *A.* |
| Rhineland | cerise-pink | 2½-*ft.* | *July–Aug.* | *H.* | 2-*ft. Sq.* | *D*3. | *A.* |
| rosea | salmon-pink | 1½-*ft.* | *June–July* | *H.* | 1-*ft. Sq.* | *D*3. | *A.* [*Pl.* 75 |
| rosea magnifica | salmon-pink | 2½-*ft.* | *June–July* | *H.* | 1½-*ft. Sq.* | *D*3. | *A.* |
| Ruby Gem | ruby-red | 5-*ft.* | *July–Aug.* | *H.* | 2-*ft. Sq.* | *D*3. | *A.* |
| Siegfried | bright rose | 2½-*ft.* | *July–Aug.* | *H.* | 2-*ft. Sq.* | *D*3. | *A.* |
| Venus | pale pink | 3-*ft.* | *June–July* | *H.* | 2-*ft. Sq.* | *D*3. | *A.* |
| Vesta | white, pink anthers | 3-*ft.* | *July–Aug.* | *H.* | 2-*ft. Sq.* | *D*3. | *A.* |
| William Reeves | dark crimson | 2½-*ft.* | *July–Aug.* | *H.* | 2-*ft. Sq.* | *D*3. | *A.* |

A. JAPONICA (Japanese) has broader leaves, divided into three parts, and bears its white plumes on stems of about two feet in length.
2-*ft.* *June.* *H.* 1½-*ft. Sq.* *D*3. *A.*

A. RIVULARIS (Growing by the brookside), W. China, creeps and runs and throws up spires of effective yellowish-white flowers.
4-*ft.* *June–July.* *H.* 3-*ft. Sq.* *D*3. *A.*

A. SINENSIS (Chinese), China, is also *A. chinensis*, and gives rise to thin, tightly packed spires of bluish pink tinged with rose.
2-*ft.* *July–August.* *H.* 2-*ft. Sq.* *D*3. *A.*

A. SINENSIS PUMILA (Small), China, is a much dwarfer type with flowers of a peculiar shade of rosy-mauve.
1-*ft.* *July–August.* *H.* 1¼-*ft. Sq.* *D*3. *A.*

**ASTRANTIA** (Umbelliferae), from G. astron—star, with reference to the star-like distribution of the flower-heads.

Though the colour of the flowers of the species is not outstanding and they cannot be said to be large, the plant has an appeal which may be attributed to its unusual appearance. Requires shaded positions in ordinary garden soil.

A. CARNIOLICA (From Carniola), S.E. Europe, has umbels of pink-rose or white, surrounded by pale-green bracts turning purple.
1-*ft.* *July–August.* *H.* 2-*ft. Sq.* *D*3. *A.*

A. MAJOR (Large), Europe, is similar but grows to a height of approximately three feet. 3-*ft.* *July–August.* *H.* 2-*ft. Sq.* *D*3. *A.*

Dianthus Emile Paré ABCEFJ

Dianthus Alicia DFJKL
Dianthus Betty Norton CFGKLO
Dianthus Highland Frazer GHMQ
Dianthus Echo MPQ

Dimorphotheca Barbarae BCFGNORS
Dimorphotheca Eklonis FGHLMOP
Rehmannia alata CDGHEPJKQU

**AUBRIETA** (Cruciferae), named after M. Aubriet, a French botanist —a name frequently and diversely misspelt.

The Aubrieta is an asset to any type of garden since it produces its colours so freely and is so easily grown. For town gardens it has few superiors. On the whole it is better grown in a light, loamy, neutral soil in a place where it gets the sunlight for at least three hours per day. Nearly all the most worth-while varieties have been given names, which are listed together with their colours. Propagation consists of tearing the plant to pieces, with or without root, and planting in prepared ground in a shaded spot in September.

*½-ft. April–June. E. 1-ft. Sq. D8–9. N.*

A. DELTOIDEA (Leaves of equilateral shape) gives us the following garden varieties:—

| *Lavender* | *Blue* | *Pink* | *Purple* | *Red* |
|---|---|---|---|---|
| Church Knowle | Aubrey Prichard | Bridesmaid | Carnival | Bonfire |
| Daybreak | Blue King | Dawn (double) | Dr. Mules | Cambria |
| J. S. Baker | Blue Queen | Gloriosa | Duke of Richmond | Double Red |
| Lavender | Prichard's A.1 | Moerheimii | Godstone | Magnificent |
| Lavender Queen | Triumphant | Mrs. L. K. Elmhirst | Gurgedyke | Mrs. Rodewald |
| Studland | | Rosea splendens | Peter Barr | Russell's Crimson |
| | | | Purple Robe | Russell Vincent |
| | | | | Vindictive |

**AURICULA** (*see* PRIMULA AURICULA).

**BEGONIA** (Begoniaceae) is named after Michel Begon, a French botanist.

A huge tropical genus, out of place in this book since its members are, without exception, tender plants. Gardeners have, however, adopted the florists' developments of B. semperflorens, and the tuberous-rooted Begonias, for decorative and bedding purposes, and some account of their growth and care is indicated. All Begonias are intolerant of draughts and drought. They are easily raised from seed, which should be sown in gentle heat in March and planted out in certain mild districts in May, but it is better to start them into growth in early April, and harden off in a cold frame in May before planting out in early June. For decorative work in the greenhouse no plant could be more apt, and provided that frost-proof storage is possible, no heat other than that required during the early stages of growth need be used. A number of attractive tuberous-rooted kinds are shown in Plates 7, 8, 9 and 10.

**BELAMCANDA** (Iridaceae) (a commemorative name).

A group of perennials of great beauty, with its attractive flowers followed by curious black seeds of great charm. They are easy to grow in rich light soils in dry positions.

B. CHINENSIS (Chinese), China and Japan, is the Leopard Flower, has leaves like the German Iris and stout spires of orange-red flowers with purple spots. Each flower is about two inches in diameter.
*2-ft. August. H. 1-ft. Sq. D3. Sd2. N.*

B. FLABELLATA (Fan-shaped), Japan, has even larger flowers of brilliant golden yellow. *1-ft. August. H. 1-ft. Sq. D3. Sd2. N.*

**BELLIS** (Compositae), from L. bellus—pretty.

The Daisies are dwarf hardy perennials, used as a rule for edgings or in the spring flower beds. The double-flowered forms are all derivatives from:—

B. PERENNIS (Perennial), Europe, which forms tufts of rounded green leaves, and produces many rounded heads of flat-petalled double flowers. Among the best varieties are B. PERENNIS ALICE, salmon-pink; B. PERENNIS DRESDEN CHINA, pink (527); B. PERENNIS DRESDEN WHITE, white; B. PERENNIS ROB ROY, red.
*¼-ft. April–June. E. ½-ft. Sq. D7. N.*

**BOCCONIA** (Papaveraceae), named after the Italian botanist Boccone.

B. CORDATA (Heart-shaped), China, is also known as *Macleaya cordata.* It makes a rosette of grey-green fig leaves which are attractively cut and lobed, and throws up long stems bearing innumerable small flowers in huge panicles of a curious pinkish-green colour. Of easy cultivation, the plant is excellent for the back of the border.
*6-ft. July–August. H. 3-ft. Sq. D3. Sd3. N.*

B. CORDATA KELWAY'S CORAL PLUME has an inflorescence of coral-pink, and is a most effective plant.
*6-ft. June–September. H. 3-ft. Sq. D3. Sd3. N.*

**BOLTONIA** (Compositae), named in memory of J. B. Bolton, professor of botany.

B. ASTEROIDES (Star-like), N. America, known as the False Starwort, is a wild Aster with clustered heads of small white daisy flowers, which makes a charming plant for the rear of the border.
*4-ft. September–October. H. 2-ft. Sq. D3. N.*

**BORAGO** (Boraginaceae), from the Low Latin borra—animal hair; a reference to the hairy nature of the leaves.

Both the leaves and flowers of the two species are edible and form an attractive addition to salads.

Helianthus hybridus "Lodden Gold" ABCDEF
Echinacea purpurea "The King" BCDFGHKLM
Chrysanthemum maximum "Mayfield Giant" HJKLMNOPQ

Aconitum Cammarum ABEFJK
Echinops bannaticus BCDGHLMQTU
Agapanthus umbellatus var. Mooreanus NOPRST

B. LAXIFLORA (With loose spikes of flowers), Corsica, makes a rosette of prickly-surfaced, round, green leaves, which throws diffuse sprays of pink buds opening to five-petalled flowers of clear pale blue. It is exceptionally easy to grow, and escapes with equal alacrity to woodland and path.

1-*ft.* *May–August.* *E.* 3-*ft. Sq.* *Sd*8. *N.* 43/1.

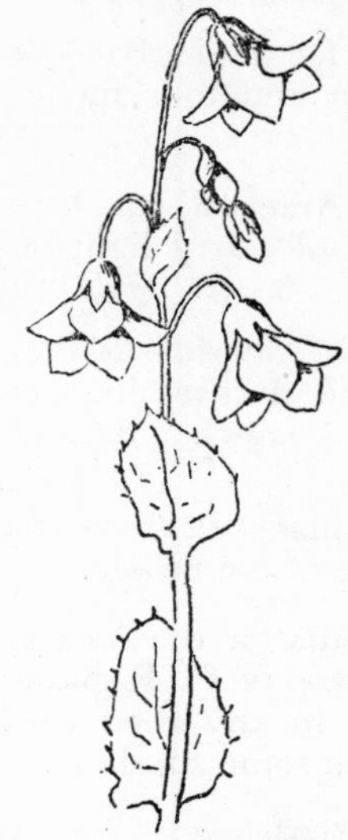

BORAGO LAXIFLORA

S. OFFICINALIS (Of the shop), Europe, has rough, green, oblong leaves, and bears sprays of bright-blue flowers reminiscent of Anchusa.

2-*ft.* *May–August.* *E.* 2-*ft. Sq.* *Sd*8. *N.*

**BUPHTHALMUM** (Compositae), from G. bous—ox, and ophthalmos—eye: from the resemblance of the centre of the flower to an ox-eye.

Both species thrive in any garden soil and are best fitted for the larger herbaceous border or the wild garden.

B. SALICIFOLIUM (Willow-leaved), Europe, spreads rapidly by means of underground runners, and bears large yellow daisy flowers with dark eyes.

2-*ft.* *June–July.* *H.* 4-*ft. Sq.* *D*3. *N.*

B. SPECIOSUM (Showy), Europe, is similar, with larger growth.

4-*ft.* *July–September.* *H.* 4-*ft. Sq.* *D*3. *N.*

**CALLIRRHOË** (Malvaceae) is named after the daughter of a mythical river god.

These are the Poppy Mallows, easily grown in good light soil in sunny sites.

C. PAPAVER (Poppy), N. America, is a plant resembling the Mallow, with large flowers of reddish-purple.
*2-ft. July–August. H. 2-ft. Sq. D3. N.*

**CAMASSIA** (Liliaceae), from Quamash, the North American Indian name for Camassia esculenta.

Bulbous plants, suitable for the herbaceous border. Bulbs should be planted three inches deep and four inches apart, and not dug up from year to year.

C. CUSICKII (comm.), N. America, has linear foliage resembling the Leek, and bears sprays of starry light-blue flowers.
*2½-ft. July. B. ⅓-ft. Sq. Sd2. ANC.*

C. ESCULENTA (Edible), N. America, is the Quamash, and is similar except for its larger and darker-blue flowers.
*2½-ft. July. B. ⅓-ft. Sq. Sd2. ANC.*

**CAMPANULA** (Campanulaceae), from Italian campana—bell, with reference to the shape of the flower.

The genus contains plants for the rock garden, the flower garden, the border and, in the case of C. Rapunculus, the kitchen garden. All grow reasonably well in any good garden soil which is not too heavy, and prefer a spot in some sunshine. *Pl.* 63.

C. ALLIARIAEFOLIA (Alliaria-leaved), Caucasus, forms basal growths of heart-shaped leaves which are green-grey, toothed, and rough in texture, and bears long sprays of pendent, creamy-white flowers. The plant runs underground and soon forms a substantial group.
*1½-ft. June–July. H. 2-ft. Sq. D3. ANC.*

C. BETONICAEFOLIA (With leaves like Betony), Asia Minor, has hairy, oval, toothed leaves and long stems carrying a few rather small purple flowers, yellow at the base.
*2-ft. July–August. H. 2-ft. Sq. D3. ANC.*

C. BURGHALTII (comm.), garden origin, is an exceptional, beautiful garden hybrid, rising to about two feet in height, with dangling bells of violet-grey. *2-ft. July–August. H. 2-ft. Sq. D3. ANC.*

C. CARPATICA (Carpathian), E. Europe, has attractive foliage of bright green which always remains neat, and sends up short stems bearing bright blue flowers of open bell shape, about two inches in diameter. It is a very suitable plant for the front of the border, where it grows a little taller than in the austerity of the rock garden. Varieties of great charm are:—C. CARPATICA ALBA, white; C. CARPATICA DITTON BLUE, blue; C. CARPATICA ISABEL, violet; C. CARPATICA RIVERSLEA, violet-blue; C. CARPATICA WHITE STAR, white.
*1-ft. June–August. H. ¼-ft. Sq. D4. ANC.*

C. COLLINA (Of the hills), Caucasus, has spear-shaped rough green leaves and runs with abandon in good loam, producing stiff, foot-high stems, each with a few intensely deep-violet hanging bell-flowers. *1-ft. June. H. 1-ft. Sq. D8. ANC.*

C. DIVARICATA (Widely spreading), N. America, has pointedly oval, notched green leaves, smooth in texture, and bears long branching spires of rather small, pale flowers.
*2½-ft. June. H. 1½-ft. Sq. D3. ANC.*

C. ELEGANS (Graceful), Siberia, produces tall spires of large pendent blue flowers from basal tufts of toothed, oval green leaves with pronounced foot-stalks. *3-ft. July. H. 1½-ft. Sq. Sd3. ANC.*

CAMPANULA CARPATICA

C. GLOMERATA (Clustered), Europe, Asia, bears large heads of somewhat small flowers clustered tightly together, and forms particularly attractive light blue patches in the border.
*1½-ft. June–July. H. 1½-ft. Sq. D3. ANC.*

C. GLOMERATA ALBA (White) has, as its name indicates, similar flowers of white.

C. GLOMERATA DAHURICA (Dahurian) has larger heads of deep violet-blue, and C. GLOMERATA SUPERBA a reputation for being even better.

C. GLOMERATA PALLIDA (Pale) has flowers paler than the type but is otherwise similar.

C. LACTIFLORA (Milky-flowered), Caucasus, has uprising leafy stems with loose sprays of open, funnel-shaped flowers of white, slightly tinged with blue. It cannot be said to be long-lived but will always be accompanied by certain seedlings which will automatically succeed it. *4-ft. June–July. H. 2-ft. Sq. Sd3. ANC.* 36/3. *Pl.* 12.

C. LACTIFLORA CAERULEA (Sky-blue) is a variative with flowers of pale blue. *4-ft. June–July. H. 2-ft. Sq. Sd3. ANC.*

C. LATIFOLIA (Wide-leaved), Europe, has wide, long, toothed, pointed leaves and bears spires of lilac-purple, funnel-shaped flowers, about one and a half inches in length, with the same perpendicular regularity as a pine wood, and with a rapidity of growth as astonishing. It is a good plant for the shady border.
*3-ft. July. H. 4-ft. Sq. D3. Sd3. ANC.*

C. LATIFOLIA ALBA (White) is similar but has white flowers.
*4-ft. July. H. 4-ft. Sq. D3. Sd3. ANC.*

C. LATIFOLIA ERIOCARPA (With woolly fruits), Europe, is a little less tall and of deep violet-blue.
*3-ft. July. H. 4-ft. Sq. D3. Sd3. ANC.*

C. LATIFOLIA MACRANTHA (Bearing large flowers), Europe, has longer and larger bell flowers of slightly paler colour.
*4-ft. July. H. 4-ft. Sq. D3. Sd3. ANC.*

C. LATILOBA (Wide-lobed), Greece, also known as *C. grandis*, forms a close mat of wide green leaves and bears large, saucer-shaped flowers of deep blue on stems of one to one and a half feet in height.
*1½-ft. July–August. H. 1½-ft Sq. D3. ANC.*

C. MEDIUM (old name), S. Europe, is the Canterbury Bell. It is biennial in its characteristics, and best raised from seed sown in May or June to produce flowering plants the next season. The variety CALYCANTHEMA (cup-flowered) is the so-called "cup-and-saucer" form. *3-ft. July. Biennial. 1¼-ft. Sq. Sd3. C.*

C. MIRABILIS (Wonderful), Caucasus, constitutes one of the most glamourful personalities in the genus, so charged with qualities of magnetic attraction that it has beguiled the gardener into a mass of misconceptions. Another monocarpic variety, it needs no other treatment than that accorded C. Medium, and though it is unthinkable that so ordinary a plant as the Canterbury Bell could exert the fascination of this fair charmer from the Orient, it must be said that its flowers are a little shorter, a little more graceful, and that they carry just that amount of extra sophistication which distinguishes the artistic from the artless. C. mirabilis forms a circular rosette of shining green leaves, waxing wider with age until, upon a time, up springs a central spire of pyramidal form clad with lavender-lilac upturned bells, and then, exhausted by its labours, it dies.
*1-ft. July. E. 1-ft. Sq. Sd5. C.* 37/3. *Pl.* 11.

C. PERSICIFOLIA (Peach-leaved), Europe, has its early leaves shaped like those of the Peach, and develops linear leaves upon its flowering stems. It bears spires of open bell-shaped flowers of bright blue.

It has given rise to the following varieties:—

| | | |
|---|---|---|
| alba | single white | 3-*ft.* |
| Backhousei | large single white | 3-*ft.* |
| Boule de Neige | double white | 3-*ft.* |
| humosa | double violet-blue | 3-*ft.* |
| Moerheimii | double white | 2-*ft.* |
| Pride of Exmouth | large double blue | 2-*ft.* |
| Telham Beauty | large China-blue | 3-*ft.* |
| The King | cup-and-saucer flowers of blue | 3½-*ft.* |
| Verdun | semi-double violet-blue | 2½-*ft.* |

*Variable. July. H. 2-ft. Sq. D3. C.*

C. PHYCTIDOCALYX (With open calyx), W. Asia, is a dwarf form of C. persicifolia, with flowers of violet-blue.
*2-ft. July. H. 1½-ft. Sq. D3. C.*

C. POSCHARSKYANA (comm.), Dalmatia, produces long sprays of starry, lavender-blue flowers, like the attenuated arms of some giant starfish. 1¼-*ft. May–October. E. 3-ft. Sq. D4. N.* 039/1.

C. PUNCTATA (Marked with dots), Japan, is also known as *C. nobilis*, and produces from a running rootstock leathery, oval, green leaves and spires of very long, creamy bells with incurved mouths, spotted within with bright red.
1-*ft. June–August. H.* 1¼-*ft. Sq. D9. N.*

C. PYRAMIDALIS (Pyramid-shaped), Europe, sends up very tall spires clad with handsome polished green leaves and bears very long spikes of open cup flowers of mid-blue. There is also a white variety. Though a perennial, C. pyramidalis is better treated for garden purposes as a biennial, and the seed sown annually in March.
5-*ft. July–September. E. 2-ft. Sq. Sd3. N.*

C. RAPUNCULOIDES (Rampion-like), Britain, is too rampant for any but the wild garden, but its graceful one-sided sprays of narrow, pendent violet-blue bells create there a glory long to be remembered.
3-*ft. June. H.* —— *D3. ANC.*

C. RAPUNCULUS (Rampion), Britain, should be reserved for the kitchen garden. 3-*ft. July. H.* 1¼-*ft. Sq. Sd3. ANC.*

C. RHOMBOIDALIS (Rhomboidal), Europe, brings us back to garden beauty, for it forms very neatly symmetrical tufts of bright-green linear foliage, and bears upon wiry stems loose sprays of deep-blue, pendent bells. Colour is variable, and a particularly attractive double-flowered form, C. RHOMBOIDALIS FL. PL., is also in cultivation.
1-*ft. June–July. H.* 1-*ft. Sq. D5. N.* 37/1. *Pl.* 11.

C. SARMATICA (Of Polish origin), Poland, spreads out its green leaves from a fleshy rootstock and produces foot-long, one-sided sprays of hanging bells of powder-blue.
1-*ft. June–July. H. 2-ft. Sq. Sd2. N.* 40/3.

C. URTICAEFOLIA (Nettle-leaved), Britain, is the Nettle Bell, suitable in the main for the wild garden only, bearing its purple-blue flowers on long, loose sprays. It is also known as *C. Trachelium.*
*3-ft. June–July. H.* —— *Sd3. N.*

**CARDAMINE** (Cruciferae), from G. cardia—heart, and damao—to subdue, with reference to the supposed medicinal properties of the plant.

Most members of the genus Cardamine flourish in damp, shady places and may therefore be used at the front of the shady border.

C. PRATENSIS (Of meadows), Europe, is a native plant with bright-green leaves and sprays of four-petalled, stock-like flowers of lilac, borne upon stems about twelve inches in height.
*1-ft. May–June. H. 1-ft. Sq. Sd3. D7. N.* 533/1.

C. PRATENSIS FL. PL. (Double-flowered) is a better garden plant since, as with most of the double varieties, its flowers persist for a long period. The large many-petalled flowers resemble those of the double Stock and are most freely borne in shady places.
*1-ft. May–June. H. 1-ft. Sq. Sd3. D7. N.* 533/1.

**CARDUUS** (Compositae), from an old L. word for Thistle.

This is the plumeless Thistle, with stemless, spiny, many-lobed leaves and typical purple thistle flowers. All species are best suited to mass effects in the wild garden.

C. ACANTHOIDES (Resembling Acanthus), Europe, has bright purple flowers and is of very easy culture.
*2-ft. July–August. H. 3-ft. Sq. Sd3. D10. N.*

C. HETEROPHYLLUS (With variable leaves), Europe, has the lovely common name "the Melancholy Thistle", and bears heads of purple upon tall, branching plants.
*4½-ft. July–August. H. 3-ft. Sq. Sd3. D10. N.*

C. NUTANS (Nodding), Europe, bears its drooping, solitary heads of deep purple upon plants of about two feet in length.
*2-ft. June–July. H. 3-ft. Sq. Sd3. D10. N.*

**CARLINA** (Compositae), named after Charlemagne, to whom—according to legend—an angel revealed the medicinal value of the plant.

Bears a family resemblance to the foregoing. The root was at one time used in the preparation of purgative medicines.

C. ACANTHIFOLIA (With leaves like a Bear's-foot), S. Europe, is an almost stemless thistle making a widespread ring of handsome spiny foliage, centred at flowering-time with a large silver thistle sitting flat upon it. *¼-ft. July. H. 1⅓-ft. Sq. Sd3. N.*

C. ACAULIS (Without stalk), S. Europe, is just as attractive but in cultivation is far from stemless, the flower being often borne on a footstalk of at least a foot in length. It is an exceptionally beautiful plant when grown in poor stony soil, its white-silvery thistles having the charm of unconscious symmetry.

*1-ft. July. H. 1⅓-ft. Sq. Sd3. N.*

C. CYNARA (Resembling the Artichoke), S. Europe, is similar in general characteristics to the other species, but the flower has a yellowish metallic look as if fashioned of brightly polished brass.

*⅔-ft. July. H. 1⅓-ft. Sq. Sd3. N.*

**CATANANCHE** (Compositae), from G. katananke—strong inducement, owing to its use in earlier days as a component of love potions.

All the species are of easy culture in good soil in a sunny situation.

C. CAERULEA (Sky-blue), Mediterranean region, is the best-known variety and has long, narrow, grey-green leaves. It bears upon long, slender stems its composite blue flowers, made up of papery bracts, which can be cut and dried and used for winter decoration.

*2-ft. June–August. H. 1½-ft. Sq. Sd3. D10. N.*

C. CAERULEA VAR. ALBA (White), Mediterranean region, is similar except that its flowers are white in colour.

*2-ft. June–August. H. 1½-ft. Sq. Sd3. D10. N.*

C. CAERULEA VAR. BICOLOR (Two-coloured), Mediterranean region, has blue ray florets turning white at the tips.

*2-ft. June–August. H. 1½-ft. Sq. Sd3. D10. N.*

C. CAERULEA MAJOR (Large) is a garden variety which produces blue flowers larger than those of the type.

*2-ft. June–August. H. 1½-ft. Sq. Sd3. D10. N. Pl. 12.*

**CELMISIA** (Compositae). The name is derived from Greek mythology and is due to Celmisius, the son of a nymph.

A large race of daisies, mostly from New Zealand, and usually possessing wide, lanceolate leaves with a silvery metallic appearance, which grow best in light, well-drained soil in sunny situations.

C. CORIACEA (Leather-like), New Zealand, makes Agave-like heads of tough, silvery-white leaves, and bears its large white flowers on heavily whitened stems.

*2½-ft. July–August. E. 2-ft. Sq. Sd3. D3. N.*

C. LONGIFOLIA (With long leaves), Australia, is very variable, but in the main the leaf surfaces are more green, and heavily felted beneath. The flower rays are white.

*1½-ft. July–August. E. 2-ft. Sq. Sd3. D3. N.*

C. SPECTABILIS (Showy), New Zealand, is still smaller but has similar leathery leaves, extremely woolly below, and has the typically felted flower-stems of the genus, carrying white daisy flowers.
*1-ft. July–August. E. 2-ft. Sq. Sd3. D3. N.*

**CELSIA** (Scrophulariaceae), named in honour of Professor Celsius.

All varieties thrive best in moderately rich, well-drained soil, in a place that the sun visits for long periods.

C. ARCTURUS (The Bear), Crete, the Bear's-tail Mullein, resembles a yellow Verbascum of dwarf habit, the flowers, centred with purple anthers, being borne in loose spikes.
*1½-ft. June–July. H. 1½-ft. Sq. Sd3. N.*

C. BUGULIFOLIA (Leaves resembling an ox-tongue), Asia Minor, makes a typical Verbascum rosette of flat green leaves, and gives rise to a spire of flowers of amber and green with crimson-purple anthers. In certain cases the amber and green are interchanged.
*1-ft. July–August. H. ½-ft. Sq. Sd2. N.*

**CENTAUREA** (Compositae) takes its name from Greek mythology as the plant which healed the Centaur Chiron's wound.

The genus bears thistle-like heads of flowers, with the outer flowers enlarged, of which the annual varieties known as Cornflowers and Sweet Sultans are typical.

C. BABYLONICA (Babylonian), Asia Minor, is a tall-growing perennial of variable height, with large, silvery-white leaves and loose sprays of yellow cornflowers. *4-ft.–8-ft. July. H. 4-ft. Sq. Sd2. N.*

C. CLEMENTEI (comm.), Spain, is probably a sub-variety of C. ragusina. It has white, woolly leaves which provide an effective contrast in the border. The flower-heads are yellow.
*3-ft. July. H. ½-ft. Sq. Sd2. C8. N.*

C. DEALBATA (Whitewashed), Asia Minor, has pinnate foliage divided into lobes, heavily whitened beneath, and bears its flowers on long stems. Flowers are red in the centre, and pass to pink or white at the margins. *2-ft. June–October. H. 2-ft. Sq. Sd2. N.*

C. GLASTIFOLIA (Woad-leaved), Asia Minor, is a tall-growing variety with cornflowers of golden-yellow.
*5-ft. July–August. H. 3-ft. Sq. Sd2. N. Pl.* 45.

C. GYMNOCARPA (Naked-seeded), Island of Capri, is possibly another sub-species of C. ragusina, and has intensely silvered foliage and small violet-rose flowers almost hidden in the leaves.
*2-ft. July–August. H. 2-ft. Sq. Sd2. C9. N.*

C. MACROCEPHALA (Large-headed), Armenia, has long, toothed, grey-green leaves and forms a much-branched plant with its very large flowers of golden-yellow, borne singly upon stout stems.
*3-ft. July–September. H. 2½-ft. Sq. Sd2. N. Pl.* 69.

Achillea Eupatorium BCFGJKN
Chrysanthemum maximum "Beauté Nivelloise" CDGHLMOPQS
Gaillardia aristata "E. T. Anderton" NRU

Gaillardia aristata "Firebrand" BCDGHM
Gaillardia aristata "Ipswich Beauty" BEFGJKL
Oenothera Fryverkii KLNOPQRSTU

C. MONTANA (Of the mountains), Europe, is the perennial Cornflower, with broad, lance-shaped leaves changing from silver to green, and bears large, bright blue cornflowers.

*1¼-ft. April–June. H. 1-ft. Sq. Sd2. N.*

C. MONTANA ALBA has white flowers; CARNEA, pink flowers; CITRINA, lemon-yellow flowers; PURPUREA, purple flowers, and ROSEA, deep-rose flowers, but in other respects they are similar to the type.

*1¼-ft. April–June. H. 1-ft. Sq. Sd2. N.*

C. PULCHERRIMA (Most beautiful), Caucasus, has long, lanceolate leaves, very grey beneath, and bears upon long stems its bright-purple flowers. *2-ft. May–July. H. 2-ft. Sq. Sd2. N.*

C. RAGUSINA (From Ragusa), S. Italy, is a dwarf, silver-leaved variety for the front of the border. The flower-heads are bright yellow.

*1-ft. June–July. H. 1-ft. Sq. Sd2. N.*

C. RUTHENICA (From Ruthenia), Europe, has lacily cut leaves with long, linear lobes, and bears its pale-yellow heads upon long, stout stems. *4-ft. June–July. H. 2½-ft. Sq. Sd2. N. Pl.* 69.

**CENTRANTHUS** (Valerianaceae), from G. kentron—spur, and anthos—flower: referring to the shape of the flower.

Centranthus ruber, the Red Valerian or Pretty Betsy, has so taken possession of many of our railway embankments and wild spots, filling them with its lurid beauty, that it must be well known to all. Thriving in any or little soil and with little or no sun, it needs but a place to grow; and even if that be not well drained, and the parent plants pass with the winter, the seedlings they produce in quantity will carry on the good work.

C. RUBER (Red), Europe, is also known as "Jupiter's Beard," and produces its sweetly fragrant, barbaric red flowers in great profusion on loose, branching spikes.

*2-ft. June–July. H. 1-ft. Sq. Sd2. N.*

C. RUBER VAR. ALBUS is an attractive variety with white flowers, and C. RUBER VAR. COCCINEUS is a less or more pleasing shade of red, according to taste. *2-ft. June–July. H. 1-ft. Sq. Sd2. N.*

**CEPHALARIA** (Dipsaceae), derived from G. kephale—head, with reference to the grouped inflorescence.

The flowers of this genus closely resemble those of Scabiosa caucasica, but grow taller and are of cream or yellow tints. All species succeed in good garden soil and in a sunny aspect.

C. ALPINA (Alpine), S. Europe, has pinnate leaves heavily cut into fine, long lobes, and grows into a tall, wide-branching plant bearing its large sulphur-yellow flowers on long, slender stems.

*5-ft. June–July. H. 4-ft. Sq. Sd2. D3. N.*

C. BALEARICA (From the Balearic Islands) has similarly cut, shining green leaves, is much more dwarf, and has flowers of deep cream.

2½-*ft.* *June–July.* *H.* 2-*ft. Sq.* *Sd*2. *D*3. *N.*

C. TATARICA (From Tartary), Russia, is another tall-growing variety, with very large flowers of deep cream.

5-*ft.* *June–August.* *H.* 4-*ft. Sq.* *Sd*2. *D*3. *N.*

**CERASTIUM** (Caryophyllaceae), from G. keras—horn, with reference to the fancied resemblance of the seed capsules of some of the species.

All the species are particularly rampant and should not be permitted to encroach where they are not wanted. They have their uses in the wilder parts of the garden, or where taste dictates their use elsewhere, and grow well anywhere under any conditions.

C. BIEBERSTEINII (comm.), Asia Minor, has short growth made up of rather wide but long, woolly, grey-green leaves over which the shining white, five-petalled flowers are freely borne.

½-*ft.* *May–June.* *E.* 1½-*ft. Sq.* *D*8. *C.*

C. BOISSIERI (comm.), Spain, is taller, more silvery in the leaf, and has large, clear white flowers.

1-*ft.* *May–June.* *E.* 1½-*ft. Sq.* *D*8. *C.*

C. TOMENTOSUM (Felted), Europe, closely resembles C. Biebersteinii but has shorter and narrower leaves.

½-*ft.* *May–June.* *E.* 1½-*ft. Sq.* *D*8. *C.*

**CHEIRANTHUS** (Cruciferae), probably derived from the Arabic kheyri (cheiri), and G. anthos—flower, applied to another sweet-smelling plant; or, perhaps, from G. cheir—hand, referring to the habit of carrying the Wallflower as a nosegay in the hand.

The Wallflower is a sweetly-scented perennial, quite frequently grown as a biennial, but can be produced from cuttings where varieties are required to be kept true to colour or to form. Sown in June or July, plants will flower the following spring.

C. CHEIRI (as above), S. Europe, is the Wallflower, of which the following varieties are of special merit:—

| | |
|---|---|
| Cloth of Gold | yellow |
| Eastern Queen | reddish-salmon |
| Emperor | red |
| Fire King | orange-red |
| Golden King | golden-yellow |
| Ivory | white |
| Phoenix | blood-red |
| Rose Queen | terracotta |
| Ruby Gem | ruby-violet |

1½-*ft.* *March–May.* *E.* 1-*ft. Sq.* *Sd*6. *Cg*8. *C.*

Gazania "Franklin" AB
Gazania "Pottsii" CDFGHL
Gazania "The Bishop" EFJKLMPQ
Gazania "Sunfire" KLOPST
Gazania "Sunspot" JKNORS
Gazania splendens PQTU

Gentiana septemfida BCDEFGJL
Gentiana Macaulayi JKLMNOPQRSTU

The following varieties are more dwarf:—

| | |
|---|---|
| Bush | crimson-red |
| Golden Mascot | gold |
| Golden Monarch | yellow |
| Golden Tom Thumb | golden-yellow |
| Primrose Dame | lemon-yellow |
| Tom Thumb | blood-red |
| Vulcan | crimson-brown |

1-*ft.* *March–May.* *E.* 1-*ft. Sq.* *Sd*6. *Cg*8. *C.*

C. Cheiri fl. pl. is the double-flowered form, variable in colour, of which C. Cheiri fl. pl. Harpur Crewe is typical.

1-*ft.* *May–June.* *E.* 1-*ft. Sq.* *Cg*6. *C.*

C. mutabilis (Subject to change), Europe, is a strange Wallflower, opening golden-yellow and changing with age to a subdued tone of Parma-violet, and having the attraction of added quaintness.

1-*ft.* *May–June.* *E.* 2-*ft. Sq.* *Cg*9. *C.*

**CHIONODOXA** (Liliaceae), from G. chion—snow, and doxa—glory, whence the common name "Glory of the Snow."

These are bulbous plants, endemic mainly in Asia Minor, whose ability to put forth their beauty under adverse circumstances, added to the brightness of their basic colour, comprises their chief charm. All flourish in a normal soil in positions of moderate sunshine.

C. Luciliae (called by a woman's name), Asia Minor, has open, bright-blue liliaceous flowers with white eyes, borne on loose sprays on stems of some four inches; C. Luciliae alba has white flowers and loses little of the charm of its coloured relative; C. Luciliae gigantea has paler colours than its parent, but all the charm of a miniature lily.

½-*ft.* *March–April.* *B.* ⅙-*ft. Sq.* *D*6. *N.* *Type* 41/1.

C. sardensis (From Sardinia) is probably only a variation of C. Luciliae with darker colouring, and no hint of white at the eye.

½-*ft.* *March–April.* *B.* ⅙-*ft. Sq.* *D*6. *N.*

**CHRYSANTHEMUM** (Compositae), from G. chrysos—gold, and anthemon—flower: a reference to the predominating colour of the flowers.

The genus Chrysanthemum is a large one, of which the perennial members may be divided roughly into four sections:—

(1) The Pyrethrums, which are all derivatives of C. coccineum, and for simplicity will be found under PYRETHRUM.
(2) The perennial border Chrysanthemums.
(3) The florists' varieties, all derived from C. morifolium, which can be employed as border plants, in which case the flowers produced will be much smaller than those from plants which have been disbudded and grown under greenhouse conditions.
(4) The Korean Chrysanthemums.

C. ARCTICUM (Arctic), Arctic regions, is a dwarf-growing, but freely spreading variety with large, single, pink daisy flowers.
1-*ft.* *May–June.* *H.* 1½-*ft. Sq.* *D*9. *N.* 427/3.

C. AZALEANUM (Resembling Azalea) is a low-growing horticultural form bearing single pink flowers on a wide plant taking the form of a cushion. 2-*ft.* *July–August.* *H.* 3-*ft. Sq.* *D*3. *N.*

C. KOREANUM (From Korea), E. China, has given rise to the following hybrids which, unless otherwise stated, are single-flowered, and form symmetrical plants producing large sprays of brightly-coloured flowers very late into the autumn. They are expectionally hardy and exhibit a resistance to frost damage much greater than that shown by the types of C. morifolium. They are propagated as described under C. morifolium, which see.

| | |
|---|---|
| Apollo | bronze-red, old gold, glowing salmon |
| Astrid | soft pink, shade apricot |
| Bubble | yellow and bronze double flowers. *Pl.* 18 |
| Carmen | rust-bronze |
| Ceres | old gold, chamois-yellow, soft coppery-bronze. [*Pl.* 13 |
| Daphne | pink |
| Diana | rose-pink |
| Fireflame | deep blood-red |
| Indian Summer | bright coppery-orange |
| Janté Wells | bright yellow, double flowers. *Pl.* 18 |
| Mars | amaranth-red |
| Mercury | salmon-red |
| Orion | canary-yellow |
| Romany | bronzy-red |
| The Moor | wine-red, double flowers. *Pl.* 16 |
| Venus | deep rose-pink, silvery lustre. *Pl.* 19 |
| Vulcan | clear red |
| Wildfire | bright rust-red |

C. MAWII (comm.), Atlas Mountains, has feathery grey, marguerite-like foliage on loose, shrubby plants and bears buds which open to bright pink daisy flowers on long, slender stalks. It flowers for a long period in hot, sunny borders.
1½-*ft.* *May–October.* *E.* 1½-*ft. Sq.* *Cg*6. *Sd*3. *N.* 429/1.

C. MAXIMUM (Largest) is the Shasta Daisy and produces very large white daisy flowers with clear golden eyes upon dwarf plants seldom exceeding three feet in height. Many varieties have been selected and given horticultural names, of which the following are the best:

ALASKA has large, glistening white flowers.

BEAUTÉ NIVELLOISE has large, single, white, fringed flowers. *Pl.* 35.

EDGEBROOK GIANT produces immense white blooms in great profusion.

ESTHER READ has large, double, white flowers.

EVEREST has large, single, white flowers.

FRINGED BEAUTY has large white flowers with fringed petals.

MAJESTIC has immense white flowers with a small yellow centre.

MARION COLYER has large white flowers with deeply-cut petals.

MAYFIELD GIANT has very large, single, white flowers. *Pl.* 33.

MOUNT SHASTA has pure-white double flowers with overlapping guard petals.

OPHELIA has sulphur buds opening to white flowers.

PEARL has snow-white flowers.

PHYLLIS ELLIOTT has white flowers with frilled petals.

PHYLLIS SMITH has very large white, fringed flowers.

C. MORIFOLIUM (With leaves like the Mulberry) is often known as *C. indicum* and is probably a cultivated variety of Chinese origin and the parent of all the variatives of the so-called florists' varieties. The month of flowering is variable, and it has seemed best to divide them into classes according to the month in which they flower.

Most of the varieties are perfectly hardy in light soils, but in heavy soil it is sometimes advisable to lift the stools of varieties which it is desired to propagate, and house them in boxes or pots of soil in cold frame or greenhouse.

Propagation of these varieties is generally done in March, when the old stools will have produced numerous fresh shoots. These, cut away when three to four inches in length, are inserted round the edges of pots filled with sandy soil, and placed in a closed frame or greenhouse, when they will rapidly produce roots.

When rooted they may be potted on into three-inch pots, using a standard potting compost, and planted out in April or May. All the varieties mentioned may be grown if desired in greenhouses in pots for interior decoration. Varieties which flower later than October *must* however be so grown.

The decorative type of Chrysanthemum can also be used in this way. The best method of procedure is to take the cuttings as they become available in December to early February, potting into four-inch pots when rooted, and then planting out in the garden in late May. When the plants reach six inches or so in height, the top is pinched out, and when the side-growths reach a similar length, they too are stopped. Unless otherwise indicated, the flower-bud which forms first is allowed to stay upon each shoot, and the side-buds are rubbed off while they are quite small. In early September they should be lifted with as little damage to the roots as possible, potted into ten-inch pots, and be taken into the greenhouse at the end of the month. No heat is required other than that needed to safeguard them against frost.

*August*

Alabaster—ivory-white
Alfreton Beauty—bronze-amber
Arctic Circle—white
Ardent—bright crimson
Autumn Gold—yellow
Bronze Précoce—terracotta
Charlotte Harley—crimson
Chastity—white
Clara Ward—scarlet-crimson
Coppelia—Indian red
Cranford—yellow
Crimson Circle—crimson
Daffodil—yellow and orange
Defiance—flame-scarlet
Early Marvel—old gold
Framfield Early White—clear white
Golden Gem—golden-yellow
Harlow—bright yellow
Hillcrest Bronze—deep reddish-orange
Immaculate—white
Kingcup—yellow
Lorna—silvery-pink
Martin Reed—yellow
Mrs. Jack Pearson—amber-bronze
Mrs. Phil Page—reddish-bronze
New Crusader—white
Peveril—rich golden-yellow
Phoenix—crimson
Pinkest—pink
Pink Gem—pink
Rose Précoce—bright rose
Shirley Bronze—bronze
Spartan—chestnut-bronze
Sunbeam—yellow
Super Page—deep copper-bronze
Titan—deep orange-bronze
Toreador—chestnut-red
Valiant—chestnut-crimson
Wendy—orange-bronze

*September*

Alcade—crimson
Almirante—deep red
Amber Utopia—golden-amber
Border White—white
Bronze Early Buttercup—bronze-yellow. *Pl.* 17
Bronze Freda—orange-bronze
Calypso—tawny-red. *Pl.* 15
Carrie—yellow
Crimson Marie Maxe—crimson
Croesus—bright orange-bronze
Cyril Coleman—bronze
Danaë—cream to blush-pink
Dr. G. Barnes—salmon-peach
Elsenham White—white
Elsie Hilder—old rose
Elstob Yellow—yellow
Excelda—fiery red
Fashion—lilac, porcelain-pink
Felicity—white
Freda—pink. *Pl.* 17
George McLeod—yellow
Goacher's Crimson—crimson
Golden Alcade—yellow
Golden Goacher—yellow
Gold Standard—golden-yellow
Halo—amber-bronze
Horace Martin—yellow
Ivanhoe—deep yellow
J. Bannister—cream
Jim Tomlinson—chestnut-crimson
Leda—mid-pink
Lichfield Pink—pink
Mary Mason—pink
Mayford Red—crimson
Mayland Flame—flaming crimson
Mayland White—white
Meridian—salmon, rose-pink
Mr. E. Crossley—deep mahogany
Mrs. W. D. Cartwright—yellow
Normandie—rose
Orange Glow—orange-bronze
Orange Queen—golden-yellow
Orpington Gem—bronze, old rose
Perle Châtillonaise—pink and cream
Pink Profusion—pink
Red Almirante—red
Red Invader—bright chestnut-crimson
Red Matador—flaming red
Reveller—chestnut-red

Gladiolus "Louis d'Or" ABEFJKLNOPRST

Gladiolus "Bit of Heaven" CDGHLMPQTU

Gladiolus "Panama" ABCEFGJKLNORS

Gladiolus "Pennlac" DHLMOPQTU

Rose Princess—rose-pink
Salmon Freda—apricot
Sanctity—white
September Glory—orange-bronze
September White—white
September Yellow—yellow. *Pl.* 17
Shirley—rose
Sincerity—clear pink
Sunlit—golden-bronze
Sunny Charm—golden-yellow
Tibshelf Glory—bronze
Tibshelf White—white
Top Score—rich yellow
Utopia—bronze
Woking Bronze—orange-bronze
Yellow Gown—yellow
Yellow Utopia—yellow
Yellow Wendy—yellow
Youth—clear pink

*October*

Apollo—terracotta-red
Arabella—pink
Betty Spatz—rose
Blanche du Poitou—white
Bridgewater Gold—golden-yellow
Bronze Cranfordian—bronze
Carisbrook—golden-yellow
Chloe—pure orange
Cranford Pink—pink
Dauntless—tangerine-orange
Dorothy Wilson—canary-yellow
Dovedale—white
Edward Page—white
Ethel Harvey—yellow
Forward—silver peach-pink
Gwen Masse—silvery-pink
Jean Pattison—bright copper-bronze
John Wearing—bright orange-bronze
La Garonne—salmon-red
Late Alcade—crimson
Mary Elizabeth—light bronze
Mayford Yellow—yellow
Mayland Yellow—yellow
Mrs. I. Godber—lemon-yellow
R. A. Roots—white
Signal—bright crimson
Uxbridge—pink
Westbourne—dark chestnut-red
Yellow Edward Page—primrose-yellow
Yellow Hammer—rich yellow

C. ULIGINOSUM (Growing in swamps), N. America, has outstanding white daisy flowers, produced upon plants of five to six feet in height, late in the year when all else has passed.
*5-ft.–6-ft. September–October. H. 3-ft. Sq. D3. N.*

**CHRYSOGONUM** (Compositae), from G. chrysos—gold, and gony—joint, knee; hence the common name Golden Knee.

C. VIRGINIANUM (Of Virginia), N. America, is a quaint composite with daisy flowers showing only five enlarged ray florets. The flowers are borne in sprays upon short stems from dwarf plants with rough, bright-green leaves. Succeeds well in good soil in either sun or shade.
*$\frac{3}{4}$-ft. May–September. E. 1$\frac{1}{2}$-ft. Sq. D4. N.* 6/1.

**CIMICIFUGA** (Ranunculaceae), from L. cimex—bug, and fugo—to flee; from the use of an extract of the plant as insecticide.

A group of plants, with white flowers borne in sprays reminiscent of the Astilbe, which succeeds in well-cultivated soil, preferably in some shade.

C. CORDIFOLIA (With heart-shaped foliage), Virginia, sends up strong stems which bear very many small white flowers arranged in symmetrical and handsome thin spikes.

*4-ft. August–September. H. 2-ft. Sq. D3. N. White.*

C. RACEMOSA (With clustered flowers), N. America, has feathery spires of flowers of creamy white, borne in branching profusion and reaching four feet in height.

*5-ft. July–August. H. 2½-ft. Sq. D3. N. White.*

CHRYSOGONUM VIRGINIANUM

C. SIMPLEX (Simple), N. America, is less tall and has slender and compact, unbranching spires of similar flowers.

*3-ft. July–August. H. 2-ft. Sq. D3. N. White.*

**CLAYTONIA** (Portulacaceae), named so after John Clayton, an American plantsman.

C. SIBIRICA (From Siberia) is a dwarf plant with bright-green, almost succulent leaves, which bears five-petalled flowers of pale pink, lined and fretted with carmine. It reproduces itself with such speed from seed as to become a weed, but is a splendid plant for wild gardens or other woodland.

*½-ft. June–September. H. 1-ft. Sq. Sd2. ANC.*

C. VIRGINICA (From Virginia), E. N. America, is a little taller and bears white flowers tinged pink, borne in loose terminal clusters, and spreads with similar vigour and is useful for the same purposes.

*1-ft. July–September. H. 1-ft. Sq. Sd2. ANC.*

**CLEMATIS** (Ranunculaceae), from G. klema—vine branch, in reference to the way in which some of the species climb.

Helenium hybridum "Madame Canivet" ABC
Helenium hybridum "Goldene Jugend" EFGH
Helenium hybridum "Wyndley" JKLMNOPQRSTU

Heliopsis patula BCFG
Heliopsis patula "Orange King" ACDEFGH
Heliopsis patula magnifica JKLMNOPQ

The few herbaceous species noted below should be treated as herbaceous perennials. They all prefer light, well-drained loam in some sunshine.

C. DOUGLASII (comm.), Rocky Mountains, has long, tubular, inverted flowers made up of four or five coloured sepals, pale purple outside, and deep purple within, borne singly upon short stems.
1½-*ft.* *May–June.* *H.* 1½-*ft. Sq.* *D*3. *Sd*2. *ANC.* 063/2–063/1.

C. FREMONTII (comm.), Montana, has somewhat smaller, hanging, bell-shaped, purple flowers borne upon stems of approximately the same length.
1½-*ft.* *May–June.* *H.* 1½-*ft. Sq.* *D*3. *Sd*2. *ANC.*

C. HERACLEAEFOLIA (With leaves like Cow-Parsnip), China, has large, coarsely serrated tripartite leaves, and bears from the leaf axils clusters of small blue tubular flowers.
4-*ft.* *July–August.* *H.* 3-*ft. Sq.* *D*3. *Sd*2. *ANC.*

C. INTEGRIFOLIA (Leaves with a smooth edge), Europe, has uncut leaves and bears its nodding, funnel-shaped flowers singly upon short stems.
1½-*ft.* *June–July.* *H.* 2-*ft. Sq.* *D*3. *Sd*2. *ANC.*

C. RECTA (Upright) bears its white, very fragrant flowers in large terminal clusters in June–July.
3-*ft.* *June–July.* *H.* 3-*ft. Sq.* *D*3. *Sd*2. *ANC.*

**CLINTONIA** (Liliaceae), an American commemorative name.

A class of liliaceous plants which spread by means of running underground rhizomes, and thrive best in leafy soil in shaded sites, preferably in woodland or shrub gardens.

C. ANDREWSIANA (comm.), California, has rosettes of polished, oval, green leaves, and bears upon a leafless stem of about a foot, a large cluster of small, rose-purple flowers, followed by blue berries.
2-*ft.* *June.* *H.* 1½-*ft. Sq.* *D*3. *A.*

C. UNIFLORA (Single-flowered), California, has leaves resembling those of the Lily of the Valley, and bears large, clear-white flowers, each upon its own stem, followed by the blue berries typical of the genus.
½-*ft.* *June.* *H.* ½-*ft. Sq.* *D*3. *A.*

**CLIVIA** (Amaryllidaceae), a name commemorating a former Duchess of Northumberland.

Clivias are not hardy herbaceous plants, but are such excellent flowering substitutes for the ubiquitous Aspidistra that they should be more widely grown. Potted in a good standard potting compost, they require little attention and will flower with freedom in a light window.

C. MINIATA (Of the colour of red lead), S. Africa, has wide green glossy leaves like those of a larger Daffodil and bears clustered heads of large lily flowers of bright orange-red, shaded yellow inside, followed by large, bright-red berries. Feeding occasionally with liquid manure or bone-meal is efficacious, but plants should be seldom re-potted. Water should be withheld after flowering in late summer and autumn. *1½-ft. June. E. ¾-ft. Sq. D8. N.*

**COLCHICUM** (Liliaceae), named from the country of origin of some of the species: Colchis in Asia Minor.

All the varieties are lovers of good soil in some sun, but will produce flowers (of a kind) without either. The leafage is lush after flowering, and the plants are better placed in good short turf, where the ample beauty of the flowers is ably set off by adequate surroundings at the time at which they flower.

C. AUTUMNALE (Autumn), Asia, is the so-called Autumn Crocus, which bears its large, goblet-shaped flowers of rosy-mauve before its leaves appear. The white variety is equally good in its chaste beauty, and many named varieties are now available, of greatly differing shades of colour:—C. AUTUMNALE ALBUM PLENUM has double white flowers, but loses some of the grace of line of its progenitor, as indeed does the double-flowered form C. AUTUMNALE FL. PL.
*½-ft. September. B. ½-ft. Sq. Sd5. N.*

C. BORNMUELLERI (comm.), Asia Minor, has even larger flowers of deep rose-lilac and produces its flowers over a considerable period of time. *⅔-ft. September. B. ⅔-ft. Sq. Sd5. N.*

C. SPECIOSUM (Showy), Asia Minor, has similar large cups of rose-claret. *⅔-ft. September. B. ⅔-ft. Sq. Sd5. N.*

**COMMELINA** (Commelinaceae), is named after J. and C. Commelin, who were early Dutch botanical writers.

The genus comprises a group of tuberous-rooted perennials with grassy foliage and jointed stems, sometimes persisting throughout the winter in moist, sheltered sites.

C. COELESTIS (Sky-blue) grows about one foot in height and bears wide-petalled flowers of bright blue. It can also be grown as an annual from seed sown in February–March.
*1-ft. July–August. H. ½-ft. Sq. Sd2. N.*

C. NUDIFLORA (With flowers without leaf bracts), N. America, is also known as *C. Sellowiana*, and has smaller flowers of bright blue, but is much more hardy. *1-ft. July–August. H. ½-ft. Sq. Sd2. N.*

**CONVALLARIA** (Liliaceae), from L. convallis—valley; the Lily of the Valley.

Should be grown in reasonably leafy loam in a partially shaded site, preferably one which does not get the early morning sun.

C. MAJALIS (Of May), Europe, is too well known to need description, but may be said to have a running rootstock, and to produce only two elongated oval leaves and a one-sided spray of very fragrant, nodding bell-shaped flowers. *⅓-ft. May. H. ¼-ft. Sq. D9. N.*

**COREOPSIS** (Compositae), from G. koris—bug, and opsis—resemblance: from which Tickseed.

The bulk of the genus, unless otherwise stated, will thrive in ordinary garden soil in a sunny spot.

C. AURICULATA (of gardens), *see* C. pubescens.

C. GRANDIFLORA (Large-flowered) has basal foliage comprising long and narrow linear leaves divided into three or five segments, and produces its large, golden-yellow daisy flowers with lobed petals on very long stems.
*2½-ft. June–August. H. 2-ft. Sq. Cg8. D3. Sd2. ANC.*

C. GRANDIFLORA AURICULATA SUPERBA (Ear-shaped), garden origin, is probably a hybrid of C. pubescens, frequently known as C. auriculata superba, and is similar but has toothed petals and a crimson patch at the base of each petal.
*3-ft. June–August. H. 2½-ft. Sq. Cg9. D3. Sd2. ANC.*

C. GRANDIFLORA MAYFIELD GIANT, which is taller-growing, reaches three and a half feet.
*3½-ft. June–August. H. 2-ft. Sq. Cg8. D3. Sd2. ANC.*

C. GRANDIFLORA PERRY'S DOUBLE is a dwarfer plant with semi-double flowers of deep yellow.
*2-ft. June–August. H. 2-ft. Sq. Cg8. D3. Sd2. ANC.*

C. LANCEOLATA (Lance-shaped), N. America, has basal tufts of lance-shaped leaves which are generally undivided, and bears upon long, slender stems its large golden-yellow sunflowers with lobed petals.
*3-ft. June–September. H. 2½-ft. Sq. Cg9. D3. Sd2. ANC. Pl. 44.*

C. PUBESCENS (Slightly hairy), Southern U.S.A., has ovate leaves with lobes, and the typical golden-yellow flowers of the type, but is stronger in growth than most of the species.
*4-ft. June–August. H. 2½-ft. Sq. Cg9. D3. Sd2. ANC. Pl. 44.*

C. ROSEA (Rose-coloured), N. America, brings a change in colour; it makes a mat of grey-green, grassy leaves produced from running underground stems, and bears upon slender stems daisy flowers of deep pink, about the size of a halfpenny, with yellow discs. It requires a damp situation.
*1-ft. August–September. H. 1½-ft. Sq. D3. A.*

C. VERTICILLATA (Whorled), Eastern U.S.A., has very fine leaves, divided into three thread-like segments, and deep-yellow flowers a little smaller than those of the grandiflora type.

*3-ft. June–August. H. 2-ft. Sq. Cg9. D3. Sd2. ANC. Pl.* 46.

**CORYDALIS** (Papaveraceae), from G. korydalos—a crested lark, referring to the shape of the flowers.

The majority of the species are dwarf in habit and grow equally well in either sun or shade. All have foliage which is attractive in colour, resembling in character that of the Maidenhair Fern.

C. CHEILANTHIFOLIA (With leaves resembling the Lip Fern), W. China, has grey-green ferny foliage, and bears loose sprays of narrow snap-dragon flowers. *1-ft. May–June. H. 1-ft. Sq. Sd4. N.*

C. LUTEA (Yellow), Europe, is the well-known Yellow Fumitory, which will grow anywhere and produce its yellow flowers with celerity and complete devotion to duty.

*1-ft. May–July. H. 1-ft. Sq. Sd4. N.* 4.

C. NOBILIS (Noble), Siberia, has very grey ferny foliage surmounted by loose spires of deep-yellow flowers with brown tips.

*1¼-ft. May–June. B. 1-ft. Sq. Sd4. N.*

C. WILSONII (comm.), China, requires for the benefit of its wonderful silky green foliage the fullest of sun, when it will become spangled with its sprays of golden-yellow flowers.

*1¼-ft. May–June. H. 1-ft. Sq. Sd4. N.*

**CRAMBE** (Cruciferae), from G. krambe—sea-kale.

The Ornamental Sea-kale thrives in rich soil in a position in which it receives some sun.

C. CORDIFOLIA (With heart-shaped leaves) is a tall-growing and wide-spreading plant with large cordate leaves and extensive clusters of small white flowers rivalling in dainty distribution those of the Gypsophila. *6-ft. June–July. H. 6-ft. Sq. Cr10. N.*

C. LACINATA (With cut foliage) has large, attractively cut foliage with similar inflorescences. *6-ft. June–July. H. 6-ft. Sq. Cr10. N.*

**CRINUM** (Amaryllidaceae), from G. krinon—lily.

Only one of the species, C. longifolium, may be regarded as being hardy, though C. Powellii may be grown out of doors in sheltered districts with success. Bulbs should be planted six inches deep in a southern aspect, well sheltered from the north and east, in soil which is both rich and well-drained.

C. LONGIFOLIUM (With long leaves), S. Africa, is also known as *C. capense* and *Amaryllis longifolia*; it has long, wide, channelled green leaves, and bears its flowers in clusters on a long stem. The individual "lily" flowers are two to three inches in diameter, and their tubes fractionally longer, and they are generally of white or pink.

*2½-ft. July–September. B. 2-ft. Sq. D3. N.*

C. POWELLII (comm.), garden origin, is a hybrid of C. longifolium with C. Moorei, and has even larger flowers of similar colours, grouped in compound inflorescences of from six to twelve.

*2½-ft. July–September. B. 2-ft. Sq. D3. N.*

**CROCUS** (Iridaceae), from G. krokos—saffron.

The grace and charm of the Crocus makes it a fitting plant for the garden both large and small, and none among the genus shows greater charm than those featured among the species before they have been "improved" by the cultivator.

C. BALANSAE (comm.), W. Asia Minor, a minute Crocus, has rounded flowers of orange and buff among a tuft of grass-green foliage, which show upon the backs of their petals the characteristic feathering of bronze. *⅙-ft. February–March. B. ⅓-ft. Sq. D6. N.*

C. BIFLORUS (Two-flowered), S.W. Europe, produces larger flowers than most of the species, of delicate silvery lavender within and of creamy buff without. The outside of the petals is feathered in purple in ways which are extremely variable but always beautiful.

*¼-ft. February–March. B. ⅓-ft. Sq. D6. N.* 038/2.

C. CHRYSANTHUS (Golden-flowered), Asia Minor, is a magnificent golden-flowering Crocus of large size and without feathering, which has produced some remarkable hybrids, among which E. A. BOWLES and E. P. BOWLES are the finest. C. CHRYSANTHUS SNOW-BUNTING is very easily grown, and is of great charm.

*⅓-ft. March. B. ⅓-ft. Sq. D6. N.* 5.

C. ETRUSCUS (Etruscan), Italy, produces goblet-shaped flowers of deep lilac-blue of extreme grace, the outer tepals having pale-yellow backs daintily feathered with purple markings.

*⅓-ft. February–April. B. ⅓-ft. Sq. D6. N.*

C. FLEISCHERI (comm.), Asia Minor, has very slender cups of snow-white, containing the orange-red wine of the anthers, all neatly nestling in a short tuft of green leaves.

*¼-ft. February–April. B. ⅓-ft. Sq. D6. N. White.*

C. IMPERATI (comm.), S. Italy, has slender tepals of deep lilac with buff backs, and a purple feathering as early as the second week in January. *¼-ft. January–February. B. ⅓-ft. Sq. D6. N.* 33/2.

C. LONGIFLORUS (Bearing long flowers), S. Europe. It is by coincidence that the earliest-flowering Crocus should be followed by the latest. The long, narrow, lavender-violet flowers are eminently fitted to contain the vermilion stigmata.

*¼-ft. November–December. B. ¼-ft. Sq. D6. N.*

C. MEDIUS (Intermediate), S. France, is one of the smallest but also one of the most glorious of all the autumn-flowering Crocuses. Its glowing goblets of bright but intense purple, coupled with their stigmata of bright scarlet, are outstanding in dull November weather, but spring into their full glory on an occasional sunny day.
*1/6-ft. October–November. B. 1/3-ft. Sq. D6. N.*

C. MOESIACUS (Bulgarian), Asia Minor, also known as *C. aureus*, has well-rounded, warm, deep orange-yellow flowers without the slightest touch of feathering, producing the effect of stored sunshine.
*1/4-ft. February–March. B. 1/4-ft. Sq. D6.* 11.

C. OCHROLEUCUS (Yellowish-white), N. Palestine, has slender-tepalled, white flowers with yellow stigmata, conveying the impression of purity beyond powers of description.
*1/4-ft. October–November. B. 1/4-ft. Sq. D6. N. White.*

C. PULCHELLUS (Beautiful but small), Greece, has small, slender flowers of lavender-lilac stained in the throat with gold. The flowers are produced before the leaves appear.
*1/4-ft. September–October. B. 1/4-ft. Sq. D6. N. White.*

C. SALZMANNII (comm.), Morocco, is another autumn-flowering species, producing from its characteristic tuft of green leaves large lilac cups in great number. *1/3-ft. September–October. B. 1/3-ft. Sq. D6. N.*

C. SATIVUS (Cultivated), Asia Minor, is the Saffron Crocus and has purple flowers with saffron stigmata which originally provided the saffron from which the plant gets its name.
*1/3-ft. October. B. 1/3-ft. Sq. D6. N.*

C. SIEBERI (comm.), Greece, is one of the most beautiful of the spring-flowering species. Its cup-shaped flowers of misty purple-blue are shaded with orange at the throat, and are surrounded with tufts of bright green. *1/4-ft. February–March. B. 1/3-ft. Sq. D6. N.*

C. SPECIOSUS (Showy), S.E. Europe, is one of the most flamboyant. Its very large flowers of extremely bright blue are feathered with purple markings which, together with the orange-scarlet stigmata, produce a picture which will remain upon the retina.
*1/4-ft. October. B. 1/3-ft. Sq. D6. N.*

C. STELLARIS (Star-spangled), garden origin. Starry orange flowers, with the tepals pencilled heavily with black markings, are borne from short tufts of green foliage.
*1/2-ft. February–March. B. 1/4-ft. Sq. D6. N.* 3/1.

C. SUSIANUS (From Susa, Iran), Crimea, is one of the best-known of the species Crocuses. Its old-gold colour is heavily pencilled with dark, shining bronze on the petals. This is the Crocus generally sold as "CLOTH OF GOLD."
*1/4-ft. February–March. B. 1/2-ft. Sq. D6. N.* 5/1.

C. TOMMASINIANUS (comm.), Serbia. Pale lavender, slender and long-stemmed flowers open to show interiors of warm mauve. Its variety

WHITEWELL PURPLE is of intense and shining purple-blue and of great beauty. It is probably the easiest of all the Crocuses to grow, reproducing itself rapidly from seed.

*¼-ft. February–March. B. ⅓-ft. Sq. D6. N.* 36/2.

C. VERNUS VAR. ALBIFLORUS (Spring-flowering; white), S. Europe, has narrow, gobleted flowers of clear white, opening to graceful six-pointed stars. *¼-ft. February–March. B. ½-ft. Sq. D6. N. White.*

C. VERSICOLOR (Changing colour), S. Europe, has rounded flowers prettily pencilled with purple-violet markings, borne from amid tufts of short green foliage.

*¼-ft. February–March. B. ⅓-ft. Sq. D6. Sd6. N.*

C. ZONATUS (Marked with a belt), Silesia, has open cups of soft lavender-blue enclosing white stigmata, produced before the appearance of the long, thin green leaves.

*⅓-ft. September. B. ⅓-ft. Sq. D6. Sd6. N.*

**CYCLAMEN** (Primulaceae), from G. kyklaminos, from kyklos—circle, probably with reference to the coiled stem which carries the seed pod, or perhaps to the rounded leaves of some of the species.

All the species establish best in slightly shaded positions in soil which is leafy but contains sufficient lime. They can only be propagated from seed, which is best sown when fresh but quite ripe, and the immature plants ensuing after germination should be kept growing as long as possible during their first year of growth. On grassy banks, under deciduous trees, in shady corners, few plants can excel the hardy Cyclamen which will grow in size and splendour from year to year.

C. AFRICANUM (African), Algeria, has large round leaves crimped at the edges, produced from the corm, with a depression in the middle at the same time as the flowers, which are made up of five long, thin, twisted, pink petals, deepening at the mouth to bright crimson. It is somewhat tender, and therefore requires a sheltered position.

*⅓-ft. September–October. B. ⅔-ft. Sq. Sd6. C.*

C. CILICIUM (From Cilicia), Asia Minor, has a well-rounded corm with a pale, light cream skin. It has green rounded leaves, purple beneath, with a heart-shaped silver mottling on the surface. The flowers, which are freely borne, have gracefully twisted petals, pale-pink, touched with bright crimson at the base.

*¼-ft. September–October. B. ½-ft. Sq. Sd6. C.*

C. COUM (From the Island of Cos), Asia Minor, has a flatter corm with a dark brown skin and produces leaves which are round and shiny deep green, and purple beneath. The typical flowers are short-petalled, rounded at the top, and of bright magenta with a crimson zone at the base of each petal. C. COUM ALBUM is white, with similar patches of crimson maroon, and C. COUM ROSEUM has glowing-pink flowers flushed from the base with crimson.

*¼-ft. January–March. B. ½-ft. Sq. Sd6. C.* 30/2.

C. EUROPAEUM (European), Europe, has a rounded corm, generally smooth but roughened in patches. The leaves are larger, green, rounded, purple beneath and lightly marbled, and the edges suggest concealed points. The sweetly scented flowers are bright crimson, becoming pale towards the tips.
*⅓-ft. July–August. B. ⅔-ft. Sq. Sd*6. *C.* 630/1.

C. GRAECUM (Greek), S.E. Europe, has a smooth round corm, with green heart-shaped leaves, and twisted-petalled pink flowers which deepen towards the base.
*⅓-ft. August–September. B. ½-ft. Sq. Sd*6. *C.*

C. HIEMALE (Winter-flowering), Anatolia, has a corm resembling that of C. coum, but the leaves, though similar in shape, are heavily marbled. The flowers, shaped like those of C. coum, are of carmine, deepening in intensity towards the base, and are produced with freedom throughout the winter.
*¼-ft. December–January. B. ½-ft. Sq. Sd*6. *C.* 28/1.

C. IBERICUM (From Transcaucasia), Caucasus, has a corm similar to that of C. coum but a little fuller, with leaves which are marbled with white. The flowers, which are similar in shape and colour to those of C. hiemale, have triangular instead of round basal colour patches. *⅓-ft. December–February. B. ½-ft. Sq. Sd*6. *C.* 28/1.

C. LIBANOTICUM (From the Lebanon), Syria, has a smooth, well-rounded corm, and grey-green leaves, rounded but roughly pentagonal, and purple beneath. The flowers, which are deliciously scented, are larger than those of any other type and are of soft rose-pink, deepening in colour towards the base.
*½-ft. March. B. ½-ft. Sq. Sd*4. *C.*

C. NEAPOLITANUM (Of Naples), S.E. Europe. The corm is generally flat, but rounded, with a rough, dark skin; the leaves are ivy-shaped and elongated, and marbled with white very variably. The leaves and flowers appear simultaneously, the latter being also variable in colour, from pale to deep pink, with a central crimson zone. *Pl.* 21. The variety C. NEAPOLITANUM ALBUM is white, and to some has even greater charm than the more colourful parent. *Pl.* 20.
*⅓-ft. September–October. B. ¾-ft. Sq. Sd*7. *C.* 30/3–30.

C. PSEUD-IBERICUM (False-Iberian), Caucasus, has a corm resembling that of C. europaeum, with a smooth skin. The leaves are marbled and rounded, but longer towards, and narrowing at, the tips. The flowers are magenta-violet and pass with age to violet.
*⅓-ft. March–April. B. ½-ft. Sq. Sd*8. *C.*

C. REPANDUM (Scalloped—the leaves), Mediterranean region, has round but flat corms with a very thin, very pale brown skin. The leaves, which are large and broad, are ivy-shaped, with undulating pointed edges. The flowers, which are borne on long stems, are

Helleborus hybridus vars.

Heliopsis gigantea ABCDEFGHJM
Coreopsis lanceolata "Perry's variety" KLMNOPQ
Coreopsis auriculata superba ORSTU

thin-petalled and gracefully twisted and shaded, from deep carmine at the base to deep pink at the tips. The white variety C. REPANDUM ALBUM (in catalogues *C. creticum*) is lovelier still.

*½-ft. April–May. B. ½-ft. Sq. Sd8. C.*

**CYNOGLOSSUM** (Boraginaceae), from G. kyon—dog, and glossa—tongue; from the shape and texture of the leaves.

C. AMABILE (Lovely), E. Asia, is monocarpic and has rough, grey-green leaves typical of the Hound's-tongue, and sends up branching sprays of intense sky-blue flowers, small in themselves but beautiful in masses. *2-ft. June–July. H. 1-ft. Sq. C2. N.*

C. NERVOSUM (Veined), Himalayas, has larger flowers, is roughly the same height and is of marine blue; add to these facts that it is a good perennial, and it becomes an exceptionally good plant to grow in moderately rich soil in full sun.

*1½-ft. June–July. H. 1-ft. Sq. C2. N.*

**CYPRIPEDIUM** (Orchidaceae), from G. Kypris—Venus, and podion—a little foot; hence Lady's Slipper.

The Lady's Slipper Orchids are among the loveliest of the orchid family, and though they cannot be said to be of the easiest of culture, they are well worth a little extra trouble, which they require to be satisfactorily grown. Their main requirement consists of a site in which they get only the evening sun and which is more or less heavily shaded for the rest of the day. The roots should be spread out like a mat just under the surface of the soil, which should be composed of well-drained but moist sandy peat. Each year they are improved by a light top dressing of leafy soil.

C. ACAULE (Without stalk), E. N. America, has only two pale-green, heavily veined leaves between which springs the stem carrying one flower with thin twisted sepals and petals like a Victorian moustache, of purple brown with a touch of rose-pink.

*⅔-ft. May. H. 1-ft. Sq. D7. A.*

C. CALCEOLUS (Little slipper), Europe, has foliage of similar appearance, similarly ribbed with a long stem which carries two flowers with twisted chocolate-brown sepals and pouches of pale yellow.

*1-ft. May. H. 1-ft. Sq. D7. C.*

C. MACRANTHUM (Long-flowered), Japan, produces a leafy stem of about a foot, and the flower has wide petals, and sepals generally streaked with crimson, and a pouch of soft carmine.

*1⅓-ft. May. H. 1-ft. Sq. D7. A.*

C. PUBESCENS (Slightly hairy), N. America, has leafy stems of about one foot in height, bearing one or two flowers made up of large brown pouches flecked at the mouth with crimson, with greenish-yellow petals and sepals with double lines and curiously twisted.

*1⅓-ft. April–May. H. 1-ft. Sq. D7. A.*

C. REGINA (Queen), E. N. America, is the *C. spectabile* of catalogues, which bears on leafy foot-high stems one to three snow-white flowers, the pouch of which is so heavily lined and tinted with rose-pink that it is more nearly that colour than that of its white base.
*1⅓-ft. May. H. 1-ft. Sq. D7. A.*

**DAHLIA** (Compositae), named after the Swedish botanist A. Dahl.

There are few hardy Dahlias, but so much is the genus used for decorative purposes in beds and borders that they cannot be omitted. Descended in the main from D. variabilis, influenced in part by D. Juarezii (said to be a hybrid) and probably, to a lesser extent, by D. Merckii, there are now so many varieties, and each year adds so many to their numbers, that they have become ponderous. The Dahlias were introduced from Mexico in the late eighteenth century, and hybridisation and mutation have produced remarkable variations.

Dahlias require rich, deep and reasonably moist soil, in a sheltered position. The young plants should not be planted out while there is any fear of frost. They should not be placed closer than five feet apart in the case of the taller-growing kinds, two feet in the case of the bedding varieties. Method of propagation is by cuttings. In the autumn tubers are lifted, and if they are heavily covered with soil they should be washed, dried and stored in a dry frost-proof place. They may be propagated from the tubers at any time from January onwards. The tubers which have been stored through the winter are placed into soil and watered and allowed to spring into growth. The young shoots are detached in late March, as close to the crown as possible, with a sharp, clean cut. They should be inserted in sandy soil in three-inch pots, in gentle heat, six to a pot, covered with a hand-light or bell-glass, and shaded from the brightest sunshine. In about ten days they will have rooted and should be potted singly into three-inch pots. From this time they should be gradually hardened off until they are ready to plant out in May.

It would seem best to deal first of all with the species varieties from which the garden varieties have sprung; of these the most important are:—

D. COCCINEA (Scarlet), Mexico, which has very slender growth, and white-petalled single flowers of bright scarlet.
*4-ft. August–September. B. 4-ft. Sq. Cg3. N.*

D. MERCKII (comm.), Mexico, is a plant of moderate height with evenly-cut foliage and small single flowers, generally with eight large ray florets of lavender-pink or lilac. It is also known with white and double flowers, and is without a doubt the hardiest of the species.
*2-ft. July–September. B. 2-ft. Sq. Cg3. N. Pl. 72.*

D. VARIABILIS (Variable), Mexico, is the forerunner of all the garden Dahlias, now much modified in its form but originally with single flowers, with eight-inch ray florets of variable colour.
*4-ft. July–October. B. 4-ft. Sq. Cg3. N.*

Centaurea glastifolia ABCDEFGHKL
Helenium hybridum "The Bishop" EFJKNOPRS
Helenium hybridum "Moerheim Beauty" LMPQTU

Asclepias tuberosa BCEFGHJLNOPQ
Coreopsis verticillata ACDEGHNOQ
Hemerocallis citrina EFGHJKLM

The Dahlias of gardens may be roughly divided into the following classes:—

Mignon single-flowered Dahlias grow to a height of from 15 to 18 inches, bear bright red, yellow or pink flowers in profusion, and are used generally for bedding purposes. The best-known variety—though probably not the best variety—is Coltness Gem, which is bright red in colour. Pink Gem is an attractive pink variety, and Scarlet Gem the best of the scarlets. Lady Eileen, deep salmon-pink. Innocence, white.

The small-flowered Paeony Dahlia grows to three to four feet in height and bears wide-petalled, semi-double flowers. Bishop of Llandaff (*Pl.* 24), with its brave show of bright red flowers and contrasting dark-green leaves, is typical of the group, of which the best are:—

Lemon Beauty—lemon-yellow
Newport Gem—scarlet
Liberty Silk—azalea pink and apricot

The large informal Decorative Dahlia has double flowers with wide petals, generally pointed at the tip, of about 7 to 10 inches in diameter. Some of the outstanding varieties are:—

Ballego's Glory—crimson, edged maroon
Electros—orange-scarlet. *Pl.* 23
Fine Limburg—orange-red
Formality—flame, lemon at tips gold
Furore—orange-scarlet. *Pl.* 25
Gladiator—orange and scarlet
John Green—scarlet
Lady Clive Wigram—salmon on pale yellow
Salmon Giant—salmon
Stuart Ogg—yellow, white tips
White Abundance—white

Medium informal Decorative Dahlias have flowers which are similar but are from 4½ to 6½ inches in diameter. Some very good varieties are:—

Astarte—nasturtium-red, 14
Heather—yellow flushed mauve
Intensity—scarlet
Janette—rose-red
Modern Times—scarlet, white tips
Peggy Andrews—scarlet
Tante Stien—orange-scarlet
Victor—cerise shaded orange

Small informal Decorative Dahlias grow from three to four feet in height, and bear similar flowers of approximately 3 to 4½ inches in diameter.

Cinnamon Gem—bright orange
England—salmon-pink and yellow
Fortune—salmon-pink and yellow
Fred Winter—orange-scarlet
Townley Orange—orange-scarlet
Townley Welcome—salmon-pink and yellow. *Pl.* 24
Winifred—orange-scarlet

Collarette Dahlias resemble single Dahlias but have an inner ring of smaller florets of a contrasting colour. Examples of this class are:—

Hussar—red and white collar
Scarlet Queen—scarlet with yellow collar. *Pl.* 24
Tuskar—rose-crimson and lemon collar

Pompon Dahlias grow generally from two to four feet in height and bear flowers which are fully double, and well and symmetrically rounded, and about 2 inches in diameter. Good modern varieties are:—

Alloway—rose-purple, 24
Andrew—rose
Blenheim—parma-violet. *Pl.* 23
Clarissa—primrose
Edwin—scarlet and yellow
Guiding Star—white
Hockley Miniature—mauve-pink, yellow base
Little Dorothy—rich yellow
Little Pat—crimson, yellow ground
Mars—scarlet
Nerissa—rose
Pauline Gibbard—crimson
Yellowhammer—bright yellow

The cactus and semi-cactus Dahlias are also variable in size and grow to a height of from 3½ to 5 feet.

The larger types have flowers up to 8½ inches in diameter, the medium type up to 6 inches in diameter, and the small up to 4½ inches in diameter.

Examples of the modern types are:—

*Large*

Alois Nolen—orange-red and Yellow
Andreas Hofer—salmon-pink
Ballego's Surprise—white
Beauty of the Garden—cerise
Bolide—orange-pink
Dr. Derrick Martin—sulphur, 1/2
Enkart Prima—apricot on yellow, 609/2
Frau O. Bracht—yellow
Golden Age—bronze-amber
Grand—turkey-red, 721
Jessie King—rose, 23/1
John Woolman—scarlet, 19 *to* 19/2
Mascotte—violet-pink
Miss Belgium—bronze
Scarlet Wonder—scarlet, 19
Snowball—white

*Medium*

Dearne's Pink Beauty—rose and yellow, 623/3 *and* 1/2
Golden Glory—golden-yellow
Madame C. Juissant—silvery lilac
Marjorie Spencer—crimson, 22
Peer Gynt—fire-red, 15
Punctueel—sulphur, 1/2
Tropic Star—orange

*Small*

Baby Royal—salmon-pink
Kendal Beauty—deep rose, sulphur base, 25/3 *to* 1/2
Little Diamond—rose Bengal, sulphur base, 25/2 *to* 4/2. *Pl.* 22
Little Dream—pink, white centre
Little Pearl—pale pink
Little Snow Queen—white
Monsieur Pierre Lunden—violet-rose and yellow
Paula Deetjen — sulphur and carmine, 21/2, 1/2
Peaceful—orange, rose-pink
Prince de Liége — pink, white centres
Sentiment—rose Bengal, 25/1 *to* 25/2
Tip—sulphur, 1/1. *Pl.* 23
Vondal—orange, tips pink, 12/1, 618

**DELPHINIUM** (Ranunculaceae) is derived from G. delphis—dolphin, from the imaginary resemblance of the flower spur to a dolphin's head.

A genus much developed by the hybrids and much confused in its nomenclature. The species vary in height from a few inches to eight or nine feet. In the main, the cultural details are similar for all varieties. They require well and deeply dug rich soil, and definitely need replanting in every third or fourth year, when they should be divided. This is better done in the spring, immediately they start into growth. They can be propagated from seeds, but where it is desired to keep a florist's variety true they can only be produced by division, or by means of vegetative reproduction. It is useful, where it is desired to prolong the period of flowering, to remove the spikes which have flowered before seed has formed. In this way the flowering period can be extended.

D. AZUREUM (Sky-blue) is likely to be a variant of any blue-flowered Delphinium of garden origin, which will be found under D. elatum hybridum.

D. BRUNONIANUM (comm.), Himalayas, has round, five-scalloped, rough hairy foliage with a short flowering stem, and rather large blue flowers varying in intensity. The flowers are musk-scented and are outstanding only in the pale-blue forms.
1½-*ft.* *June–July.* *H.* 1-*ft. Sq.* *C2.* *N.*

D. CARDINALE (Scarlet), S. California, has very finely-cut leaves and bears in very open sprays long-spurred flowers of bright scarlet with yellowish petals. 2½-*ft.* *July–August.* *H.* 1½-*ft. Sq.* *C2.* *N.*

D. ELATUM HYBRIDUM is the name given to horticultural forms of the Delphinium generally known by proprietary names. There is a true D. hybridum but it is probably not now in cultivation. The D. hybridum of gardens has been developed in part from D. cheilanthum and D. elatum. Neither of these two varieties is particularly outstanding in its wild form, and the garden varieties which have been developed from them are in most cases much superior to the wild ones. The hybrid Delphiniums known as the belladonna group show the influence of D. cheilanthum to a larger extent than that of their other parent, and the tall-growing varieties the predominance of D. elatum. The outstanding examples of the hybrids are listed below, preceded by a separate section devoted to those of the belladonna class.

The belladonna Delphinium is generally shorter than the hybridum or elatum types, with a more branching habit, has smaller and more diffusely spread flowers upon less imposing spikes, but has an added grace and is less formal in appearance than these types.

BELLADONNA has large, single flowers of beautiful sky-blue. 3-*ft.*

BELLADONNA SEMIPLENUM is a semi-double form of the above, which is free-flowering. 2½-*ft.*

BLUE BEES has flowers of pale forget-me-not blue, with a small bluish eye. 3½-*ft.*

ISIS has flowers of deep purplish-blue and graceful habit. 2½-*ft.*

LAMARTINE is deep sky-blue with a pure-white centre. 3½-*ft.*

MOERHEIMII has pure-white single flowers and is of free branching, vigorous habit. 4½-*ft.*

MRS. J. S. BRUNTON is a good, strong grower with deep sky-blue, single flowers. 4½-*ft.*

MRS. THOMSON is of fine clear blue and of good habit of growth. 3-*ft.*

MUSIS SACRUM has semi-double flowers of pale sky-blue. 4-*ft.*

NAPLES is of rich gentian-blue, with a faint mauve flush and a small purplish-blue eye. 3-*ft.*

ORION has large, clear-blue flowers with white eye. 4-*ft.*

PERSIMMON has single cornflower-blue flowers on branching spikes. 4-*ft.* *Pl.* 26.

THEODORA is bright pure gentian-blue, with a brown eye. 4-*ft.*

WENDY has flowers of bright cobalt-blue with white eyes and is of branching habit. 4-*ft.* *Pl.* 26.

D. ELATUM HYBRIDUM.

A. J. MOIR has semi-double flowers of bright sapphire-blue tinged with mauve at the eye. 6-*ft.*

ANDREW CARNEGIE has large, lavender, double flowers with lilac centres.

BETTY WELLS has pale gentian-blue flowers, flushed with mauve, and inner petals of mauve with small white eyes. 4½-*ft.* *June.*

BLUE BIRD has tall, well-made spikes with semi-double flowers of good deep blue. 5-*ft.*

BLUE DANUBE has bright forget-me-not-blue flowers, flushed with pale pinkish-mauve with small pale buff eyes. 7-*ft.* *July.*

BLUE GOWN has semi-double, true ultramarine flowers with very small black eyes. 6-*ft.* *June.* *Pl.* 29.

BLUE SPIRE has rich forget-me-not-blue flowers, with faint tinge of mauve and small pale brown eyes. *June.*

B. M. GURTEEN, with pale-mauve flowers, outer petals tinged pale blue, and eyes dark brown and mauve, is exceptionally fine. *June.*

CAMBRIA. The spikes are long and fully clothed with large-semi-double flowers of clear heliotrope, centred with Venetian blue, with white eyes. 5-*ft.* *July.*

CHARLES GREEN has very pale sky-blue flowers, flushed with pale mauve, and delicate mauve inner petals, with brown eyes. *June.*

CLARISSA has its bright forget-me-not-blue flowers with its inner petals tinged pale mauve at tips. *June.*

Hemerocallis hybrida CEFGHJKLMNORS
Alstroemeria aurantiaca ABCDHLMOPQSTU

Iris germanica, varieties

COMMANDANT CHAPUIS is of very striking bright sky-blue with semi-double flowers, with creamy-white eyes. 6-*ft.*

COSSACK has bright, clear blue, single flowers, with bronze centres, and long tapering spikes. 5-*ft.*

DAWN produces medium-sized spikes of sky-blue with a mauve sheen, and has flowers with brown eyes. 5½-*ft.*

DONALD ALLAN has slightly tapering spikes, gentian-blue flowers, lightly flushed with mauve, and small white eyes. *June.*

DUCHESS OF PORTLAND has its semi-double flowers of rich deep gentian-blue, with inner petals flushed with deep mauve with white eyes. 5½-*ft.* *June.* *Pl.* 30.

EDWARD BROMET has rich deep purple, semi-double flowers with white eyes. 5-*ft.*

ELIZABETH RICKETT is rich gentian-blue with the inner petals of purplish-mauve, with a dark-brown large eye. *June.*

EVELYN RICHIE is of deep rich forget-me-not blue, with a small white and mauve eye. *June.*

F. W. SMITH has spikes of large gentian-blue flowers with white eyes. 5½-*ft.*

GRAHAM SETON has semi-double flowers of rich ultramarine shaded with rosy purple. 5-*ft.* *June–July.* *Pl.* 30.

HARRY SMETHAM has rosette-like flowers of ultramarine, shading to lavender in the centre.

HUNSDEN DELL is forget-me-not-blue with its inner petals lightly flushed pale mauve, with a small eye. 5-*ft.*

INNOCENCE has white, semi-double flowers in bold, tightly-packed spikes. 5-*ft.* *Pl.* 28.

ISLA is sky-blue with Parma-violet shading, with large round flowers with white eyes. *Pl.* 27.

ITALIA has semi-double flowers of bright gentian-blue with delicate mauve flush, with small white eye.

JOAN CARTER is semi-double, with lavender-mauve flowers and white eyes. 5-*ft.*

KING GEORGE has bright-blue single flowers with white eyes. 4½-*ft.*

LADY AMY is violet-purple with the tips of the outer petals of azure-blue.

LADY CLARA has delicate pale-mauve outer petals with a faint pale sky-blue flush. The eye is large. 5½-*ft.*

LADY DIANA has outer petals of very sky-blue, tinged with pale mauve, and inner petals of pale pinkish-mauve.

LADY DOROTHY has forget-me-not-blue flowers with the inner petals pale pinkish-mauve, zoned pale blue at the large black eye.

LADY ELEANOR has sky-blue flowers shaded with pale mauve. The flowers are double, and the inner petals effectively waved.

LADY ELIZABETH, with flowers of Cambridge blue, has its inner petals of pale mauve, centred by large brown eyes.

LADY GRACE has large, single, ultramarine flowers.

LADY GUINEVERE has a pale pinkish-mauve flower, centred with pale forget-me-not blue, and a small eye.

LADY HOLT, with flowers of pale forget-me-not blue, has inner petals faintly tinged mauve at the tips, with white eyes. 6-*ft.*

LILIAN BISHOP has bright gentian-blue flowers with its inner petals flushed mauve, small eye, and is resistant to mildew. 5-*ft.*

LIZE VAN VEEN has large single flowers of Cambridge blue, lightly touched with lilac-rose.

LORD DERBY, with large flowers of rich deep rosy-mauve, is both a strong-growing plant and free-flowering. 4½-*ft.* *July.*

LORENZO DE' MEDICI has large, circular, rosy-mauve, semi-double flowers. 5-*ft.*

MADGE has flowers of forget-me-not-blue, with their inner petals of light pinkish-mauve, and very small white eyes.

MARY WELLS. Large, semi-double flowers of electric-blue, with inner petals of rosy-mauve, make this a most attractive variety. 5-*ft.* *July.*

MILLICENT BLACKMORE has large and well-formed semi-double flowers of rich blue and mauve with black centres. 5½-*ft.* *July.*

MRS. COLIN MCIVER is a most pleasing shade of heliotrope with large semi-double flowers. 6-*ft.*

MRS. H. KAYE has large semi-double flowers of rich indigo-blue flushed with light purple. 5-*ft.*

MRS. H. J. JONES has single flowers of azure-blue with white eyes.

MRS. NEWTON LEES is a delicate mauve, lightly shaded with pale blue, and has large semi-double flowers. 5-*ft.*

MRS. PAUL NELKE is a wonderful colour: a bright semi-double unshaded cornflower-blue, with a small white eye. 5½-*ft.*

MRS. SHIRLEY is a most beautiful variety, of lovely lilac-mauve, with white and sulphur eye, with semi-double flowers. 6-*ft.*

MRS. T. CARLILE is Parma-violet with pink shading, with a semi-double flower with a white eye. 5-*ft.*

MRS. TOWNLEY PARKER is a beautiful sky-blue, single, large pip, with white eye. 5½-*ft.* *Pl.* 27.

NATALIE is cornflower-blue, with Parma-violet shading. *Pl.* 29.

NORA FERGUSON has flowers of pale blue, flushed soft pink, with white eyes; the flowers are semi-double. 5-*ft.*

PHILIP BUTLER has semi-double, deep blue flowers. *June–July.*

PRINCE GUSTAV has large semi-double flowers of dark violet-blue, shading to pure violet towards the central grey eye. 5-*ft.* *June.*

PURPLE SPLENDOUR is exceedingly tall with large spikes of rich cornflower-blue flowers shaded amethyst. The eye is brown. 5-*ft.* *July.*

Inula Helenium ABCDEFG

Aster acris LMOPQ

Inula Royleana EFGHJKLMNO

Lilium auratum ABCEFGHJKLMOPQ
Lilium Henryi NOPRSTU

RANDOLPH has flowers of gentian-blue, flushed with purplish-mauve; white eye banded purplish-mauve. 6-*ft.* *July.*

REV. E. LASCELLES sends up bold spikes of large double flowers with distinct blue and white centres. 5-*ft.*

ROBBIE has flat flowers of pale sky-blue. The inner petals are pale pinkish-mauve, with a large central brown eye.

ROMEO, with flowers of gentian-blue, has a light mauve flush and a small eye.

SIR NEVILLE PEARSON has flowers of light gentian-blue, with the inner petals purple, with large eye. 5½-*ft.*

SMOKE OF WAR has semi-double flowers of reddish-purple, on long spikes. 4½-*ft.*

SPLENDOUR is light mauve shaded rose, and has semi-double flowers. 5-*ft.*

STATUAIRE RUDE produces enormous spikes of soft pale heliotrope. 6-*ft.*

THE BISHOP has large, navy-blue, semi-double flowers with bold white eyes. 6-*ft.*

VIOLET ROBINSON, with flowers of violet tinged with purple, has its inner petals of rich violet-purple. 4-*ft.*

VISCOUNTESS HARCOURT has flowers of pale sky-blue, tinged pale pinkish-mauve, and large eyes.

WALES. Single flowers of unshaded royal-purple, with small white centres, are borne on long, tapering spikes.

W. B. CRANFIELD has large semi-double flowers of gentian-blue and rosy-mauve, with white eyes. 5-*ft.* *Pl.* 28.

WELSH BOY is gentian-blue, flushed with deep mauve, with inner petals of purple. 4-*ft.*

WILD WALES has flowers of deep forget-me-not blue, broadly tinged with pinkish-mauve, and small black eyes. 5½-*ft.*

WILL SHAKESPEARE is of azure-blue, with inner petals of mauve, and with pale brown eyes.

D. GRANDIFLORUM (Large-flowered), China, is often known as *D. sinense* or *D. chinense*. It has very finely cut green foliage and bears large sky-blue flowers in short open spikes. There are numerous varieties, of which D. GRANDIFLORUM ALBUM has white flowers and a pale blue form which masquerades under the name of "AZURE FAIRY," but in all probability the finest of all is the spurless variety, with dark blue open flowers, sometimes called GRANDIFLORUM CINERARIA, or even CINERIA. 1-*ft.* *June–July.* *H.* 1-*ft. Sq.* *C2.* *N.* 31.

D. MACROCENTRON (Large-spurred), Kenya, has bright-green flowers marked with bright blue, with green upright spurs. The solidity of the flowers is redeemed from stolidity by the amazing blending of blue and green. The plant flowers normally in November, and is likely to be of great value in the production of new hybrids.
1½-*ft.* *October–November.* *H.* 1-*ft. Sq.* *C2.* *N.*

D. NUDICAULE (Bare-stemmed), Oregon, is another small variety with three-parted leaves, and very short spires of brilliant-scarlet flowers with long straight spurs. The variety D. NUDICAULE LUTEUM has bright-yellow flowers; D. NUDICAULE CHAMOIS has flowers of pale apricot. The root is tuberous, and the plants are best grown from seed; they will flower during their first year of growth.

*1-ft. June–August. H. 1-ft. Sq. C2. N.*

D. PANICULATUM (With tufts of flowers), N.W. America, is a pleasant, bright violet-blue counterpart of Gypsophila paniculata, with gracefully distributed flowers, open and airy, and the delightful propensity of broadcasting itself freely and widespread from the seed which it produces with abandon.

*1½-ft. July–August. H. 1-ft. Sq. Sd3. ANC. Pl. 76.*

D. RUYSII (comm.), garden origin, is a hybrid of appearance suggesting the influence of D. nudicaule, and produces loose branching sprays of light rose-pink flowers. Known as PINK SENSATION, it is an unusual and attractive plant for the border.

*4-ft. June–September. H. 2-ft. Sq. D3. N. Pl. 26.*

D. SULPHUREUM (Yellow), Persia, is also tuberous-rooted and bears a single stem about eighteen inches in height, and has small bright yellow flowers. *1½-ft. July–August. H. 1-ft. Sq. C2. N.*

D. TATSIENENSE (From Tatsien), China, is a dwarf branching plant with dark green, finely cut foliage, distinct white spots in the notches of the leaves, bearing much-branched sprays of long-spurred flowers of variable blue. *1½-ft. June–July. H. 1-ft. Sq. C2. N.*

D. WELBYI (comm.), Abyssinia, is a comparatively tall-growing plant with huge pale-blue flowers, with extremely long spurs. Distribution of the flowers in this case is so wide as to bear no resemblance to the tight heads of elatum hybridum.

*2½-ft. July–August. H. 1-ft. Sq. C2. N.*

**DIANTHUS** (Caryophyllaceae), from G. Dios—of Jupiter, and anthos—flower, that is, the Divine Flower, is said to have been named so by Theophrastus for its fine fragrance.

The Dianthus family is one of very wide scope, comprising tufted, fragrant plants known as Pinks, Sweet Williams, and Carnations. They are of easy cultivation, but as a rule are short-lived and benefit by being re-propagated, generally by vegetative means every second or third year. The flowers may be either single or double, and it can be stated as a general rule that though the single flowers last for a shorter period than the double ones, they are produced in greater quantity. There is no hard and fast rule for successful growth for every type of Dianthus, so that cultural details for the various varieties are stated.

D. Alicia (comm.), garden origin, is a very hardy hybrid of D. caryophyllus, and produces pale-pink, double, sweetly-scented flowers with great persistence under normal border conditions.

1-*ft.* *June–October.* *E.* 1-*ft. Sq.* *Cg*7. *N.* *Pl.* 31.

D. arboreus (Tree-like), S.E. Europe, is a pink with hard woody stems and pale-green grass-like foliage, and bears long stems with clusters of buds opening one by one into large single flowers of bright pink. It grows to about six feet in height, and requires a sheltered position at the back of the border.

5-*ft.*–6-*ft.* *May–October.* E. 4-*ft. Sq.* *Sd*2. *N.*

D. atrorubens (Dark-red), Europe, is a clustered-headed Pink with thin, dark green leaves and wiry stems, bearing at their ends small heads like those of a bright crimson-scarlet Sweet William.

⅔-*ft.* *July–September.* *E.* 1-*ft. Sq.* *Sd*2. *N.*

DIANTHUS BARBATUS

D. barbatus (Bearded), Eurasia, is the Sweet William, with broad, flat, green leaves, and bearing its flowers in large, flat, composite heads. Though perennial, it is better treated as biennial in most of its garden forms. It has the disadvantage of not sharing the scent of the other varieties, but has many delightful hybrids, some of which have long ceased to resemble in any way the parents and have regained the scent of the more attractive members of the family.

1½-*ft.* *June–July.* *E.* 1-*ft. Sq.* *Sd*2. *N.* 30/1.

D. barbatus Atkinsonii (comm.) has exceptionally large, single flowers of bright crimson-scarlet, borne in branching sprays on six-inch stems. Foliage is wide and green.

¾-*ft.* *June–August.* *E.* 1-*ft. Sq.* *Cg*7. *A.*

D. barbatus fl. pl. (Double), garden origin, is a very dwarf, double, red Sweet William which has the advantage of remaining neat in growth. It should be re-propagated annually.

⅓-*ft.* *June–August.* *E.* 1-*ft. Sq.* *Cg*7. *N.*

D. BARBATUS NAPOLEON III (comm.), garden origin, bears some resemblance to D. Atkinsonii in habit, but has barbaric double crimson flowers. *½-ft. June–July. E. ⅔-ft. Sq. Cg7. N.*

D. BARBATUS SPARK, garden origin, has wide, bright-green leaves and deep-crimson single flowers, deepening in colour towards the centre.
*½-ft. June–July. E. ⅔-ft. Sq. Cg7. N.*

D. BETTY NORTON (comm.), garden origin, is another attractive hybrid with large single flowers of deep rose-pink with outstanding maroon eyes. The most notable characteristic of the type of hybrid is their ability to flower continuously.
*1-ft. June–October. E. 1-ft. Sq. Cg7. N. Pl.* 31.

D. CAESIUS (Grey-blue), Europe, is the Cheddar Pink, and a delightful plant for the front of the border. It is argued that by priority its name should be *D. gratianopolitanus*, but it is so well known now under its later name that it would be a sin indeed to change it. Above very short tufts of blue-grey foliage, the sweetly scented, fringed, rose-pink flowers are produced in great quantity.
*½-ft. June–July. E. 1-ft. Sq. Cg7. C.* 630/1.

D. CARYOPHYLLUS is the Clove Pink or Carnation, its tufted, smooth grey-green foliage varying in height from two to three feet, producing its flowers either alone or a few on each stem. It comes, in the first place, from Europe and Asia, and has given rise to a large number of horticultural variatives differing in shape, colour and size.

The hardy border carnations are of easy cultivation in good loamy soil. In soils which are too rich they become too luxuriant; in others which are too light they fail. They are best planted in groups of from six to two dozen, and it is wise to keep one's stock going each year by producing freshly-rooted layers or cuttings. It is necessary as a rule to perform the operation of layering when the plants are in flower, and for this purpose reserves of plants should be kept so that those flowering in the border should not be adversely affected. They may be raised from seed, if a good strain is selected, and may also be produced from cuttings or layers.

Cuttings should be taken in July, should be about four inches in length and taken just below a joint. A cut is then made through the joint up the middle of the stem, and the cuttings inserted in sandy soil with the cut open—a small stone in each cut is often effective. The boxes or pots in which the cuttings are placed should be stored in a sheltered cold frame and be kept moist by being occasionally syringed.

Layering takes place in July. The soil is drawn away from around the plant from which the layers are to be made, and a mixture of two-thirds loam, one-sixth sand, and one-sixth leaf-mould substituted to a depth of about two inches. The lower leaves are stripped off the shoots to be layered, and a cut made up the middle of the stem so that half the stem still remains attached to the parent plant. Each layer is then pinned down with a hairpin, at a point just above the cut so that the tongue is kept open, and fixed firmly into the soil. An inch of the prepared compost should be added, and the layers kept moist in dry weather. Rooting takes from five to six weeks, and the new plants may then either be potted on, or transferred to reserve borders to grow on.

A number of exceptionally good border carnations are listed below.

BETTY THAIN, sulphur ground, broad-petalled, flaked towards the margins with cerise. 2-*ft.* *July.*

BLUSHING BRIDE, pink. 2-*ft.* *July.*

BOOKHAM BEAU, flowers of white ground flaked with scarlet, petals broad. 1½-*ft.* *July.*

CORONATION SCARLET, bright rich scarlet, broad-petalled, clove-scented flowers. 2-*ft.* *July.*

COTTAGE CRIMSON, crimson. 2-*ft.* *July.*

COTTAGE FANCY, white ground edged and flaked crimson-maroon, petals broad, crenate, free-flowering. 2-*ft.* *July.*

COTTAGE ORANGE, flowers of mandarin-red banded geranium-lake, petals broad and crenate-fringed. 1½-*ft.* *July.*

COTTAGE SCARLET, bright rich scarlet, petals broad. 1⅓-*ft.* *July.*

DARKIE, rich crimson, petals broad. 2-*ft.* *July.*

DELICIOSA, pale rose-pink, petals broad and slightly fringed. 2-*ft.* *July.*

DOWNS BEAUTY, primrose-yellow, flaked and edged with scarlet, petals broad. 2-*ft.* *July.*

DOWNS DELIGHT, orange-apricot, flushed and flaked with maroon. 2-*ft.* *July.*

DOWNS MAID, white ground edged with geranium-lake. 2-*ft.* *July.*

DOWNS MIST, purplish heliotrope flaked scarlet, vigorous growth. 1½-*ft.* *July.*

EGLANTINE CLOVE, rich scarlet-cerise, petals broad, flowers freely produced. 1½-*ft.* *July.*

ETTRICKDALE, yellow self. 2-*ft.* *July.*

FIREFLY, primrose-yellow ground, edged with rosy-purple, slightly fringed. 2-*ft.* *July.*

FIRETAIL CLOVE, apricot ground heavily flushed with scarlet, clove-scented. 2-*ft.* *July.*

FLAMBEAU, scarlet. 2-*ft.* *July.*

FRANCES KINNAIRD, white ground lightly flaked with rose. 1⅓-*ft.* *July.*

GALAXY, white ground.

GRENADIER, scarlet. 2-*ft.* *July.*

HAPPINESS, primrose-yellow edged with geranium-lake, slightly fringed. 1½-*ft.* *July.*

IDA GRAY, bright cerise banded and striped with pale heliotrope. 1½-*ft.* *July.*

INEZ, white. 2-*ft.* *July.*

INNOCENCE, pink. 2-*ft.* *July*

JOAN WARDALE, crimson. 2-*ft.* *July.*

JULIA B. WELLS, primrose-yellow flaked and edged with Bengal rose. 2-*ft.* *July.*

JUNO, pale sulphur ground flaked and lightly flushed with cerise. 2-*ft.* *July.*

LADY GAY, white ground flaked and striped with scarlet. 1½-*ft.* *July.*

LADY MILNE-WATSON, white ground flaked with wine-purple, clove-scented. 1½-*ft.* *July.*

LAVENDER CLOVE, mauve. 1½-*ft.* *July.*

LIMPSFIELD WHITE, white self, petals broad and of thick texture. 2-*ft.* *July.*

LORD LONSDALE, yellow ground marked and pencilled crimson-scarlet. 1½-*ft.* *July.*

MADONNA, creamy white. 1⅓-*ft.* *July.*

MAISIE THORBURN, apricot ground, edged and flaked with cerise. 2-*ft.* *July.*

MARGARET DAY, flowers of creamy-white, centres open and petals broad. 2-*ft.* *July.*

MONTROSE, scarlet. 2-*ft.* *July.*

MRS. EVELYN LAKE, crimson. 2-*ft.* *July.*

NAUTILUS, light rose. 1½-*ft.* *July.*

PINK BRAES, white ground edged with rose-pink. 2-*ft.* *July.*

RED ROVER, bright scarlet, petals broad and flowers freely produced. 2-*ft.* *July.*

R. J. DAY, primrose-yellow edged and flaked with deep rosy-red, open centres, and freely produced flowers. 2-*ft.* *July.*

SCARLET CLOVE, scarlet, clove-scented. 1½-*ft.* *July.*

SINCERITY, white with a creamy tint, slightly fringed. 1½-*ft.* *July.*

SUSSEX GEM, light pink lightly edged with deeper shade. 1¼-*ft.* *July.*

TALISMAN, bright rose-cerise. 2-*ft.* *July.*

YELLOW BEAUTY, yellow self. 2-*ft.* *July.*

D. ECHO, garden origin, is of the hybrid type called Allwoodii alpinus, and has salmon-rose single flowers with a deeper eye, produced with continuity throughout the season.

½-*ft.* *June–October.* *E.* ¼-*ft. Sq.* *Cg7.* *N.* 25/1. *Pl.* 31.

D. EMILE PARÉ (comm.), garden origin, is a hybrid of barbatus parentage with wide, green leaves and attractive, small, double flowers of soft salmon-pink, borne in small clusters on good stems.

1-*ft.* *June–September.* *E.* 1½-*ft. Sq.* *Cg7.* *N.* *Pl.* 31.

D. Highland Frazer, garden origin, is another hybrid of perpetual flowering habit, with prettily tartaned, single, pink flowers.

*½-ft. June–September. E. ¾-ft. Sq. Cg7. N. Pl. 31.*

D. inodorus (Without scent), Europe, is the *D. sylvestris* of catalogues, forming a grassy tuft of foliage with thin, bending stems and large clear-pink flowers. *⅔-ft. June–July. E. ½-ft. Sq. Sd2. C.*

D. Knappii (comm.), S.E. Europe, in habit resembles D. atrorubens but has foliage much more green. At the end of long whip-like stems it bears cluster-heads of clear yellow flowers. In some ways it reminds one of an advertisement of the furniture removers who used to advertise "Why pay rent? Move," and should be kept going annually from the seed which it produces with great freedom.

*1-ft. June–July. E. 1-ft. Sq. Sd2. N.*

D. Noëanus (comm.), Balkans, is so sweetly scented as to convey some consolation for the discomfort occasioned by its very prickly foliage; it has the added merit of bearing fringed white flowers in a pattern of perfect symmetry.

*½-ft. June–August. E. ½-ft. Sq. Sd2. N.*

**DIASCIA** (Scrophulariaceae), from G. diaskeo—to adorn, a reference to the dainty appearance of the flowers.

D. Barberae (comm.), S. Africa, is a good running plant with short spires of double-spurred rosy-pink flowers borne in short but open sprays. A perennial which is hardy only in the mildest winters and requires to be propagated annually from cuttings or from seed; it may be treated, if desired, as an annual.

*1-ft. June–October. H. 1-ft. Sq. Cg3. Sd2. N.*

D. Salmonae (comm.), Africa, is a particularly pleasing variant with similarly shaped flowers of salmon-pink.

*1-ft. June–October. H. 1-ft. Sq. Cg3. Sd2. N.*

**DICENTRA** (Papaveraceae), from G. di—double, and kentron—spur, with reference to the two spurs of the corolla; is also known as Dielytra.

The plants survive well in light, leafy soil, preferably in some shade.

D. Cucullaria (Resembling Monkshood), N. America, is very dwarf, with very small, green, much-tufted foliage, and hanging white flowers like pearls. Also known as Dutchman's Breeches, it is one of the most charming of all the dwarf garden plants.

*½-ft. May–June. H. ½-ft. Sq. D7. A. White.*

D. eximia (Choice), New York, has finely-divided, very green, ferny foliage, and bears hanging flowers of pink with short round spurs in multiple sprays. *1-ft. May. H. 1-ft. Sq. D7. A. 30/2.*

D. SPECTABILIS (Showy), Japan, is larger in every way than D. eximia, to which it otherwise bears a very close resemblance, except that it has rather redder flowers, borne in unbranching sprays.

*2-ft. May. H. 1-ft. Sq. D7. A.* 30/1.

DICENTRA EXIMIA

**DIERAMA** (Iridaceae), from G. dierama—a funnel, from the shape of the flowers.

D. PULCHERRIMUM (Most beautiful), S. Africa, grows with stiff, tough, Iris-like foliage to about two feet in height and bears long, slender wands of hanging bright-purple flowers in drooping sprays. It is also known as *Sparaxis pulcherrima*.

*4-ft. July–September. E. 3-ft. Sq. Cg2. N. Pl.* 75.

**DIGITALIS** (Scrophulariaceae), from L. digitus—a finger, the flowers resembling the finger of a glove.

Foxgloves are easily grown in light, leafy soil, generally in a partially shaded site. Most varieties propagate easily from seed. The Common Foxglove, D. purpurea, is often biennial in its characteristics and should be raised annually from seed. The other varieties are good perennials.

D. DUBIA (Doubtful), Balearic Islands, is a miniature pink foxglove with heavily netted or felted foliage. The flower sprays seldom exceed twelve inches in length, and it forms a delightful subject for light soil at the front of the border.

*1⅓-ft. July–August. E. ¾-ft. Sq. Sd2. N.* 630/2.

Kniphofia species ABCDEFGHKM
Physostegia virginiana DFGHJKMNP
Nerine Bowdeni LNOPQRSTU

Lupinus polyphyllus, hybrid seedlings

D. ferruginea (Rust-coloured), Spain, has quaint rusty-yellow flowers with pouting lips, borne in densely-packed spires of at least two feet in height. *2-ft. June–July. E. 1½-ft. Sq. Sd2. N.*

D. Mariana (Maryland), Spain, is a taller-growing variety with green lanceolate leaves with tightly packed spires of pink flowers, each with a long, protruding white lip. It requires similar cultivation. *1½-ft. June–July. E. 1-ft. Sq. Sd2. N.*

D. obscura (Dull), Spain, forms a hard woody stem, and makes a shrubby base of rosettes of narrow green leaves which produce short sprays of brown flowers heavily spotted and marked with orange. *1½-ft. July–August. E. 1-ft. Sq. Sd2. N.*

D. orientalis (Eastern), Asia Minor, has flowers borne upon freely-produced branching long spikes, of buff or orange, with similarly protruding lips, in tightly-packed spires. *2½-ft. June–July. E. 1½-ft. Sq. Sd2. N.*

**DIMORPHOTHECA** (Compositae), from G. di—two, morphe—form, theke—seed; referring to the forms of seed produced by some of the plants.

D. Barbarae (comm.), S. Africa, is a shrub more suited to the herbaceous border than the shrub garden. The branching woody stems bear linear leaves which are aromatic, and large pink daisy flowers with buff backs. *2-ft. June–September. E. 2-ft. Sq. Cg3. N. Pl. 32.*

D. Eklonis (comm.), S. Africa, is a little more tender, a little wider in the leaves, and bears white flowers, purple at the backs, with blue stamens. In some winters both of these plants will survive without difficulty, but care should be taken that some rooted pieces are removed to a place of safety in the early autumn. *2-ft. June–September. E. 2-ft. Sq. Cg8 and 3. N. Pl. 32.*

**DIPLARRHENA** (Iridaceae), from G. diploos—double, arren—male, two stamens only being perfect.

D. Moraea (comm.), Australia, is a plant with Iris-like leaves which are thin and very stiff, throwing up wiry stems which carry three-petalled white flowers, feathered with pale blue and centred with gold. *1-ft. July. D. 1-ft. Sq. D3. A. White.*

**DODECATHEON** (Primulaceae), from G. dodeka—twelve, and theos—divinity, that is, "the flower of the twelve gods."

These plants comprise the American Cowslips or Shooting Stars, and have Cyclamen-like flowers, borne in loose clusters at the top of long stems. They are most at home in well-drained but moist soil, preferably in a place where there is some shade. The species are extremely variable in colour, nearly all of them varying from white to magenta. Propagation is comparatively easy from seed and, when established, from division of the root broken off at the collars of the crown.

D. Clevelandii (comm.), California, has rather small, neat leaves, and bears clusters of purple flowers with reflexed petals and a yellow base with the anthers standing out like a cone in the centre.
1¼-*ft.* *May–June.* *H.* 1-*ft. Sq.* *D*8. *A.* 31.

D. Hendersonii (comm.), California, is very similar in appearance but has purple anthers, and is most frequently found in cultivation with lilac flowers. 1¼-*ft.* *May–June.* *H.* 1-*ft. Sq.* *D*8. *A.*

D. Jeffreyi (comm.), N.W. America, has larger, more upstanding leaves, flowers of reddish-purple and a prominent cone of dark purple. 1½-*ft.* *May–June.* *H.* 1-*ft. Sq.* *D*8. *A.*

D. Meadia (old name), N.W. America, has smaller leaves but has very strong growth, carrying spikes of the typical flowers, variable in colour but generally of rose with a white base.
2-*ft.* *May–June.* *H.* 2-*ft. Sq.* *D*8. *A.*

## DORONICUM (Compositae), derived from Arabic doronigi or doronakh.

The Doronicum produces some of the earliest colour in the herbaceous border; it is comparatively easy to grow in ordinary garden conditions, and can be increased by periodic division.

D. austriacum, Austria, has hairy, rough, toothed leaves and produces its yellow, narrow-petalled daisy flowers, usually singly, upon long pliable stems. 2-*ft.* *May.* *H.* 2-*ft. Sq.* *D*10. *N.*

D. Clusii (comm.), S. Europe, has oval, toothed leaves and bears its large, single, deep-golden, sharply-petalled daisy flowers on slender stems. 1¼-*ft.* *March–May.* *H.* 1½-*ft. Sq.* *D*10. *N.*

D. plantagineum (Plantain) has tuberous roots, dull-green toothed leaves and produces its golden-yellow sunflowers on long, slender stems. 4-*ft.* *April–May.* *H.* 2-*ft. Sq.* *D*10. *N.*

D. plantagineum excelsum "Harpur Crewe" is a variety seldom exceeding two feet in height, with flowers large and of bright gold.
2-*ft.* *April–May.* *H.* 1½-*ft. Sq.* *D*10. *N.*

## DRACOCEPHALUM (Labiatae), from G. drakon—dragon, and kephale—head, because of the shape of the flowers.

Bears flowers resembling those of the Monkshood in shape, and prefers, in the main, good garden soil and plenty of sun. It can be propagated with equal ease from either seed or cuttings of the stem.

D. argunense (Boat-shaped), China, makes a plant of about one foot in height, bearing spikes of bluish-purple flowers.
1-*ft.* *July–August.* *H.* 1-*ft. Sq.* *Sd*2. *Cg*6. *N.*

D. GRANDIFLORUM (Large-flowered), Siberia, has hyssop-like foliage and bears its intense-blue, hairy flowers on short spikes.

*1-ft. June–July. H. 1-ft. Sq. Sd2. Cg6. N.*

D. ISABELLAE (comm.), W. China, grows taller, has leaves divided into narrow segments and large violet-blue flowers in long spikes.

*2-ft. July–August. H. 1-ft. Sq. Sd2. Cg6. N.*

D. RUYSCHIANUM (comm.), China, has short spikes of closely-packed flowers of purple-blue.

*1½-ft. July–August. H. 1½-ft. Sq. Sd2. Cg6. N.* 40/1.

**ECCREMOCARPUS** (Bignoniaceae), from G. ekkremes—pendant, and karpos—fruit, the seed vessels being pendulous.

This is in reality a climbing plant, somewhat tender, but perfectly at home rambling through bushes with persistent tops, or upon walls which are slightly protected. The vine-like growths have pinnate leaves terminating in tendrils. It is easily grown in any normal garden soil.

E. SCABER (Rough), Chile, will climb to twelve feet in height, but will also flower while quite small and during the first year of its growth from seed. The flowers are small, tubular, and orange-red, and borne in clusters up to four inches in length.

*10-ft. July. H. 1-ft. Sq. Sd2. N.*

**ECHINACEA** (Compositae), from G. echinus—hedgehog.

Echinacea requires good garden soil and should not be divided too frequently.

E. PURPUREA (Purple), E. N. America, is also known as *Rudbeckia purpurea*, and produces large daisy flowers of purple-crimson on long stems. Flowers sometimes reach four inches in diameter.

*3½-ft. July–September. H. 2-ft. Sq. D3. N.*

E. PURPUREA THE KING, garden origin, has flowers larger in size and deeper and more attractive in colour.

*3½-ft. July–September. H. 2-ft. Sq. D3. N. Pl.* 33.

**ECHINOPS** (Compositae), from G. echinus—hedgehog, and opsis—like, alluding to the bristly spines which surround the flowers.

These are fine bold plants, very effective in the border, the metallic blue colour having great charm in such a setting. They are of easy cultivation in normal garden soil and exceptionally hardy.

E. BANNATICUS (From the Banat), Hungary, has rather thin thistle-like leaves, green above and whitish beneath, bearing globular, bristling heads of metallic blue, opening to show lavender-blue flowers.

*3-ft. July–August. H. 2½-ft. Sq. Sd10. Cr2. D3. N. Pl.* 34.

E. Ritro (old name), S. Europe, is usually represented in the garden by *E. sphaerocephalus*, but the true plant is comparatively dwarf, has white stems, the leaves are green above and woolly-white beneath, resembling those of the Acanthus. The flower-heads are globular and of pale heliotrope.
*2-ft. July–August. H. 2-ft. Sq. Sd3. N. Pl.* 12 *&* 65.

E. sphaerocephalus (Round-headed), S. Europe, grows much taller, has leaves which are rough green above, clothed with occasional hairs, and woolly-white beneath, with very large heads of silver-white flowers. *5-ft. July–August. H. 2-ft. Sq. Sd3. N.*

**EOMECON** (Papaveraceae), from G. eos—dawn, and mekon—poppy: the Dawn Poppy.

E. chionantha (Snow flower) bears pale grey-green, heart-shaped leaves on long stalks, rising from a rhizome which runs in a hot, dry but leafy soil in sun. The milky-white poppy flowers are borne on stems of about a foot.
*1-ft. May–June. H. 3-ft. Sq. D8. N. White.*

**EPIMEDIUM** (Berberidaceae), from G. epi—upon, and Media—the land of the Medes.

Not only do the flowers of this genus provoke the interest of the observer by their fancy flights of pendent flowers, but the beauty of line and colour of the leaves combine also to attract. Add to this their ability to grow in shady corners, and one has indeed the almost perfect plant.

E. × rubrum (Red), garden origin, produces its eccentric flowers of deep red, and ornaments them with a pale yellow centre.
*1-ft. May. H. 1-ft. Sq. D9. N.*

E. × versicolor var. sulphureum (Changing colour; sulphur), garden origin, is just as beautiful, just as useful, but of colour pale-yellow. *1-ft. May. H. 1-ft. Sq. D9. N.* 601/1.

**EREMURUS** (Liliaceae), from G. eremos—single, and oura—tail, with reference to the solitary nature of the flowering spikes.

This is the Giant Asphodel, with roots resembling an octopus in appearance. It forms tufts of sword-shaped leaves, from the centres of which rise stately spires of flowers sometimes reaching five to six feet, or even more, in height. It should be planted in well-dug, deep, but light loam, in a sunny border, and the crown of the plant protected during the winter with bracken or straw.

E. Bungei (comm.), Persia, is one of the dwarfer of the species and has green sword-shaped leaves about one foot long. The slender and graceful flowering stems, which vary from eighteen inches to three feet in height, are closely packed with small bright-yellow lily flowers with green centres. *3-ft. June–July. H. 3-ft. Sq. Sd3. N.*

E. ELWESII (comm.), Asia, has grey-green leaves and larger, more upstanding spikes of pink flowers each with a deeper band down the centre. *6-ft. June–July. H. 3-ft. Sq. Sd3. N.*

E. HIMALAICUS (From the Himalayas), N. India, is a tall, white-flowered species, similar in appearance to the foregoing, with the terminal spikes of flowers of at least four feet in length upon stems varying up to seven or eight feet in height.
*7-ft. May–June. H. 3-ft. Sq. Sd3. N.*

E. ROBUSTUS (Robust), Central Asia, has even longer and wider spikes of bright-pink flowers borne in stately splendour over tufts of grey-green sword-shaped leaves. *8-ft. June. H. 3-ft. Sq. Sd3. N.*

**ERIGERON** (Compositae), from G. eri—early, and geron—old man; possibly alluding to the appearance of the leaves of some of the species in the spring, or to the hoary tasselled seed-heads which resemble the head of an old man.

The Fleabanes are of exceptionally easy cultivation in good garden soil in a sandy position in the border. Nearly all the varieties can be produced with some ease either from seed or from division. The kinds suitable for the border which are in general cultivation are:—

E. AURANTIACUS (Orange), Turkestan, makes a tuft of wide, green leaves, from which spring several stems bearing many large, bright-orange, multiple-rayed flowers.
*1-ft. June–July. E. 1-ft. Sq. Sd2. D3. N.* 27/2.

E. AURANTIACUS ASA GRAY, garden origin, is a variative with flowers of buff-yellow, quite unlike any other colour to be found in the garden. *1-ft. June–July. E. 1-ft. Sq. Sd2. D3. N.*

E. GLABELLUS (Hairless), Rocky Mountains, produces heads of from one to three flowers, of violet-blue or purple, on long stems rising to about fifteen inches in height. The colour is variable; the varieties in cultivation are generally deep lavender.
*1¼-ft. May–June. H. 1½-ft. Sq. D3. N.*

E. GLABELLUS B. LADHAMS, garden origin, is similar but has flowers of bright coppery-pink. *1¼-ft. May–June. H. 1½-ft. Sq. D3. N.*

E. GLAUCUS (Grey-blue), N. America, has very wide rosettes of grey-green, rounded leaves bearing radiating stalks carrying a number of large lavender-blue flowers.
*1-ft. July–October. E. 1-ft. Sq. Sd2. D2. N.* 636/3.

E. HYBRIDUS (Hybrid), garden origin, is the name which is given to a host of variable plants under proprietary names. Of these, BEAUTY OF HALE, with lavender-blue flowers, and MERSTHAM GLORY, with semi-double flowers of violet-blue, are two feet in height. ELSTEAD PINK, with rose-pink flowers, MRS. H. BEALE, with violet-blue flowers with golden centre, and ELSIE, of rose-pink, seldom exceeding one foot in height, are among the best of their kind.

E. MACRANTHUS MESA GRANDE (Large-flowered) has large, deep violet-blue flowers, with an outstanding yellow boss—a pleasing contrast, asking for emulation! 2-*ft.* *May–June.* *H.* 1½-*ft. Sq.* *D*3. *N.*

E. PHILADELPHICUS (From Philadelphia), E. N. America, bears clusters of rather small, many-rayed flowers of bright pink for a very long period. 1-*ft.* *May–October.* *H.* 1½-*ft. Sq.* *D*3. *N.*

E. SPECIOSUS (Showy), W. N. America, grows to a height of about two feet, and has large flowers with many narrow petals of bright violet-blue, borne several in a head. Many horticultural forms exist in this plant, and varieties GRANDIFLORUS, MAJOR, SUPERBUS, ROSEUS, GRANDIFLORUS SUPERBUS will be found, most of which vary but slightly from the type. 2-*ft.* *June–July.* *H.* 1½-*ft. Sq.* *D*3. *N.*

**ERIOPHYLLUM** (Compositae), from G. erion—wool, phyllon—leaf, from the white, woolly appearance of the leaves.

E. CAESPITOSUM (Grown in tufts), N. W. America, is known in catalogues also as *Bahia lanata*, and is one of the most striking of all perennials for using at the front of the border: its combination of silvery-grey leaves, with the added warmth of its multiplicity of golden flowers, making it a perfect plant for any forward position.
1-*ft.* *June–September.* *H.* 1½-*ft. Sq.* *Cg*6. *D*3. *N.*

**ERYNGIUM** (Umbelliferae), from G. eryngano—to vomit; a reference to the supposed medicinal properties of the plant.

The roots of certain of the species are edible and tasty and have medicinal qualities. This is particularly so in the case of E. maritimum, a well-known native plant. All the plants are of easy culture in good garden soil in a sunny position.

E. AGAVIFOLIUM (With leaves like Agave) is one of the tallest of the species, growing to a height of about five feet; it has Agave-like leaves of grey-green, and forms large branching tops carrying pale blue or white spiky heads rather like those of the Teazle.
5-*ft.* *July–August.* *H.* 3-*ft. Sq.* *Sd*2. *N.*

E. ALPINUM (Alpine), Europe, has attractively cut grey-green foliage, often touched with metallic-blue, and bears clusters of oval, spiny heads of steel-blue, widely spread flowers.
2½-*ft.* *July–September.* *H.* 2-*ft. Sq.* *Sd*2. *N.*

E. amethystinum (Like amethyst), Asia Minor, has branching heads of light blue, very small and spiny, with the stems and bracts generally of the same colour.

*1½-ft. July–September. H. 1½-ft. Sq. Sd2. N.*

E. Bourgati (comm.), Mediterranean region, is roughly the same height, has its light-blue flower stems shielded with spiny bracts, and bears light-blue flower-heads.

*1½-ft. July–September. H. 1½-ft. Sq. Sd2. N.*

E. ebracteatum (Without bracts), Brazil, grows to about two feet in height, and has long, strap-like leaves on wiry stems which carry small thistle heads of jet-black.

*2-ft. July–September. H. 2-ft. Sq. Sd2. N.*

E. Oliverianum (comm.), E. Europe, probably a natural hybrid, grows to about three feet in height and has rounded leaves cut into four or five segments, and large blue heads sheathed with stiff, straight bracts. *3-ft. July–September. H. 2½-ft. Sq. Sd2. N.*

E. Oliverianum Springhill Seedling is larger and stronger, and produces giant heads of steel-blue colour.

*4-ft. July–September. H. 3-ft. Sq. Sd2. N.*

E. planum (Flat), Europe, has small blue thistle-like flowers rigidly borne on diffuse and branching sprays, the stems of which are also coloured blue. E. planum Violetta is similar but has double, violet-blue flowers, and is probably the darkest blue of all.

*3-ft. July–September. H. 2-ft. Sq. Sd2. N. Pl. 70.*

**ERYTHRONIUM** (Liliaceae), from G. erythros—red; the species which was discovered first having had flowers of reddish colour.

These are the Dog's-tooth Violets, delightful in shape and in colour. They are exceptionally easy to grow in deep leafy soil in a position in which they get a reasonable amount of shade. For shady borders nothing can be more apposite. They are easily increased from seed, which will germinate readily, but if the bulbs are to be stored they must not be allowed to become parched.

E. californicum (Californian) has silvery, mottled green, lily-like leaves, and creamy-white flowers with the segments bent back in graceful fashion. *1-ft. March–April. B. ¼-ft. Sq. Sd7. A.* 601/3.

E. Dens-canis (Dog's-tooth), Europe, is the Dog's-tooth Violet, bearing similar flowers of variable colour shading from lavender to rose, the segments of the flowers being similarly reflexed.

*½-ft. March–April. B. ¼-ft. Sq. Sd7. A.* 630/2.

E. grandiflorum (Large-flowered), Western U.S.A., has plain unmottled lily-like leaves with large yellow flowers usually growing two or more on a spray, with the petals much reflexed. The variety Snow Queen is typical of E. grandiflorum, with its white flowers and yellow centres. *1½-ft. March–April. B. ½-ft. Sq. Sd7. A.*

E. Hendersonii (comm.), Oregon, has heavily mottled leaves of pale green and brown, and bears reflexed-petalled flowers of deep lavender marked with maroon at the base.
¾-*ft.* *March–April.* *B.* ¼-*ft. Sq.* *Sd7.* *N.*

E. revolutum (With petals rolled back), British Columbia, has mottled leaves and can be distinguished by the rather narrow and thinner petals, rather more turned back than those of the other varieties. E. revolutum Johnsonii has flowers of dark rose. E. revolutum albiflorum or Watsonii has white flowers with a maroon base and is much the strongest grower of this group.
¾-*ft.* *March–April.* *B.* ½-*ft. Sq.* *Sd7.* *N.* 030/1.

**EUPATORIUM** (Compositae) is named after Mithridates Eupator, King of Pontus, who found among its species an antidote for poison.

A few species only are suitable for growing in the wilder places of the garden, where they flourish in almost any kind of soil.

E. Fraseri (comm.), sometimes called *E. urticaefolium* or *E. ageratoides*, E. N. America, grows to four feet in height and has round, coarsely-toothed, large leaves, and bears in large flat heads masses of small white flowers. 4-*ft.* *August–September.* *H.* 5-*ft. Sq.* *Sd3.* *N.*

E. purpureum (Purple), E. N. America, produces branching heads of crimson-purple flowers in open convex heads.
6-*ft.* *August–September.* 5-*ft. Sq.* *Sd2.* *N.*

**EUPHORBIA** (Euphorbiaceae), named after Euphorbus, who was physician to a King of Mauretania.

The Spurges, which are easily grown in any garden soil, generally have the fault of being invasive. They owe their usefulness to the effectiveness of their prettily coloured bracts, stems, and leaves, and are propagated by division.

E. Cyparissias (Resembling Cypress), Europe, is an invasive plant, reminiscent of the Cypress in its growth, bearing bright yellow bracts, and having its leaves changing in colour to orange and dull red. It is quite useful for covering banks where nothing else will grow.
1½-*ft.* *April–May.* *H.* 3-*ft. Sq.* *D3.* *ANC.*

E. epithymoides (Resembling a parasite of Thyme) is sometimes known as *E. polychroma*, and has wide, somewhat oval leaves surrounding flowers turning bright yellow. It forms a bushy and symmetrical plant about eighteen inches in height, and is probably about one of the best of the genus for a place in the border.
1½-*ft.* *July–August.* *H.* 2½-*ft. Sq.* *D3.* *N.* *Pl.* 74.

E. polychroma (*see* E. epithymoides).

Lupinus polyphyllus, Russell seedlings

Lupinus polyphyllus "Princess Elizabeth" BEFGJKLOP
Lupinus polyphyllus "Mrs. Penry Williams" HLMPQ

**FRITILLARIA** (Liliaceae), from L. fritillus—dice box, hence by analogy to the chequer-board from the resemblance of the markings of the flowers.

Fritillaries as a whole require sandy, peaty soil, and plentiful water while in growth, but otherwise to be kept reasonably dry.

F. CAMCHATCENSIS (From Kamschatka), N. W. America, throws up a stem like that of a small lily and produces a large hanging bell of purple-black. 1-*ft.* *May.* *D.* ¼-*ft. Sq.* *Scales* 8. *A.*

F. IMPERIALIS (Imperial), Persia, is the Crown Imperial, and has a stout stem rising to over two feet in height, resembling that of the lily, clothed with bright-green leaves, and produces at the top a large cluster of hanging bells on grooved stems, generally of yellow, red, or orange. It thrives best in good leafy loam, when planted deeply and left undisturbed. It has the drawback of having a repulsive odour. 3-*ft.* *July–August.* *B.* 1-*ft. Sq.* *Scales* 8. *N.*

F. MELEAGRIS (Speckled like a guinea-fowl), Europe, is the Snake's-head Fritillary, a particularly beautiful native frequently found growing wild in Oxfordshire, with hanging flowers of wine-purple, chequered with white. The white variety F. MELEAGRIS ALBA, which predominates, is equally lovely. Large patches should be naturalised wherever possible.
1-*ft.* *April–May.* *B.* ⅓-*ft. Sq.* *Scales* 8. *A.*

F. PYRENAICA (From the Pyrenees), Spain, grows to a height of about eighteen inches and has hanging flowers somewhat smaller than those of F. Meleagris, of brownish-purple without, and amber and green within. Caught with the sun upon it, it is one of the loveliest subjects in the whole garden, and is, in addition, probably the easiest of the species to grow. 1½-*ft.* *May.* *B.* ¼-*ft. Sq.* *Scales* 8. *A.*

**FUNKIA** (Liliaceae), named after Dr. H. Funk, a German botanist.

It is commonly called the Plantain Lily and is grown mainly for the decorative effect of the striking foliage, though the flowers themselves, which are borne in one-sided spikes, are also particularly attractive. They are very useful in shady borders, and are sometimes known by the alternative name of HOSTA.

F. FORTUNEI (comm.), Japan, has blue-green, long, wide, multiple-ribbed leaves, and bears its pale-lilac flowers in one-sided sprays in July and September. 2-*ft.* *July–September.* *H.* 1½-*ft. Sq.* *D*3. *N.*

F. JAPONICA (Japanese), Japan, is also known as *F. lancifolia* and *F. lanceolata*, and has much narrower green foliage with only six or eight veins and bears pale lilac flowers, on somewhat shorter stems.
1½-*ft.* *July–September.* *H.* 1½-*ft. Sq.* *D*3. *N.*

F. JAPONICA ALBA MARGINATA (White; edged) is similar but has its leaves edged with white.
$1\frac{1}{2}$-*ft.* *July–September.* *H.* $1\frac{1}{2}$-*ft. Sq.* *D*3. *N.*

F. SIEBOLDII (comm.), Japan, has very long, very wide leaves of glaucous colour and bears long one-sided sprays of extremely pale lilac flowers in August. $2\frac{1}{2}$-*ft.* *August.* *H.* 2-*ft. Sq.* *D*3. *ANC.*

FUNKIA FORTUNEI

**GAILLARDIA** (Compositae) is named after a French botanist, Gaillard.

The garden varieties appear to be hybrids of the one perennial species and, like all the Composites, are liable to sport considerably from seed. They may be propagated from cuttings in the summer, or by division of the root in the spring, and flourish in a sunny position in good garden soil.

G. ARISTATA (Awned), W. N. America, has spathulate long leaves, sometimes pinnately cut, and bears heads of orange-yellow daisy flowers up to four inches in diameter. The following named varieties are of outstanding appearance:—

| | |
|---|---|
| Dazzler | scarlet with yellow margin |
| E. T. Anderton | very large yellow. *Pl.* 35 |
| Firebrand | large lacinated flowers of red with a wide yellow margin. *Pl.* 36 |
| Ipswich Beauty | ruby red, golden margin. *Pl.* 36 |
| Lady Rollison | yellow, with a deeper eye |
| Mrs. H. Longster | bright yellow, crimson centres |
| Tangerine | tangerine-orange |
| The King | deep red, with gold |

2-*ft.* *June–October.* *H.* 2-*ft. Sq.* *D*3. *Cg*6. *ANC.*

**GALANTHUS** (Amaryllidaceae), from G. gala—milk, anthos—flower.

The Snowdrops are both the earliest and the latest of all hardy flowers, beginning to flower in November and flowering throughout the winter until March. All multiply readily from seed.

G. BYZANTINUS (From Constantinople), E. Europe, is a pretty little Snowdrop of white and green which starts to flower in November and carries on during January.
*⅓-ft. November–January. B. ¼-ft. Sq. C4. N.*

G. ELWESII (comm.), Asia Minor, is a quaint Snowdrop with large, very handsome outer petals of white, with the inner segments of green. *1-ft. January–February. B. ¼-ft. Sq. Sd4. N.*

G. NIVALIS (Growing near the snow) is the Common Snowdrop, available in many variable forms. The general characteristics, however, are that the leaves are from six to nine inches long and about a quarter of an inch wide. The flowers, which are borne upon six-inch stems, are white, with the inner segments green along the edges. There are double-flowered forms, and forms which vary considerably in the size of the flowers, all of which are undoubtedly beautiful. Snowdrops should be planted three inches deep in reasonably good soil. *½-ft. January–February. B. ¼-ft. Sq. Sd4. N.*

**GALEGA** (Leguminosae), from G. gala—milk; with reference to an old idea that the herbage encouraged production of milk in herds.

The genus Galega is commonly called Goat's Rue, and has pinnate leaves and bears blue and white pea flowers in clusters. Propagation is by seed sown early in the year or by the division of the roots in the spring.

G. OFFICINALIS (Of the shop), Spain, grows to a height of three feet, and has clusters of purplish-blue flowers. Its variety ALBA has white flowers, and G. CARNEA has pretty flesh-pink flowers. The variety HARTLANDII has lilac flowers and variegated flowers. LADY WILSON has flowers of rosy-lavender. HER MAJESTY has flowers of soft blue, and NIOBE has attractive flowers of clear white.
*2-ft. June–July. H. 2-ft. Sq. Sd2. D3. N.*

**GAZANIA** (Compositae), from G. gaza—riches, alluding to the large, brightly-coloured flowers, is commonly known as the Treasure Flower.

These are also perennials, produced freely from cuttings taken either late in the autumn or during the winter, but which are only hardy in the winter in maritime districts. Though the hardiest species is probably G. montana, all are worth a place in the border in a sunny position. The modern hybrids are particularly beautiful both in colour and shape.

**GAZANIA (continued)**

G. MONTANA (Mountain), Natal, has narrow, grassy leaves, silvery beneath, and bears creamy-white flowers with a greenish back to the petals. It can be propagated by division.
*½-ft. June–September. E. 1-ft. Sq. D9. N.*

G. NIVEA (Snowy), S. Africa, has wider leaves and wider petals, and white flowers. *½-ft. June–September. E. 1-ft. Sq. Cg9. N.*

G. PAVONIA (Peacock), S. Africa, has extremely large bright flowers of orange-yellow, with leaves divided into pinnate segments, shiny green above and woolly-grey beneath.
*1½-ft. June–September. E. 1½-ft. Sq. Cg9. N.*

G. RIGENS (Stiff), S. Africa, has green leaves, wide and woolly beneath, and sometimes pinnately divided, and large orange-yellow flowers with brown-black spots, with white eyes at the base of each of the petals. *½-ft. May–September. E. 1-ft. Sq. Cg9. N.*

G. SPLENDENS (Shining), natural hybrid, has flowers of orange with black and white spots at the base of the petals.
*⅓-ft. May–September. E. 1-ft. Sq. Cg9. N. Pl. 37.*

GAZANIA HYBRIDS.—Some of the best-known hybrids are noted below:

BLACKCAP has deep-cream flowers with black spots at the base of the petals.

DAINTY is clear yellow, with dainty black and white squares at the base of the petals.

FRANKLIN has cream flowers, grey-backed, with dark spots at the base of the petals. *Pl. 37.*

HALO has flowers of pale orange with white basal patches.

POTTSII is the largest variety, with huge full orange flowers. *Pl. 37.*

RED CHARMER is a dwarf mahogany-red.

SUNFIRE is mahogany-red. *Pl. 37.*

SUNGOLD is a deep mahogany-red.

SUNSPOT is deep orange-red. *Pl. 37.*

TANGERINE is tangerine-orange.

THE BISHOP is a deep orange-yellow. *Pl. 37.*

*½-ft.–⅔-ft. June–October. E. 1-ft. Sq. Cg9. N.*

**GENTIANA** (Gentianaceae), said by Pliny to have been brought into use by Gentius, King of Illyria.

The genus Gentiana is a very large one, comprising upwards of 800 known species, the number of which is being increased each year. In addition, since the more general cultivation of Gentians in the garden, many hybrids of great beauty are being added, so that the already lovely genus has the tendency to become even more beautiful. The colour range is very large, for, while the colour of the genus as a whole must be said to be blue, there are also white Gentians, for example G. saxosa, of New Zealand, the Yellow Gentian, Gentiana lutea, and even the scarlet of G. scarlatina.

The best-known of the species is undoubtedly G. acaulis, which is by no means the most beautiful of all Gentians, though there are few better. It can be either a good plant or a bad one in the garden, flowering with great freedom in some locations, but proving quite intractable and difficult to flower in others for no seeming reason. Recent investigations suggest that there is a bacteriological reason for its failure to flower in certain gardens, and it would be wise for the gardener not to accept his failure to grow G. acaulis as a test of his ability to make other Gentians flower. Unfortunately, very few of the plants comprising the genus Gentiana may be said to be pre-eminently fitted to grow in the herbaceous border, but many of the species are so grown with success. Recently I have seen kitchen gardens in which the edges of the beds were made beautiful with G. acaulis, and at least two others I know have G. sino-ornata growing in similar places with the virility of weeds. These two species are certainly fitted by adoption to the purpose.

G. ACAULIS (Stemless), Europe, is, as indicated above, one of the species which can be grown with success in the border, and produces tubular deep blue flowers on stems of an inch or so, from mats of glossy-green broad-pointed leaves. It should be planted in moderately heavy loam in a fully sunny exposure, and can be propagated by means of division, the divisions being planted very firmly.

*⅓-ft. March–June. E. 1-ft. Sq. D6. C.* 41.

G. AFFINIS (Similar), N. W. America, grows to about one foot in height, bearing its narrow blue funnel-shaped flowers at the tops of the stems, and in the axils of the leaves. It grows best in a moist site in some sun. *1-ft. August. H. ¾-ft. Sq. Sd2. A.*

G. ASCLEPIADEA (Resembling the Swallow-wort), Europe, throws up long arching stems, bearing willow-like leaves, to a height of some two feet, and carries azure-blue tubular flowers in groups of two or three in the leaf axils. The colour is variable, white, pale-blue and violet varieties all existing. It is best grown either in a soil which is moderately moist or in a partly shaded site.

*2½-ft. August–September. H. 2-ft. Sq. Sd2. N.* 40. *Pl.* 67.

G. LINEARIS (Of uniform width), N.W. America, grows to about one foot in height, bears clusters of blue tubular flowers with erect lobes, and grows best in deep open soil in a sunny position.

*1-ft. July–August. H. 1-ft. Sq. Sd3. N.*

G. LUTEA (Yellow), Europe, is a yellow-flowered Gentian which grows to upwards of three feet in height. It forms a wide rosette of long broad basal leaves and bears its flowers in the leaf axils of its leafy stems in groups of from three to one dozen. The flowers are pale-yellow and have no folds between the petal segments. It grows well in any deep soil in a sunny place.

*3-ft. July–August. E. 2½-ft. Sq. Sd2. N.*

G. MACAULAYI (comm.), garden origin, is a hybrid of G. Farreri with G. sino-ornata, and is one of the most easily grown of all the Gentians, forming a loose and open tuft of very narrow green foliage and producing large turquoise-blue tubular flowers, striped on the back with pale green and violet. It grows well in any good garden soil in a sunny position. *½-ft. July–August. H. ⅔-ft. Sq. D3. N. Pl.* 38.

G. MAKINOI (comm.), Japan, grows from a central rootstock and has foot-high leafy stems with polished green foliage. The pale-blue to violet-blue flowers, which are heavily speckled with small spots, are borne at the tops of the stems, and at the topmost leaf axils. It thrives in a sunny, lime-free soil.
1-*ft. July–August. H.* 1-*ft. Sq. Sd*2. *N.*

G. PNEUMONANTHE (Lung flower), Europe, is also a native of Great Britain, and is of variable height with large flowers of deep blue, heavily speckled with green spots in distinct bands. It requires a lime-free soil and a position in which it obtains more than ordinary moisture. 1-*ft. August–September. H. ¾-ft. Sq. Sd*2. *A.*

G. SCEPTRUM (Resembling a sceptre), N. America, grows to about fifteen inches in height, has green spoon-shaped leaves and bears rounded buds in groups of two or three at the tips of the shoots or in the leaf axils. It seems never to open its flowers, which vary from blue to blue-green, as its lobes stand upright. It is best grown in a damp place in the sun. 1¼-*ft. August. H.* 1-*ft. Sq. Sd*2. *N.* 43/2.

G. SEPTEMFIDA (Divided into seven parts), S.W. Asia, is probably one of the easiest of the Gentians to grow, rising to a height of about one foot, with leafy stems clothed with pointed, shining leaves. The flowers, which are of soft blue, are produced in clusters at the tops of the stems and in the uppermost leaf axils. It grows well in any sunny position in good garden soil.
1-*ft. August. H.* 1-*ft. Sq. Sd*2. *N.* 41. *Pl.* 38.

G. SINO-ORNATA (Chinese, decorative), W. China, is the finest of all autumn-flowering Gentians, making a central tuft of grassy leaves from which other stems radiate freely and root at the nodes. They bear at their tips tubular royal-blue flowers of about an inch in diameter, striped without with blue and greeny-yellow. It must be grown in a good deep lime-free soil, and have plenty of summer moisture. It can be propagated with ease by division.
*½-ft. September–November. H.* 1-*ft. Sq. D*2. *A.* 42.

G. TRICHOTOMA (With the divisions in threes), W. China, has become progressively easy in cultivation, grows to about two feet in height, with leafy stems and somewhat long green leaves. The flowers, which are borne in threes at the tops of the stems and in the leaf axils, vary from sea-blue to deep blue and are white within. It needs deeply-dug soil which is free from lime.
1½-*ft. June–August. H. ½-ft. Sq. Sd*2. *A.*

**GERANIUM** (Geraniaceae), from G. geranos—a crane, the seed capsules resembling the head and beak of the bird.

A group of almost indispensable and exceptionally free-flowering plants which thrive in light, well-drained soil in a sunny place.

G. ARMENUM (From Armenia), Armenia, is also known as *G. psilostemon*, and has deeply cut, five-lobed leaves which turn crimson in autumn. The large crimson-magenta flowers are spotted with black at the base. 2-*ft.* *May–August.* *H.* 1½-*ft. Sq.* *D*3. *N.*

G. ENDRESSII (comm.), Pyrenees, has small, five-lobed, grey-green leaves and bears clusters of bright rose-pink flowers in great profusion, growing well in any position and being a convenient plant for shady places. 1-*ft.* *June–August.* *H.* 1-*ft. Sq.* *D*3. *N.* *Pl.* 80.

G. ERIOSTEMON (With woolly stamens), Siberia, also known as *G. platyanthum*, bears, above large palmate velvety five-lobed leaves, loose clusters of large violet-blue flowers in profusion. 1½-*ft.* *July–August.* *H.* 1½-*ft. Sq.* *D*3. *N.*

G. GRANDIFLORUM (Large-flowered), N. Asia, has green leaves deeply cut in five lobes, and has very large, round, flat flowers of bright purple-blue. 1-*ft.* *June–August.* *H.* 1-*ft. Sq.* *D*3. *N.*

G. IBERICUM (Georgian), S.W. Asia, has large violet flowers veined with red and is a strong garden type with attractive seven-lobed leaves which turn a pleasing crimson in late autumn. 1½-*ft.* *July–August.* *H.* 1½-*ft. Sq.* *D*3. *N.*

G. MACRORRHIZUM (With long roots), S. Europe, forms a mat-like structure of thick roots bearing light green five- to seven-lobed leaves which are heavily scented. The flowers, which, though small, are very attractive, are of rosy-purple, and borne in clusters. 1¼-*ft.* *July–August.* *H.* 3-*ft. Sq.* *D*3. *N.*

G. PHAEUM (Dusky), Great Britain, has deeply lobed small green leaves and bears clusters of almost black flowers upon long slender stems. Late in the season the flowers change to white, heavily veined with purple. It grows well in shaded sites and in woodland. 1½-*ft.* *July–August.* *H.* 1-*ft. Sq.* *D*3. *N.*

G. PRATENSE (Growing in meadows), Great Britain, is the wild blue Crane's-bill of the wayside, growing to about three feet in height, bearing green leaves cut into seven lobes, and purple-blue flowers of about ¾ inch in diameter. The variety G. PRATENSE ALBUM has white flowers, and G. PRATENSE FL. PL. has attractive double flowers of violet-purple. 3-*ft.* *July–September.* *H.* 1½-*ft. Sq.* *D*3. *N.*

G. (TRAVERSII) RUSSELL PRICHARD (comm.), garden origin, has the good habits of G. Endressii, with a deeper and more intense colour, accompanied by greener leaves. ¾-*ft.* *June–August.* *E.* 2-*ft. Sq.* *D*3. *N.* *Pl.* 80.

**GERBERA** (Compositae), named after a German naturalist.

Gerberas can at best only be said to be half-hardy perennials, but in milder winters will survive out of doors with some surface protection, which can be provided by means of bracken, straw or ashes.

G. Jamesonii (comm.), Transvaal, has long hairy leaves, woolly beneath, bearing large daisy flowers with perfectly patterned petals of flaming orange. G. Jamesonii hybrida covers hybrids with flowers of variable shades and colour, from white to yellow and red to purple. The plants may be grown with facility in a cold house which is frost-proof, in a mixture of equal parts of loam peat or leaf-mould, and sand. Propagation may be done either from seed or from cuttings made from the basal shoots in April.
1½-*ft.* *July–September.* *H.* 1½-*ft. Sq.* *Sd*2. *Cg*4. *N.*

**GEUM** (Rosaceae), from G. geuo—to flavour, the roots of some of the species being pleasant to the taste.

This group of attractive and colourful plants is exceptionally useful, since, in the main, they will flower well in any good garden soil in either a sunny or shady site.

G. Borisii (comm.), Bulgaria, is said to be a hybrid of G. reptans and G. bulgaricum, and makes a tuft of rough bright green foliage, and bears its orange-scarlet flowers in diffuse sprays on foot-high stems.
1-*ft.* *May–August.* *E.* 1½-*ft. Sq.* *Sd*2. *D*3. *N.*

G. chiloense (From Chile), is the *G. coccineum* of gardens and has leaves made up of one large rough green terminal leaflet with many small laterals. The flowers, which are borne in clusters upon long, slender stems, are of bright scarlet. The variety Fire Opal has large scarlet flowers touched with orange. Lady Stratheden has semi-double, golden-yellow flowers. Mrs. Bradshaw has similar flowers of bright scarlet. Orange Queen, Orangeman, Prince of Orange all have flowers of orange-yellow, while Princess Juliana has large double flowers of tawny-yellow.
2-*ft.* *June–September.* 1½-*ft. Sq.* *Sd*2. *D*3. *N.*

G. Heldreichii (comm.), Greece, is said to be a form of G. montanum and has flowers of rich orange, on longer and more upstanding stems. 1½-*ft.* *May–October.* *H.* 1½-*ft. Sq.* *D*3. *Sd*2. *N.*

G. rivale (Of brooks), Europe, has rough, green, much-divided leaves, carries nodding flowers of terracotta-red in purple calyces, and seems to be in flower almost the whole year through, being met with sometimes in November, and again in early January. It is available in the form of a number of hybrids, of which Leonard's variety, with flowers of old rose, is as attractive as a host of others.
1-*ft.* *May–October.* *E.* 1-*ft. Sq.* *D*3. *Sd*2. *N.* 636/3.

Lupinus polyphyllus "Rapture" AEJNORSMPQT
Lupinus polyphyllus "General Holditch" CFGKLOPST
Lupinus polyphyllus "Maud Tippets" MPQTU

Oenothera rivularis ABCDFGHLM
Aster Novae-Angliae "Barr's Violet" EJ
Lychnis chalcedonica rubra plena FGJLMNOPRS
Aster Thompsonii OPQSTU

**GLADIOLUS** (Iridaceae), from L. gladius—sword, from the shape of the leaves of the plants.

Few of the original species or wild types of Gladioli are now grown by the amateur. The modern Gladiolus is pre-eminently an example of the art of the hybridist; from the species G. cardinalis, which was introduced at the end of the eighteenth century, and G. psittacinus sprang G. gandavensis with its long dense spike of medium size, flowers bright red in colour and splashed with orange, which is one of the earliest of the garden types. From this sprang the types known as Lemoinei, nancieanus, Childsii, and others, but it was not until after the introduction of G. primulinus in 1902 that the amazing range of colours and diversity of size was obtainable in the resultant hybrids which have submerged the parent species, probably with a very large measure of justification. As a result there are two main types of Gladioli, the large-flowered type and the primulinus or small-flowered type, all of which are available in a large range of colours, and in named varieties.

Cultivation of Gladioli is best undertaken in a moderately rich sandy loam, though successful cultivation can be assured in any moderately rich soil. If the soil, however, is poor, it should be well manured in the autumn before the corms are planted in the spring. For border purposes these are best planted in clumps and at least six inches apart and three to four inches in depth. In June, feeding should take place, but should not be heavy. As a rule, after flowering the corms mature in about six weeks, and at the first advent of yellowing of the foliage they should be lifted, the tops cut off and the corms spread out to dry and stored throughout the winter in a cool but frost-proof place. There are few of the older species still in general cultivation.

G. BYZANTINUS (Byzantine) grows to a height of two feet and has reddish-purple flowers, and is probably one of the hardiest of the species. *2-ft. August. B. ½-ft. Sq. Sd3. Offsets. N.*

G. HYBRIDUS (Hybrid), garden origin, covers all the large-flowered Gladioli which have sprung as the result of the hybridisation of the species, and may be divided into two sections—the large-flowered hybrids, and the primulinus hybrids with smaller hooded flowers, soft colours, and slender and graceful habit of growth.

Examples of the large-flowered type are:—

AMERICA—shell-pink, 3-*ft.*, late-flowering.

AVE MARIA—violet-blue, 3½-*ft.*, early-flowering.

BARON JOSEPH HULOT—purple-blue, 3½-*ft.*, mid-season.

BIT OF HEAVEN—orange-yellow, 3-*ft.*, mid-season. *Pl.* 39.

BLUE BEAUTY—light blue edged violet, 3½-*ft.*, mid-season.

CAPTAIN BOYTON—mauve-lilac, 3½-*ft.*, late.

COMMANDER KOEHL—fiery-scarlet, 4-*ft.*, mid-season.

CRIMSON GLOW—crimson-scarlet, orange centre, 4-*ft.*, mid-season.

EMPRESS OF INDIA—dark claret, 3-*ft.*, mid-season.

FATA MORGANA—pale pink, primrose throat, 3-*ft.*, early.

GLADNESS—fiery scarlet, 3½-*ft.*, early.

LOUIS D'OR—fiery gold, 3-*ft.*, mid-season. *Pl.* 39.

MOORISH KING—dark crimson-maroon, 3½-*ft.*, mid-season.

MRS. VAN KONIJENBURG—lavender-blue, 4-*ft.*, mid-season.

ORANGE PRINCESS—salmon-orange, crimson throat, 3½-*ft.*, mid-season.

PANAMA—salmon-red, 3-*ft.*, mid-season. *Pl.* 40.

PELEGRINA—dark-blue and purple, 4-*ft.*, early.

PFITZER'S TRIUMPH—salmon with orange-scarlet, 4-*ft.*, late.

PRINCE OF WALES—salmon-pink with primrose, 3½-*ft.*, early.

TIP TOP—cerise-scarlet, 4-*ft.*, mid-season.

YELLOW HAMMER—yellow, 3½-*ft.*, mid-season.

Primulinus hybrids:—

ALICE TIPLADY—orange-salmon, 2-*ft.*, early.

APRICOT GLOW—apricot, buff throat, 3-*ft.*, mid-season.

COPERNICUS—orange and scarlet, 3-*ft.*, early.

GOLDEN FRILLS—yellow, marked red, 3½-*ft.*, early.

HERMIONE—buff salmon, 3-*ft.*, early.

MAIDEN'S BLUSH—blush-rose, cream throat, 2½-*ft.*, early.

MYRA—salmon-rose, cream centre, 3-*ft.*

ORANGE BRILLIANT—orange buff, 2½-*ft.*, mid-season.

PENNLAC—soft salmon-pink, white stripe, 3-*ft.* *Pl.* 40.

ROSE LUISANTE—bright rose and cream, 3½-*ft.*, early.

SALMON BEAUTY—salmon, yellow throat, 3-*ft.*–4-*ft.*, mid-season.

SCARLET CARDINAL—crimson-scarlet, 3-*ft.*, early.

SCARLETTA—rose-scarlet, 3½-*ft.*, early.

SOUVENIR—rich yellow, 4-*ft.*, mid-season.

TOPAZ—orange-salmon, chamois centre, 3-*ft.*, early.

TROUBADOUR—deep purple, 3½-*ft.*, mid-season.

WHITE BUTTERFLY—white, 2½-*ft.*, mid-season.

**GUNNERA** (Haloragidaceae) is named to commemorate J. E. Gunner, a Swedish botanist.

The two species which follow are natives of South America, where the thick stems of the leaves are eaten by the natives. They are grown mainly for the benefit of their huge rhubarb-like leaves, which are often more than six feet in diameter, and are borne upon prickly stems upwards of five feet in length.

G. CHILENSIS, from Chile, is also known as *G. scabra*, grows to at least six feet in height and produces giant rhubarb-like leaves which provide an attractive feature near the waterside or in a large border. The root requires protection during winter with bracken or straw, and the club-shaped flower-head should be cut out before it matures.

*6-ft.* — *H.* *12-ft. Sq.* *D3.* *N.*

G. MANICATA (Sleeved), Brazil, is similar, with large foliage shaped like a shield, and has its thick stems covered with red hairs. It requires similar treatment and situation.

*8-ft.* — *H.* *12-ft. Sq.* *D3.* *N.*

**GYPSOPHILA** (Caryophyllaceae), from G. gypsos—chalk, and phileo—to love.

Most of the species prefer a soil containing chalk and thrive well in the border in any good garden soil which is alkaline.

G. ACUTIFOLIA (With pointed leaves), Caucasus, grows to three feet in height with many-branching flowering stems clad with sharply-pointed long leaves up to an inch in width, and producing diffuse sprays of lilac flowers larger than those of G. paniculata.

*3-ft.* *July–September.* *H.* *4-ft. Sq.* *Sd2.* *N.*

G. OLDHAMIANA (comm.), garden origin, resembles G. paniculata, with flowers of very pale pink.

*3-ft.* *July–September.* *H.* *4-ft. Sq.* *Sd2.* *N.*

G. PACIFICA (From the Pacific region) is similar with large flowers of clear rose-pink. *3-ft.* *July–September.* *H.* *4-ft. Sq.* *Sd2.* *N.*

G. PANICULATA (Panicled), Europe, has an attractive common name, "Baby's Breath," and forms a cloud of tiny white flowers upon stiff thread-like branching stems. The taproot is reminiscent of the horse-radish and requires deeply-dug soil. The variety G. PANICULATA PLENA has tiny double-white flowers and is probably even more attractive than the single-flowered variety.

*3-ft.* *August–September.* *H.* *4-ft. Sq.* *Sd2.* *C.*

G. REPENS ROSEA PLENA (Creeping; pink; double), garden origin, is a hybrid from G. repens, with extremely attractive double flowers of rose-pink. The height seldom exceeds eighteen inches, but the spread of the plant is up to three-foot square, which makes it a very useful plant for the front of the border.

*1½-ft.* *August–September.* *H.* *3-ft. Sq.* *Sd2.* *C.* *Pl. 76.*

**HELENIUM** (Compositae) is named after Helen of Troy, its flowers, it is said, having sprung from her tears.

Heleniums will do well in the border in any moderately rich soil in a sunny position, and require little out of the ordinary in the way of cultivation.

H. AUTUMNALE (Of the autumn), N. America, is also known as *H. grandiflorum*. It grows to a height of about three feet, and bears high-centred, crinkled, wide-rayed flowers of lemon-yellow in the utmost profusion. *3-ft.* *August–September.* *H.* *3-ft. Sq.* *D3.* *N.*

H. AUTUMNALE CHIPPERFIELD ORANGE has orange flowers striped with red. $2\frac{1}{2}$-*ft.* *August–September.* *H.* $2\frac{1}{2}$-*ft. Sq.* *D3.* *N.*

H. AUTUMNALE PUMILUM is a dwarf variety seldom exceeding two feet in height, with deep-yellow flowers. A very attractive variation called CRIMSON BEAUTY has bronze-red flowers and is of the same height and habit. 2-*ft.* *August–September.* *H.* 2-*ft. Sq.* *D3.* *N.*

H. AUTUMNALE RIVERTON BEAUTY, garden origin, has lemon-yellow flowers with a dark-brown centre.
$2\frac{1}{2}$-*ft.* *August–September.* *H.* $2\frac{1}{2}$-*ft. Sq.* *D3.* *N.*

H. AUTUMNALE RIVERTON GEM, garden origin, has old-gold flowers which turn rose. $2\frac{1}{2}$-*ft.* *August–September.* *H.* $2\frac{1}{2}$-*ft. Sq.* *D3.* *N.*

H. AUTUMNALE RUBRUM has flowers of mahogany crimson.
$2\frac{1}{2}$-*ft.* *August–September.* *H.* $2\frac{1}{2}$-*ft. Sq.* *D3.* *N.*

H. BIGELOVII (comm.), N. America, grows to two and a half feet in height and has deep-yellow crinkled and crenate petals surrounding a very dark-brown disc. $2\frac{1}{2}$ *ft.* *July–August.* *H.* $1\frac{1}{2}$-*ft. Sq.* *D3.* *N.*

H. HOOPESII (comm.), U.S.A., is the earliest-flowering of all Heleniums, grows to a height of about two feet and produces its large, yellow, wide-petalled daisy flowers in groups of two or three on long stems.
2-*ft.* *May–June.* *H.* $1\frac{1}{2}$-*ft. Sq.* *D3.* *N.*

H. HYBRIDUM (Hybrid), garden origin, consists mainly of garden varieties, one of the parents of which is H. autumnale. The outstanding varieties are MOERHEIMII (MOERHEIM BEAUTY), which has even darker and very attractive flowers borne upon a plant which is tall. THE BISHOP has attractive golden-yellow flowers with a particularly dark brown eye, and the third one, WYNDLEY, very large yellow flowers centred with bronze. GOLDENE JUGEND has attractive golden-yellow flowers and a brown eye, and MADAME CANIVET is an exceptionally floriferous variety bearing large numbers of rather small flowers of bright yellow with a dark brown eye.
4-*ft.* *August–September.* *H.* 2-*ft. Sq.* *D3.* *N.* *Pl.* 41 *&* 45.

**HELIANTHUS** (Compositae), from G. helios—sun, and anthos—flower.

This is the Sunflower, which is made up in part of annual plants, and of the following perennial species. From the point of view of the border they are grown for the benefit of their large, attractive golden flowers. One of the species, H. tuberosus, the Jerusalem Artichoke, is probably as attractive in the border as it is useful in the kitchen.

H. DECAPETALUS (Having ten petals), N. America, has chrome-yellow flowers up to about three inches in diameter, with a yellow disc. A garden variety developed from this species is the bigger-flowering variety known as SOLEIL D'OR, with double-quilled rich-yellow flowers. 5-*ft.* *August–September.* *H.* 3-*ft. Sq.* *D3.* *N.*

H. DECAPETALUS FL. PL. has double flowers but is otherwise similar, as also is H. GRANDIFLORUS. H. DECAPETALUS MAXIMUS has large flowers with pointed ray florets, and grows to eight feet in height.
*8-ft. August–September. H. 3-ft. Sq. D3. N.*

H. HYBRIDUS LODDEN GOLD, garden origin, is a fine, upstanding plant with large, double, golden-yellow flowers, freely borne.
*5-ft. August–October. H. 3-ft. Sq. D3. N. Pl. 33.*

H. ORGYALIS (A fathom, or six feet, in height) has long, narrow leaves, and produces many clusters of small yellow sunflowers above its graceful arching foliage.
*7-ft. September–October. H. 3-ft. Sq. D3. N.*

H. SCABER (Very rough), N. America, also known as *H. rigidus*, bears its solitary flowers of golden-yellow, with a brown disc, on eight-foot stems with rough, hairy leaves. The variety MISS MELLISH is a development of this species and has attractive orange-yellow flowers.
*6-ft. July–August. H. 3-ft. Sq. D3. N.*

H. SPARSIFOLIUS (With scattered leaves), Virginia, is also known as *H. atrorubens*. It has large semi-double orange flowers, borne on stems of at least six feet in length.
*6-ft. September–October. H. 2½-ft. Sq. D3. N.*

H. TUBEROSUS (Tuberous) is the Jerusalem Artichoke, growing six to eight feet in height and producing yellow sunflowers about three inches in diameter with a yellow disc.
*6-ft.–8-ft. August–September. H. 3-ft. Sq. D3. N.*

**HELIOPSIS** (Compositae), from G. helios—sun, and opsis—resemblance, hence sun-like; the common name is the Orange Sunflower.

Heliopsis bears flowers similar to those of the Sunflower, and of use for the same purpose.

H. GIGANTEA (Giant) has exceptionally large flowers of orange-yellow made up of many quill-like petals.
*4-ft. July–September. H. 2-ft. Sq. D3. N. Pl. 44.*

H. LAEVIS (Smooth) has attractive semi-double flowers of golden-yellow. *5-ft. July–September. H. 2-ft. Sq. D3. N.*

H. PATULA has single flowers of deep orange-yellow. H. PATULA ORANGE KING has larger semi-double orange-yellow flowers, and H. PATULA MAGNIFICA has many-petalled flowers of the same colour.
*4-ft. July–September. H. 2-ft. Sq. D3. N. Pl. 42.*

H. SCABRA (Rough), N. America, differs from H. laevis mainly by having its golden-yellow flowers borne singly on long, rough, hairy stems. H. SCABRA EXCELSA has nearly double bright-yellow flowers; H. SCABRA GRATISSIMA has pale-yellow flowers; H. SCABRA IMBRICATA is much dwarfer than the type, has large flowers of golden-yellow; and H. SCABRA ZINNIAEFLORA has very double bright-orange flowers.

**HELLEBORUS** (Ranunculaceae), from G. helein—to kill, and bora—food, some of the species being poisonous.

The Hellebores should be grown in rich, well-drained soil in a sunny place; they should not be disturbed until they become too tightly packed to succeed further. *Pl.* 43.

H. COLCHICUS (From Colchis), Russia, has five-petalled flowers of deep purple, surmounting five-parted leaves of deep, glossy green.
1½-*ft.* *January–March.* *H.* 1½-*ft. Sq.* *Sd*2. *N.*

H. LIVIDUS (Livid) has leaves divided into three lobes of glossy, deep green, veined with cream, and bears curious greenish-yellow flowers early in the year. 1½-*ft.* *April–May.* *H.* 1½-*ft. Sq.* *Sd*2. *N.*

H. NIGER (Black), Italy, has deep-green leaves divided into seven leaflets and produces its large clear-white flowers with creamy anthers from December until March. The variety ALTIFOLIUS throws its leaves higher than those of the type and has flowers which are normally larger. 2-*ft.* *December–March.* *H.* 2-*ft. Sq.* *Sd*2. *N.*

H. ORIENTALIS (Eastern) is the so-called Lenten Rose, which bears similar flowers to those of H. niger, in various shades of purple, pink and white from February to April. Of this, SNOWDRIFT is the best white, and LARISSA a good deep-pink.
1-*ft.* *February–April.* *H.* 1-*ft. Sq.* *D*4. *Sd*8. *N.*

H. VIRIDIS (Green), Pyrenees, is another green-flowered Christmas Rose, bearing its flowers in clusters, and is said to be sweetly-scented, though one would need to be exceptionally discerning to find even a trace of this latter quality.
1½-*ft.* *March–April.* *E.* 1½-*ft. Sq.* *Sd*2. *N.*

**HEMEROCALLIS** (Liliaceae), from G. hemera—day, and kallos—beauty; with reference to the short life of the flowers.

The Day-lily is easily grown in any ordinary garden soil which has been deeply dug and is rich in character. It thrives in a fully sunny aspect, but upon light soil is better grown in some shade. Propagation is by means of division, which should take place in the late autumn.

H. AURANTIACA (Orange-yellow), Japan, has strap-like channelled leaves and bears upon stout stems its large lily flowers of burnt orange. 3-*ft.* *June–July.* *H.* 3-*ft. Sq.* *D*10. *N.*

H. CITRINA (Lemon-coloured), China, forms a clump of similar leaves to those of H. aurantiaca, and has creamy-yellow flowers with long narrow petals, which are very fragrant, but seldom open fully in the brightest daylight.
3-*ft.* *July–August.* *H.* 3-*ft. Sq.* *D*10. *N.* *Pl.* 46.

H. FLAVA (Pure yellow), Europe, bears its large, sweetly-scented, clear-yellow flowers on open, slender sprays.
3-*ft.* *July.* *H.* 3-*ft. Sq.* *D*10. *N.*

H. FULVA (Reddish-brown) has shorter and wider leaves and bears sprays of rusty orange-red flowers on stout, packed spires. H. FULVA VAR. KWANSO is similar but has semi-double flowers produced upon a somewhat stouter scape.

*3½-ft. July–August. H. 2½-ft. Sq. D10. N.*

H. HYBRIDA comprises hybrids of the species, of which the following are good examples:— *Pl. 47.*

| | | |
|---|---|---|
| Apricot | apricot-yellow | *2½-ft.* |
| Golden Bell | golden-yellow | *2½-ft.* |
| Hyperion | yellow | *2½-ft.* |
| Orangeman | deep orange | *1½-ft.* |
| Sir Michael Foster | lemon-yellow | *3½-ft.* |
| Sovereign | deep yellow | *1½-ft.* |

**HESPERIS** (Cruciferae), from G. hesperos—evening, alluding to those species which scent the evening air.

H. matronalis (the Sweet Rocket) will grow well in any sunny position in good garden soil, division only taking place when the plants are known to be failing.

H. MATRONALIS (Matron's), Europe, has long sprays of large, fragrant, white, lilac or pale-purple flowers borne in profusion in early summer. The attractive double form is known as H. MATRONALIS FL. PL.

*2½-ft. June. H. 1½-ft. Sq. D3. N.*

**HEUCHERA** (Saxifragaceae) commemorates Professor J. H. Heucher

Heuchera prefers a soil of light, well-drained loam, and is admirably fitted for any sunny place at the front of the herbaceous border. It can be propagated by division in the late autumn.

H. BRIZOIDES is a doubtful name given to a number of varieties which are more properly varieties of H. sanguinea.

H. SANGUINEA (Blood-red), N. America, has crenate, heart-shaped leaves and bears long sprays of hanging bell-shaped flowers of variable colour, the forms generally to be met being bright red. Hybrids in cultivation vary in colour from white to dark crimson; the following are varieties which are particularly attractive:—

| | |
|---|---|
| Bloom's var. | coral-red |
| Countess of Warwick | deep scarlet |
| Edgehall | rose-pink |
| Honey Bell | light rose |
| Oxfordii | bright scarlet |
| Pluie de Feu | red |
| Rose Cavalier | rose |
| Rufus | red |
| Saturnale | crimson |
| Scarlet Beauty | scarlet |

*2-ft. June–August. H. 1½-ft. Sq. D3. N.*

H. TIARELLOIDES (Resembling Tiarella), garden hybrid, is really a hybrid between H. sanguinea and Tiarella cordifolia, and bears arching sprays of attractive pale-pink flowers.
*1-ft. May–July. H. 1-ft. Sq. D3. N.*

**HOSTA** (*see* FUNKIA).

**INCARVILLEA** (Bignoniaceae) is named to commemorate Père Incarville, a Jesuit and botanist.

These are tuberous-rooted plants with highly polished, pinnate leaves, and are best propagated from seed, which germinates very freely.

I. DELAVAYI (comm.), China, makes a rosette of feathered, polished, green leaves from which rise high, stout stems carrying clusters of large, rose-purple, trumpet-shaped flowers with yellow tubes.
*3-ft. May–June. H. 1½-ft. Sq. Sd3. N.*

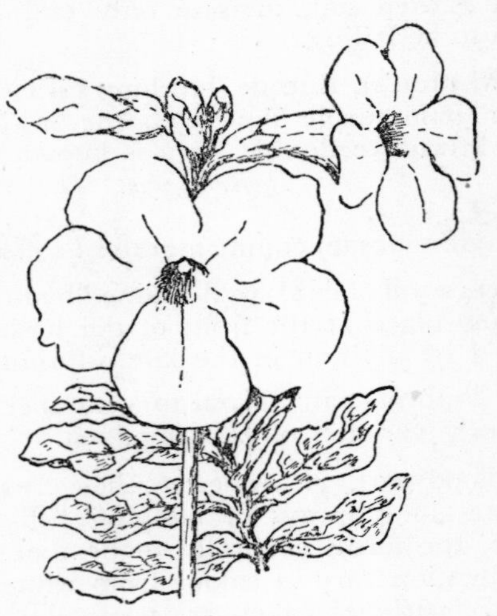

INCARVILLEA GRANDIFLORA

I. GRANDIFLORA (Large-flowered), China, is another tap-rooted species with similar attractive foliage, bearing extremely large rose-pink gloxinia flowers in clusters of two or three. It is as easily propagated from seed as the previous species and is attractive (if only for a short period) at the front of the border.
*1-ft. May–June. H. 1-ft. Sq. Sd2. N.*

I. GRANDIFLORA BEES' PINK is similar except that it bears flowers of clear soft pink of exceptional size, more subdued and less flaunting than the type. *1-ft. May–June. H. 1-ft. Sq. Sd2. N.*

Mimulus hybridus "Plymtree"

Paeonia chinensis

I. GRANDIFLORA BREVIPES (Short-stalked) has large rose-purple flowers conspicuously marked with white in the throat, borne upon very short stalks in large clusters.

*1½-ft. May–June. H. 1½-ft. Sq. Sd2. N.*

**INULA** (Compositae); probably derived from a corruption of the name Helenium, from the G. helenion.

I. GLANDULOSA (Having glands), Caucasus, is also known as *I. orientalis*, and is a dwarf plant producing shaggy-petalled saffron-yellow sunflowers upon dwarf symmetrical plants.

*2-ft. July–August. H. 2-ft. Sq. D3. N.*

I. HELENIUM (Resembling Helenium), Britain, has large, roughly-surfaced foliage, smooth to the touch beneath, bearing ragged, yellow sunflowers about four to six inches in diameter, and is attractive at the back of the border.

*6-ft. June–August. 4-ft. Sq. D3. N. Pl. 49.*

I. ROYLEANA (comm.), Himalayas, has huge foliage soft to the touch beneath, and bears attractive black buds which open to show huge ragged orange-yellow sunflowers, brassy but not brazen.

*2-ft. June–September. H. 2-ft. Sq. D3. Sd2. N. Pl. 49.*

**IRIS** (Iridaceae), from G. iris—a rainbow, with reference to the varied colours of the flowers of the species.

The Iris makes up a very large genus of hardy plants which have either perennial rhizomes or bulbs. Those which grow from rhizomes have normally leaves shaped like a sword. The bulbous Irises have normally narrow, channelled leaves; they vary in height from a few inches to six feet, in time of flowering from January to the late autumn, and in colour from white, yellow, bright blue to nearly crimson.

Irises which have a thickened root-stem, or rhizome, may be divided mainly into three types: tall bearded, dwarf bearded, and the beardless kinds. The beard, when it is present, will be found in the outer petals or falls, where a thick line of hair stretches down the lower half of the petal. The botanical name given to the section of bearded Irises is pogon, and the botanical name given to the beardless section, in which the falls are not bearded and do not bear protuberances, is apogon. The horticultural forms of the bearded Iris are very numerous, and are often known under the collective name of Iris Germanica or German Irises.

The bulbous Irises may be divided into three groups: firstly, the Juno Irises, in which the bulbs bear fleshy roots from the base while resting; the Xiphium section, in which the flowers have large and erect standards and the bulbs have no roots in the resting stage; and the reticulatas, which have a netted covering to the bulbs, in opposition to the smooth bulbs of the Xiphium section.

The apogons or beardless Irises have normally narrow, grass-like leaves, and are widespread throughout the world. The bearded or pogon Irises are native to South and Central Europe and Western China. Cultivation of the different types varies considerably, and cultural notes for each type will be found under its appropriate name.

I. ALATA (Winged), Juno section, Mediterranean region, has light-green channelled and pointed leaves, and flowers which vary from deep lavender to violet-blue, with dark-violet marking on the falls, which also bear long golden crests. It thrives best in rich limy soil and should be kept dry in summer.
1-*ft.* *November–January.* *B.* ½-*ft. Sq.* *D*7. *C.*

I. APHYLLA (Leafless), pogon section, E. Europe, has grey-green leaves and bears purple flowers with white beards on stems of a foot or so in height. It requires the normal cultivation of the bearded section, with its rhizome kept near to the surface of the ground, in good, well-drained soil and a sunny site.
1¼-*ft.* *April.* *H.* 1-*ft. Sq.* *D*7. *N.*

I. BAKERIANA (comm.), reticulata section, Asia Minor, bears fragrant flowers with the standards of deep lilac with falls of violet, spotted with white. The leaves are typically those of the reticulata section, long, cylindrical and hollow, eventually rising to over a foot in height. 1½-*ft.* *January.* *B.* ½-*ft. Sq.* *D*6. *N.*

I. BARBATA (Bearded) is the name sometimes given to the tall bearded Irises which are hybrids of I. Germanica.

I. BLOUDOWII (comm.), pogon section, has stiff, wiry leaves with pale-yellow flowers, sometimes veined with brown, with a yellow beard, thriving in sun-baked soil. ½-*ft.* *June.* *E.* ½-*ft. Sq.* *D*7. *N.*

I. BUCHARICA (From Bokhara), Juno section, Turkestan, has channelled foliage resembling that of a Leek, and bears a spray of flowers the falls of which are gold and yellow with small standards of clear white. On the whole, it would appear to be one of the easiest of this section to cultivate in any moderately open soil in a sunny site.
1-*ft.* *April–May.* *B.* ½-*ft. Sq.* *D*7. *N.*

I. BULLEYANA (comm.), apogon section, W. China, has long, narrow, stiff leaves, and bears upon a stem of some eighteen inches one or two flowers with the falls of purple-blue and cream, and the standards of lavender-blue. It is easy to cultivate in good garden soil in a position where it is not wet in the summer months.
1½-*ft.* *June–July.* *H.* 1-*ft. Sq.* *D*8. *N.*

I. CHAMAEIRIS (On the ground—i.e. dwarf), pogon section, N.W. Italy, is generally taller than I. pumila and has a flower-stem as long as the tube of the flower; in addition, the foliage is persistent during the winter months. Many sub-varieties of I. Chamaeiris exist; the characteristics of the flowers are the rounded falls and wide standards. The flowers may be either blue, reddish-purple, white or yellow, usually with a contrasting beard. I. CHAMAEIRIS CAMPBELLII has flowers with deep-violet falls and sky-blue standards. I. Chamaeiris cretica has smoky purple flowers. In catalogues I. Chamaeiris is generally much confused with I. pumila.

*½-ft. April–May. E. 1-ft. Sq. D6. N.*

I. chrysographes (Veined with gold), apogon section, W. China, is exceptionally hardy, with long, green, narrow leaves bearing, upon slender stems, two or three deep-blue flowers with long narrow falls, heavily netted with gold. The variety Purple Robe has similar flowers of intense purple. *1¼-ft. July. H. 1-ft. Sq. D8. N.*

I. cristata (Crested), Evansia section, Southern U.S.A., makes a mat of short but rather wide leaves with wide soft-blue flowers with a crest spotted with gold and white. It is best grown where the sunlight is interrupted, and divided and replanted immediately after flowering, any good garden soil sufficing for its normal growth.

*¾-ft. June–July. H. 1-ft. Sq. D7. N.*

I. Delavayi (comm.), apogon section, China, grows to five feet in height with wide, very long, sword-shaped, grey-green leaves with rounded violet-blue falls, with a white patch and markings. The standards are small and pointed.

*5-ft. June. H. 2-ft. Sq. D8. N.*

I. ensata (Sword-shaped), apogon section, China, has graceful flowers varying from lilac to white, with the standards deeper in colour than the falls, borne above a tight tuft of narrow, green, sword-shaped leaves. It thrives well in any good garden soil in a sunny position.

*1¼-ft. June. H. 1½-ft. Sq. D8. N.*

I. foetidissima (Worst-smelling), apogon section, native, is commonly known as the Stinking Gladwyn, from the evil odour of its leaves when bruised. It grows to about eighteen inches in height, with bright-green, wide leaves, and may have purplish-grey, small, inconspicuous flowers, or yellow flowers of the same kind. The flowers are followed by large seed-pods opening in autumn to show clusters of striking orange-scarlet seeds. It is of easy cultivation in any good garden soil. *1½-ft. June. E. 2-ft. Sq. D3. N.*

I. Forestii (comm.), apogon section, S.W. China, has slender, narrow, glossy leaves with graceful narrow-petalled flowers of deep creamy-yellow, sometimes with purple veins. It thrives in either a position in which it is in full sun and kept reasonably moist, or in a partly shaded site. *1½-ft. June. H. 1-ft. Sq. D7. N.*

I. Gatesii (comm.), Oncocyclus section, Asia Minor, is probably the largest-flowered of any Iris, the individual falls and standards sometimes reaching five inches across. The basic colour is greyish-white, and the flowers are heavily netted with grey-purple, and are borne on stems of approximately eighteen inches with glaucous leaves of about ¾ inch in width. It should be grown in a well-drained light, but rich soil, and water should be withheld entirely during the summer months. *2-ft. April. H. 1-ft. Sq. Sd10. N.*

I. GERMANICA (German), pogon section, is also known as *I. vulgaris*, and gives rise to the horticultural forms known as the Bearded or German Iris. The general characteristics are the long glaucous leaves, sword-patterned, about one and a half inches in width, and the rounded falls and the standards of purple blue, with a white beard, tipped with yellow. Cultivation is not difficult, well-drained good garden soil sufficing, preferably in a dry sunny spot. The rhizomes should not be buried.

2-*ft.*–3½-*ft.* *May.* *H.* 1-*ft.* *Sq.* *D*7. *ANC.* *Pl.* 48.

Here follows a list of the horticultural varieties developed from this Iris.

IRIS GERMANICA HYBRIDA.

AFTERGLOW has flowers of lavender and yellow. 3-*ft.*

ALBICANS has large white flowers tinged with lavender. 2½-*ft.*

ALCAZAR has violet-blue standards shaded with bronze, with purple falls. 3-*ft.*

ALINE is a fragrant untinted lavender-blue. 2½-*ft.*

AMBASSADOR is a tall variety with standards of reddish-bronze, with falls of crimson with bronze veins. 4-*ft.*

AMBER is of bright, unmarked yellow, with flowers of medium size. 3-*ft.*

ANGELUS has flowers of bright pink shaded with lavender, with a yellow beard. 3-*ft.*

AUREA is bright gold. 2½-*ft.*

BEAUTÉ D'ARGENT is white with the falls streaked with violet. 2-*ft.*

BEOWULF is maroon with a bright orange beard. 3-*ft.*

BLACK PRINCE is of dark purple with white markings on the falls. 2½-*ft.*

BLACK WINGS is violet with black wings. 3-*ft.*

BLENHEIM is mahogany-red with the standards tinged with violet. 3-*ft.*

BLUE BOY has violet-blue standards with falls of deep purple. 2-*ft.*

CAPRICE has claret standards and rose-red falls. 2-*ft.*

CATERINA is soft lavender-blue, veined in the throat. 4-*ft.*

CLEMATIS combines with its lavender standards falls of violet-blue. 2½-*ft.*

CORDELIA sets off its lilac-pink standards with red-purple falls. 2-*ft.*

DOGROSE is an unshaded rich pink. 2½-*ft.*

DORÉ has immense flowers of lemon-yellow with ivory falls which have gold veining and orange beards. 3-*ft.*

ED. MICHEL is claret-red. 3-*ft.*

ELTA is pale-lilac, with falls of violet edged with lilac. 2½-*ft.*

FLAMING SWORD has falls of purple and edges and standards of gold. 3-*ft.*

FLAVESCENS is primrose-yellow. 2-*ft.*

FLORENTINA is white with a lavender tinge and a sweet scent. 3-*ft.*

GAGUS combines brown falls with canary-yellow. 2-*ft.*

GAZELLE is lavender and white. 3-*ft.*

GOLD CREST is violet-blue with golden beards. 2½-*ft.*

GRACCHUS has pale-yellow flowers with the falls heavily netted with purple. 2-*ft.*

GUDRUN is probably the largest white-flowered variety. 3-*ft.*

HAMILCAR combines blue with deep purple. 3-*ft.*

HELENA is attractively clad in light purple. 3-*ft.*

KNYSNA uses red-brown and deep yellow in attractive combination. 3-*ft.*

MINERVA blends two shades of mauve. 3½-*ft.*

MOONLIGHT is pale-yellow with orange beards. 3-*ft.*

OZONE has an insidious charm composed of rosy-lavender flowers centred with coppery-orange. 3-*ft.*

PALLIDA DALMATICA is pale lavender. 3-*ft.*

PALLIDA MINOR has small, soft-lilac flowers. 1½-*ft.*

PALLIDA VARIEGATA has variegated foliage and lavender-blue flowers. 2-*ft.*

PETREA is bright mahogany-red. 2½-*ft.*

PLUMIERI has copper-red standards with reddish-violet falls. 2½-*ft.*

QUAKER LADY has bronzy-lavender standards with deeper falls. 2½-*ft.*

RAMESES combines a most delicate yellow and amethyst-pink, centred with sunshine-yellow. 3-*ft.*

RICHARD II has white standards, with its purple falls edged with white. 3-*ft.*

ROTA is carmine-red. 2½-*ft.*

SIERRA BLUE has the clearest blue flowers of all, and rises to four feet in height. 4-*ft.*

SOUVENIR is yellow, heavily netted with bronze. 2½-*ft.*

SUNSET: old gold, copper, yellow flushed with violet are all combined. 2-*ft.*

VIOLA is deep violet-blue. 3-*ft.*

WILLIAM MOHR combines a delicacy of tiny leaves with immense flowers of pale lilac, deepening in parts and veined with deepest violet. 3-*ft.*

I. GORMANII (comm.), apogon section, N. America, makes a tight tuft of stiff foliage, above which are borne the flowers of pale straw-yellow. 1-*ft.* *June.* *H.* 1-*ft.* *Sq.* *D7.* *A.*

I. GRACILIPES (Slender-stalked), Evansia section, Japan, has very thin, pointed, frail foliage and slender stems, and yellow-crested, pinkish-mauve flowers. It should be grown in a well-drained but shady, moist, leafy soil. 1-*ft. June. H.* ½-*ft. Sq. D*7. *N.*

I. GRAMINEA (Grassy), spuria section, S. Europe, makes a tight mat of narrow, green-ribbed, sword-like leaves, amid which are borne the violet-blue and purple, heavily veined and greengage-scented flowers.
1-*ft. June. H.* 1-*ft. Sq. D*7. *N.* 30/2.

I. HOOGIANA (comm.), regelia section, Turkestan, has large purple-blue flowers with thick golden-brown beards, on long upstanding stems, in groups of from one to three. Easier to grow than most of the section, it is best placed in good fertile soil under the protection of a deciduous tree, by which means it may be completely deprived of the summer moisture which usually proves fatal to this class.
2-*ft. May. H.* 1-*ft. Sq. D*8. *N.*

I. INNOMINATA (Unnamed), apogon section, N.W. America, has thin, sword-like leaves with golden-yellow flowers netted with chocolate on the falls. A second form with flowers of lavender and purple is equally attractive, and both plants will grow equally well in good soil in a sunny position.
1-*ft. May–June. H.* 1-*ft. Sq. Sd*8. *N.* 5/2.

I. JAPONICA (Japanese), Evansia section, Japan and China, is also known as *I. chinensis* and *I. fimbriata*, and bears its flowers on branching, many-flowered stems, resembling those of some of the Odontoglossum orchids. The falls have toothed edges and are white, heavily bordered with mauve, and the crest is touched with orange. It grows well in any good garden soil in a warm and sheltered spot.
1½-*ft. June–July. H.* 1½-*ft. Sq. D*7. *N.*

I. JAPONICA LEDGER'S VAR. has larger and even more attractive flowers of deeper colour. 1⅓-*ft. June–July. H.* 1½-*ft. Sq. D*7. *N.*

I. KAEMPFERI (comm.), apogon section, is the Japanese Iris, and is generally supposed to be derived from I. laevigata and I. setosa. The flowers of the different varieties vary considerably in size and may be as large as nine inches in diameter. The general appearance of the flowers appears to be flatter, larger, and more symmetrical than those of the other Irises. To be well grown, I. Kaempferi should be planted either in a moist site or in a soil retentive of summer moisture, that is to say, containing a large quantity of peat-mould or leaf-mould. The site chosen should be one in full sun, and propagation should be undertaken regularly from seed, and the sub-standard varieties destroyed. The named varieties in general cultivation are listed below.
2½-*ft. July–August. H.* 1½-*ft. Sq. Sd*2. *N.*

I. Kaempferi.

Bluebird has gracefully-formed flowers of an even shade of bright blue.

Catherine Perry has double flowers of soft blue, veined and overlaid with purple.

Chosei-den is white-centred and heavily veined with reddish-purple.

Columbia has double flowers of bright blue, veined with white and with yellow centres.

Dominator has indigo-blue flowers with narrow white stripes, paling in the centre.

Doris Childs has double white flowers veined with rose-red stripes.

Eleanor Parry has double flowers of claret-purple.

Fascination has double flowers of mauve-pink veined with white.

Gei-sho-Ui has a yellow centre and is tinted and veined with lilac.

Gei-sho-no-Kagoroma has large blue flowers centred with yellow.

Gekko-no-Nami is the largest and purest white.

Habu-hina is still another attractive white variety.

Hatsushima is a fine clear white variety.

Koki-no-Iro is deep red-purple with yellow eyes.

Kuro-no-uye has double violet flowers shading to white.

La Favorite has large white flowers veined with blue and centred with purple.

La Tosca has large, double, white flowers faintly shaded with blue.

Lavender Giant has really immense flowers of lavender-blue.

Mahogany has large double flowers of deep mahogany-red.

Navarre has large lilac flowers veined with purple.

Oku-Banri has grey flowers veined with purple.

Oshokum is royal purple flushed with blue.

Purple and Gold has double flowers of deep violet-purple, with white immature petals flecked with violet, and golden throats.

Queen of the Blues has six-petalled flowers of pale delft-blue.

Rose Anna has extremely large, double flowers of light mauve, heavily veined with intense purple.

Sir John Franklin has white flowers striped with red.

Tokio is lilac in colour, and is pencilled with violet.

Tora-Odori is lavender, veined with purple and mauve.

Warei-Botei has large purple flowers.

Yoshima has double flowers, white, spotted with violet.

I. lacustris (Of the lake), Evansia section, Shores of the Great Lakes, N. America, is a diminutive form of I. cristata, tighter in growth and similar in its cultural requirements.

*½-ft. June–July. H. 1-ft. Sq. D7. A.*

I. LONGIPETALA (Long-petalled), apogon section, California, grows to a height of about two feet, has bright-lilac flowers veined with orange on the central ridge, and forms a tight tuft of many narrow leaves.
*2-ft. June. H. 1¼-ft. Sq. D8. N.*

I. MACROSIPHON (Long-tubed), apogon section, N.W. America, is larger and stiffer than I. innominata, which it somewhat resembles, and exists in two forms of similar colours.
*1-ft. June. H. 1-ft. Sq. D6. N.*

I. MILESII (comm.), Evansia section, Himalayas, grows to a height of three feet, with very wide sword-like leaves. The flowers, which are rather small, are of reddish-purple with darker veins, and have orange crests. *3-ft. June. H. 2-ft. Sq. D8. N.*

I. OCHROLEUCA (Yellowish-white), apogon section, Asia Minor, grows to three feet in height, with long, narrow leaves, and bears large flowers with the falls touched with gold and the standards tinged with yellow. *3-ft. May–June. H. 2-ft. Sq. D7. N.*

I. PRISMATICA (Prismatic) has narrow, slender leaves and, above three-foot stems, violet-blue flowers veined with yellow.
*3-ft. May. H. 2-ft. Sq. D7. N.*

I. PSEUDACORUS (Sham Acorus), apogon section, Europe, is the Water Flag, generally found growing near ponds or at the waterside, and has bright-yellow flowers, borne in May and June, upon stems of two and a half feet. It is worthy of any damp place which can be provided for it in the garden.
*2½-ft. May–June. H. 2-ft. Sq. D7. N.*

I. PUMILA (Dwarf), pogon section, Europe, is the Dwarf Bearded Iris so often found at the front of the border. It has little or no flower stem, does not retain its foliage in winter, and grows well in any hot dry spot, with a limy soil, seldom exceeding half a foot in height. It is available in a large number of colours varying from white to violet-blue. *½-ft. April–May. H. 1-ft. Sq. D6. C.*

I. RETICULATA (Netted—viz. the bulb), reticulata section, Caucasus, has four-sided leaves which are just in evidence as it flowers, and bears upon a long tube its sweetly-scented, deep-violet flowers marked with orange. It is available in a large number of varieties, of which I. RETICULATA KRELEGEI has reddish-purple flowers, and I. RETICULATA CANTABRIGIENSIS has pale-blue flowers.
*1-ft. February. B. ¼-ft. Sq. D6. N.*

I. RUTHENICA (Russian), pogon section, Asia, has wide, grassy leaves with violet-blue flowers, with the falls netted with white and sweetly scented. It is best planted in a soil which does not become too dry, and divided immediately after having flowered.
*½-ft. May–June. H. 1-ft. Sq. D7. N.*

Papaver orientale

Phlox decussata "Mrs. Askew" ABCDGH
Phlox decussata "Sam Pope" EFJKLNORS
Phlox decussata "Leo Schlageter" LMOPQST

I. SAMBUCINA (Elder-scented), pogon section, resembles a tall bearded Iris, with yellow standards and claret falls, and with a very attractive scent. *2-ft. June–July. E. 1½-ft. Sq. D9. N.*

I. SIBIRICA (Siberian), apogon section, Siberia, has narrow green leaves above which are borne, upon long upstanding stems, twofold spires each carrying from two to five flowers of deep lilac-blue. It is variable, and there are a number of forms of which I. SIBIRICA ATROSANGUINEA with flowers of violet, I. SIBIRICA EMPEROR of cornflower-blue, EMPRESS OF CHINA of blue, PERRY'S BLUE of sky-blue, and SNOW QUEEN, milk-white, are the best. I. SIBIRICA CAESAR'S BROTHER has flowers of intense, deep pansy-violet.
*3-ft. June–July. H. 2-ft. Sq. D3. N.*

I. SINDJARENSIS (comm.), Juno section, Syria, has channelled glossy-green leaves and bears its fragrant flowers, varying from violet-blue to blue-grey, in groups of from three to four. It should be grown in well-drained soil in a sunny position where it is perfectly dry in summer. *1-ft. March. B. ½-ft. Sq. Sd6. N.*

I. SISYRINCHIUM (Resembling Sisyrinchium), Gynandrus section, grows to a height of one foot and produces evanescent small flowers of lilac-blue with a small white patch.
*1-ft. May–June. B. ½-ft. Sq. D7. N.*

I. SPURIA (False), apogon section, is extremely variable in colour and habit, but may be said to approximate to about one foot in height, with the flowers borne slightly above the leaves, and of purple-blue or lilac. It flowers under any good garden conditions.
*1¼-ft. May. H. 1-ft. Sq. D7. N.*

I. STYLOSA (Long-styled), apogon section, Algeria, has narrow, tough, linear leaves and bears large bright-lilac and deep-lilac flowers on very long flower tubes, generally in the middle of winter. It is also known as *I. unguicularis*. I. STYLOSA SPECIOSA is deeper in colour. I. STYLOSA ALBA has flowers of clear white. All the varieties should be planted in a spot where they will become sun-parched in summer. The most usual place in which to find them is at the foot of a sunny wall in hard, poor soil.
*1¼-ft. January–February. E. 1-ft. Sq. D4. N.*

I. SUSIANA (From Susa), Oncocyclus section, Persia, is the Mourning Iris, growing to about one and a half feet in height, with large, silvery-grey flowers heavily overlaid with purple-black veins, with a broad brownish beard. It thrives best if grown in a light, chalky soil in as sunny a place as is possible.
*1½-ft. May. H. 1-ft. Sq. D6. C.*

I. TECTORUM (Of roofs), Evansia section, China, an Iris which is grown upon thatched roofs of houses in Japan, reaches a height of one and a half feet, and has deep-lilac or purple-blue flowers netted with darker colour and a white crest. It is best grown in a hot, sunny place, where it gets little summer moisture. There is also a very fine white form with a golden crest.

*1-ft. May. H. 1-ft. Sq. D6. N.*

I. TENAX (Tough), apogon section, W. America, has large flowers of bright lilac-purple with a yellow stripe on the falls. It thrives under any good garden conditions.

*1-ft. June–July. H. 1-ft. Sq. D7. A.* 437/1.

IRIS STYLOSA

I. TUBEROSA (Tuberous), also known as *Hermodactylus tuberosus*, grows to about one foot in height, has narrow-petalled green and black Iris-like flowers, and produces a finger-shaped tuberous root. It is best grown in rich sandy soil in a sheltered place.

*1-ft. March–April. H. 1-ft. Sq. D9. N.*

I. VERSICOLOR (Changing colour), apogon section, Canada, has leaves of grey-green over two feet in length and about an inch in width, with purplish-blue flowers with a green spot at the base.

*2-ft. May–June. H. 1-ft. Sq. D7. N.*

I. WILSONII (comm.), apogon section, China, has flat grey-green leaves about two feet in length, with yellow flowers marked with reddish-brown, and narrow, upright standards of yellowish-white.

*2-ft. May–June. H. 1½-ft. Sq. D7. N.*

I. XIPHIOIDES (Resembling Gladiolus segetum), Xiphium section, is a bulbous Iris, known as the English Iris, with a stem of about eighteen inches and flowers of deep ultramarine-blue with a golden patch on the falls. Originally hailing from the Pyrenees, the species has now become submerged by a large number of hybrids of variable colours, all of which undoubtedly exert considerable charm. The bulbs are planted in groups in October in ordinary garden soil, three to four inches deep and eight inches apart, and are allowed to remain undisturbed unless deterioration takes place, when they should be lifted and replanted.

*1½-ft. April–May. B. ⅔-ft. Sq. D9. N.*

I. XIPHIUM (*Gladiolus segetum*), Xiphium section, Spain, now comprises the Spanish and Dutch Irises which grow to a height of eighteen inches, with thin, channelled leaves and purple-blue flowers with a long oval stem joined to each fall with a rounded blade. It is now available in a large range of colours, and requires similar cultivation to I. xiphioides, except that its bulbs should be planted two or three inches deep and a little closer together.

*2-ft. May–June. B. ½-ft. Sq. D9. N.*

**ISATIS** (Cruciferae), from the ancient G. name for woad, once used for dyeing. Woad was obtained from a native plant, I. tinctoria, and was once of great importance in Great Britain, for a blue dye was obtained from its leaves, similar to indigo.

The only species much used in the garden is:—

I. GLAUCA (Sea-green), Asia Minor, produces large, diffuse panicles of mustard-yellow flowers, reminiscent of a larger Gypsophila.

*4-ft. July–August. H. 3-ft. Sq. Sd10. N.*

**IXIA** (Iridaceae), from G. ixia—bird-lime, because of the sticky juices exuded from the stems.

Ixias are natives of South Africa and are produced from corms. They may be planted out of doors from September to October in a light soil, three inches deep and two inches apart. They must, however, be lifted when the leaves have died down if their qualities are seen to deteriorate. Most of the Ixias now grown are hybrids of the following species:—

I. COLUMELLARIS (Pillar), S. Africa, grows to one foot and has star-shaped flowers of lilac or mauve-purple.

I. LUTEA (Yellow), with starry flowers of deep yellow, borne in long spikes.

I. MACULATA, with yellow flowers, but bearing in cultivation a very large range of variable colours.

I. SPECIOSA (Showy) is similar, with flowers of deep crimson.

*1-ft. May–June. B. ⅙-ft. Sq. D9. N.*

**IXIOLIRION** (Amaryllidaceae), from G. ixia—the Corn Lily, and leirion—lily; from its resemblance to that plant.

Another bulbous plant which requires light, well-drained soil and a sunny position.

I. MONTANUM (Of the mountains), Siberia, bears sprays of starry-lilac flowers in June. *1-ft. June. B. ¼-ft. Sq. D9. N.*

I. PALLASII (comm.), S. Russia, has similar but longer sprays of violet-blue. *1½-ft. June. B. ¼-ft. Sq. D9. N.*

**KIRENGESHOMA** (Saxifragaceae): a name of Japanese origin, the meaning of which is obscure.

K. PALMATA (Hand-shaped), Japan, is an attractive plant with wide and large dentate leaves with soft-yellow bell-shaped flowers borne in small clusters. It thrives in a shady place in light, leafy soil and may be propagated by division in the spring.
*2-ft. August–September. H. 1½-ft. Sq. D3. A.*

**KNIPHOFIA** (Liliaceae). The name is commemorative of J. H. Kniphof, a German professor of medicine.

A group of plants extremely useful in the border for their outstanding value in flowering late in the year. They are sometimes known as the Torch Lilies or Poker Plants. They thrive in any good ordinary garden soil which is well drained. The flowers, which are borne in long poker-like spikes, are particularly striking. They may be propagated by periodic division and from seeds. *Pl.* 51.

K. CAULESCENS (Long-stemmed), S. Africa, has exceptionally fine grey-green foliage resembling that of the Aloe, produced upon stout woody stems. It produces outstanding spikes of salmon-red flowers which turn greeny-yellow towards the base.
*4-ft. September. E. 3-ft. Sq. D3. Sd10. N.*

K. CORALLINA (Coral-red), garden origin, is a hybrid of K. Macowanii and K. Uvaria, grows to two feet in height and has coral-red flowers.
*2-ft. August–September. H. 1½-ft. Sq. D3. N.*

K. FOLIOSA (Leafy) has long, channelled, green leaves and bright-yellow poker heads made up of tubular flowers about an inch in length, with protruding stamens.
*3-ft. August–September. E. 3-ft. Sq. D3. N.*

K. MACOWANII (comm.), S. Africa, is smaller than most of the species, with narrow leaves less than two feet in length, and red and orange flowers, borne upon stems of one and a half feet, in tight brush-like heads. *2-ft. July–September. E. 2-ft. Sq. D3. N.*

K. MULTIFLORA (Many-flowered), S. Africa, is a grand outstanding plant with seven-foot stems and flowers of pale silver.

*7-ft. October–November. E. 6-ft. Sq. D3. N.*

K. NELSONII (comm.), S. Africa, has exceptionally narrow leaves up to two feet in length, slender stems and bright scarlet flowers, tinted orange, in loose heads about three inches in length.

*2-ft. August–September. E. 2-ft. Sq. D3. N.*

K. PAUCIFLORA (Few-flowered) has narrow leaves about two feet in length and bears slender stems and bright-yellow flowers in short and dainty racemes. *2½-ft. July–September. H. 2-ft. Sq. D3. N.*

K. RUFA (Reddish), Natal, has narrow, channelled leaves up to eighteen inches in length, and yellow flowers, tinted red at the top of the spike, with long yellow protruding stamens.

*3-ft. July–September. E. 2-ft. Sq. D3. N.*

K. TUCKII (comm.), S. Africa, has wider channelled long green leaves, and bears its spire-like stems in profusion, topped with bright-red flowers passing with age to yellow.

*4-ft. June–August. E. 2½-ft. Sq. D3. N.*

K. UVARIA (Clustered), S. Africa, has still longer channelled green leaves with scarlet flowers turning yellow with age, borne upon extremely stout and long stems in great profusion.

*4-ft. August–September. E. 3-ft. Sq. D3. N.*

K. UVARIA GRANDIFLORA is taller, and has bolder flowers of deep orange-crimson.

K. UVARIA NOBILIS grows between six and eight feet in height and has exceptionally large flowers of crimson-scarlet.

K. UVARIA PRAECOX is an earlier-flowering form.

The horticultural forms of hybrids of garden origin have the attractions common to the species.

EGYPT has buff-yellow flowers, fading paler. *3½-ft. July–August.*

EXPRESS has upstanding spikes of salmon-orange flowers produced in great quantity. *4-ft. July–August.*

GOLD ELSE has tapering spikes of soft-yellow flowers in *July–September. 1½-ft.*

GOLDEN SCEPTRE has three-foot spikes of saffron-yellow flowers. *3-ft. June–July.*

JUNE GLORY has very bright-scarlet heads, and flowers most freely. *4-ft. June.*

LACHESIS is very tall, with large heads of honey-coloured flowers tipped with bronze. *6-ft. September.*

LEMON QUEEN has soft lemon-yellow heads very freely borne. *3½-ft. July–September.*

MAJESTIC has very rich-red flowers. 5-*ft.* *September.*

MRS. SAMUEL SMITH has extremely tall spikes of lemon-yellow and scarlet flowers. 4-*ft.*–5-*ft.* *July–September.*

MT. ETNA (*see* The Rocket).

ORANGE PRINCE is a very dwarf variety with slender spikes of bright orange. 2½-*ft.* *July–September.*

PRIMROSE BEAUTY produces graceful spikes of primrose-yellow flowers, slightly arched. 2½-*ft.* *June.*

ROYAL STANDARD has bright-yellow flowers at the base of the spike, changing to scarlet at the top. 3-*ft.* *August–September.*

RUSTLER'S GOLD is similar, except that its flowers are of golden-yellow. 3-*ft.* *June–August.*

SIR K. BUTLER combines in its strong, tall spikes sulphur-yellow and light-red. 5-*ft.* *July–August.*

SPRINGTIME has flower spikes of rich coral-red fading to ivory-yellow on the lower half. 3-*ft.* *July.*

SULPHUR SPIRE produces flowers of a clear pale-yellow. 5-*ft.* *July–August.*

SUMMER SUNSHINE has flame-red flower spikes, freely produced. 3-*ft.* *July.*

THE ROCKET is also known as Mt. Etna, and has extremely tall spires of brilliant terracotta-scarlet, produced in profusion in *August–September.* 6-*ft.*

VANILLA is a small, free-flowering variety with pale-yellow flowers. 2-*ft.* *June.*

WHITE FAIRY is another small and prolific variety with pure white blossoms. 2-*ft.* *June.*

**LACTUCA** (Compositae), from L. lac—milk, referring to the milky juice excreted by the plant when cut.

This is the Lettuce family, which contains among its number one or two species attractive in the herbaceous border. Cultivation is simple in any good garden soil. It is also known as MULGEDIUM. The species most commonly found in the herbaceous border is:—

L. BOURGAEI (comm.), Mediterranean region, which has green bristly leaves the colour of those of the Lettuce, with loose clusters of lilac daisy flowers. 6-*ft.* *July–August.* *H.* 2-*ft. Sq.* *Sd*2. *N.*

**LAVATERA** (Malvaceae) commemorates two Swiss botanists named Lavater.

L. CACHEMIRIANA (From Cashmir), Himalayas, grows to six feet in height and bears loose sprays of bright-rosy flowers, resembling those of the brilliant Hollyhock, upon long branching stems.
6-*ft.* *July–August.* *H.* 3-*ft. Sq.* *D*3. *N.*

**LEWISIA** (Portulacaceae), named after Captain Lewis, American traveller.

These are succulent-leaved plants with fleshy roots which are edible, and require to be kept reasonably dry during the winter. The species which are deciduous—L.L. brachycalyx, oppositifolia, and rediviva—are best grown in a sunny place where they become sun-baked in summer, whereas the evergreen species are best in a partially shaded site. The plants, though not necessarily alpine, are normally found growing in the rock garden, but can be grown with some success in the herbaceous border, where they are particularly striking. The best types for this kind of work are undoubtedly L.L. Cotyledon, Finchii, and Howellii, though these by no means complete the species.

L. Cotyledon (Resembling Cotyledon), Oregon, makes a large rosette of clean-edged leaves and bears many spires made up of clusters of salmon-pink flowers, each petal striped with pink.
*1-ft. June–July. E. 1-ft. Sq. Sd2. N.*

L. Cotyledon var. Heckneri (comm.), California, has notched margins to the leaves, and pink flowers striped with white in a similar fashion. *1-ft. June–July. E. 1-ft. Sq. Sd2. N.*

**LIATRIS** (Compositae) (derivation unknown).

A group of perennials with thick woody roots, thriving well in good garden soil and propagated with ease from seed. The flower sprays, which are compound, have unusual characteristics, the uppermost flowers opening before those lower on the spike. The common names of the species are: Blazing Star, Gay Feather or Button Snake-root. The species in general cultivation are:—

L. pycnostachya (Dense-spiked), U.S.A., has long linear leaves and bears, for a long period, dense spikes of purple flowers arranged in small groups. *3-ft. August–October. H. 1½-ft. Sq. Sd2. N. Pl. 73.*

L. scariosa (Dry, not green), E. N. America, has pointed, oblong leaves up to one foot in length, and bears interrupted spikes of bluish-purple flowers. *3-ft. August–October. H. 1½-ft. Sq. Sd2. N.*

L. spicata (Spiked), E. N. America, has narrow leaves, and bold, wide spikes of flowers of rosy-purple in groups of from six to twelve.
*3-ft. August–October. H. 1½-ft. Sq. Sd2. N.*

**LIBERTIA** (Iridaceae), named after Madame A. Libert, Belgian botanist.

Libertias require good garden soil in a sheltered position in a sunny place.

L. formosa (Beautiful), Chile, has long, stiff, sword-shaped leaves and bears spikes of white starry flowers, borne amid greenish-brown bracts. *3-ft. June–August. H. 2-ft. Sq. D3. N.*

L. GRANDIFLORA (Large-flowered), New Zealand, is the New Zealand Satin Flower, and is similar in appearance, with Iris-like foliage, and larger flowers of clear satiny white.
*2½-ft. May–June. H. 2-ft. Sq. D3. N.*

**LILIUM** (Liliaceae), from the L. name for Lily which is common to most European languages.

Most Lilies are of easy cultivation and comparatively hardy, though thriving as a rule in light, fertile, loamy soil to which some leaf-mould has been added, and prefer a partially shaded site not unduly exposed to wind or sun. They do vary considerably, however, and where any variation from these conditions is required it is noted under the name of the species.

The genus varies widely in characteristics and geographical distribution. The bulbs vary greatly in size: those, for instance, of L. tenuifolium are seldom larger than a small marble, whereas those of L. giganteum are often larger than a tennis ball. In range of height and size of the flower, the variation is just as marked. L. elegans var. alutaceum seldom exceeds nine inches in height, whereas L. giganteum will grow to a height of ten feet.

Lilies are best planted in the autumn, and should be set as a rule upon a layer of coarse sand in such a way that moisture does not collect within the bulb. The soil should be lime-free unless otherwise noted, and of the texture suited to the growth of Rhododendrons. The depth at which the bulb should be planted varies: L. auratum, L. Henryi, and L. sulphureum are stem-rooting types which produce roots from the base of the bulb, and from the stem in addition, and should be planted with at least six inches of soil covering the bulb; on the other hand, L. candidum does not require such a deep covering. As a rule, it may be said that unless the Lilies are stem-rooting, shallow planting is preferable.

Lilies may be propagated by division of the offsets, when the stems have died down. They may be produced also by scaling the bulbs or by means of the aerial bulblets which are produced in the leaf axils, and some of the species will generally produce flowering plants in from two to three years. Lilies raised from seed are subject to considerable variations, but most of the species can be raised from seed in standardised compost.

L. AMABILE (Lovely), Korea, is a stem-rooting Lily and should be planted six inches deep in a sandy, lime-free loam. It bears flowers like the Turk's-cap Lily, with much-reflexed petals of red spotted with black.
*3-ft. July. B. 1-ft. Sq. Bulblets 7, offsets 10, scaling 10, seed 3. A.*

L. AURATUM (Golden-rayed), Japan, is a stem-rooting Lily best grown in lime-free soil and planted to a depth of eight inches in a place where the lower half of the stem will be shaded. The large flowers, which are borne in open sprays, are up to twelve inches in diameter, and variable in their markings, but always white in their basic colour.

Phlox decussata "Caroline Vandenberg" ABEF
Phlox decussata "Ethel Pritchard" CDGHLM
Phlox decussata "Daily Sketch" JKLMNOPQRSTU

Phlox decussata "Newbird" ABEFG
Phlox decussata "Graf Zeppelin" CDGHLMPQ
Phlox decussata "Le Mahdi" JKNO

The type generally known as L. auratum has white flowers with each segment with a yellow stripe, spotted variably with small crimson spots. L. AURATUM VAR. PICTUM has the tip of the central band of crimson, and in VAR. RUBRUM the whole band is crimson. L. AURATUM VAR. PLATYPHYLLUM has broader leaves and very few spots, and VAR. WITTEI (sometimes known as VIRGINALE) has practically no yellow band and but faint yellow spots.

*6-ft. August. B. 1-ft. Sq. Bulblets* 7, *offsets* 10, *scales* 10, *seeds* 3. *A.* [*Pl.* 50.

L. BOLANDERI (comm.), California, is the Thimble Lily, and is stem-rooting, requires lime-free leafy soil, and bears open sprays of reddish-purple flowers, approximately two inches in length, with spots of dark purple and paler shades.

*3-ft. June–July. B. 1-ft. Sq. Bulblets* 7, *offsets* 10, *scales* 10, *seeds* 3. *A.*

L. BROWNII (comm.), China, has large trumpet-shaped flowers which are orange-purple outside and creamy-white within. It is a stem-rooting Lily which will grow well in any good garden soil. L. BROWNII VAR. COLCHESTERI has very sweetly scented, funnel-shaped flowers of similar colour.

*4-ft. July. B. 1-ft. Sq. Bulblets* 7, *offsets* 10, *scales* 10, *seeds* 3. *N.*

L. BULBIFERUM (Bulb-bearing), S. Europe, has orange-red upright flowers spotted with purplish-black, and with a yellow centre. It will grow in ordinary garden soil in a sunny or partially shaded site, and is stem-rooting and should therefore be planted deeply. It obtains its name from its habit of producing bulblets in the leaf axils, and can be easily propagated by this means.

*4-ft. June. B. 1-ft. Sq. Bulblets* 7, *offsets* 10, *scales* 10, *seeds* 3. *N.*

L. CALLOSUM (With a hard skin), Japan, is a stem-rooting Lily which will grow in ordinary well-drained garden soil in a sunny place. It has bright scarlet flowers, spotted with purple-black, about two inches in diameter, with the petals turned back.

*2-ft. August–September. B. Offsets* 10, *scales* 10, *seeds* 3. *N.*

L. CANADENSE (Canadian), Canada, is a woodland Lily which thrives in partial shade and bears sprays of drooping orange-yellow to red flowers spotted with brown, about three inches in diameter. It should be planted six to eight inches deep in a lime-free soil.

*5-ft. July. B.* $1\frac{1}{2}$*-ft. Sq. Bulblets* 10, *offsets* 10, *scales* 10, *seeds* 3. *A.*

L. CANADENSE COCCINEUM OR RUBRUM is similar but has flowers of orange-red.

L. CANADENSE FLAVUM has lemon-yellow flowers.

*5-ft. July. B.* $1\frac{1}{2}$*-ft. Sq. Bulblets* 10, *offsets* 10, *scales* 10, *seeds* 3. *A.*

L. CANDIDUM (Pure white), S.W. Europe, is the Madonna Lily, thrives best in limy soil, only roots from the base, and should be planted quite shallowly with the top of the bulb only about an inch below the surface of the ground. It is practically evergreen; as soon as the flowering stems have died down they are replaced by new stems. It should be left undisturbed as long as possible, and if divided should be thus treated in either August or September. The flowers are of clear white, unmarked, and borne in tight sprays with the flowers held horizontally; VAR. MACULATUM has its flowers streaked on the outside with purple, and VAR. SPECIOSUM has black stems.

4-*ft.* *June–July.* *B.* 1-*ft. Sq.* *Offsets* 9, *scales* 9, *seeds* 3. *C.*

L. CARNIOLICUM (From Carniola), S.E. Europe, grows to three feet in height, with small, nodding, sweetly scented, orange-red flowers with turned-back petals, spotted with purple-black.

2-*ft.*–3-*ft.* *June.* *B.* 1-*ft. Sq.* *Bulblets* 10, *offsets* 10, *scales* 10, *seeds* 3. *N.*

L. CAROLINIANUM (From Carolina), N. America, is the Meadow Lily of the South, similar in appearance to L. canadense. It is orange-scarlet in colour, spotted with purple-brown, and has slightly fragrant, drooping flowers borne in open racemes on stems of some three to four feet. It thrives best in a shady place in a moist, well-drained, peaty soil. The bulb is curious and looks like a miniature dumb-bell, and should not be broken when it is planted.

4-*ft.* *July.* *B.* 1½-*ft. Sq.* *Bulblets* 10, *offsets* 10, *seeds* 3. *A.*

L. CENTIFOLIUM (Hundred-leaved), China, grows to six feet in height, has flowers which are greenish-white outside, and produces, in numbers from ten to twenty, large trumpet-shaped flowers each about six inches long. It is a stem-rooting Lily, and the bulbs should be planted about eight inches deep in light loamy and leafy soil in partial shade.

6-*ft.* *August.* *B.* 1½-*ft. Sq.* *Bulblets* 10, *offsets* 10, *scales* 10, *seeds* 3. *A.*

L. CHALCEDONICUM (From Chalcedonia), Greece, is the Scarlet Turk's-cap Lily. It has vermilion-scarlet flowers hanging in open racemes of from five to eight flowers, each about three inches in diameter, and with the petals much reflexed and with a rather nauseous odour. It thrives well in a sunny position in a limy soil, but is liable not to flower the first year after planting.

4-*ft.* *June–July.* *B.* 1-*ft. Sq.* *Bulblets* 10, *offsets* 10, *scales* 10, *seeds* 3. *C.*

L. CONCOLOR (Of uniform tone), China, has erect, slightly fragrant, vermilion flowers about one and a half inches in length, produced in clusters upon stems of about two feet in height. It is not stem-rooting and grows well in any sandy, leafy soil in a sunny place.

2-*ft.* *June–July.* *B.* 1-*ft. Sq.* *Bulblets* 10, *offsets* 10, *scales* 10, *seeds* 3. *N.*

L. CONCOLOR VAR. PULCHELLUM is similar except that the vermilion flowers are spotted with purple.

L. CROCEUM (Saffron), S.E. Europe, is the Orange Lily, and is suitable to grow in a heavy loamy soil, thriving with equal vigour upon limy or lime-free soil. The flowers, which are borne in clusters, are orange spotted with crimson, approximately three inches in length, and borne erect. It is stem-rooting and should be planted about six inches deep.

6-*ft.* *June–July.* *B.* 1½-*ft. Sq.* *Bulblets* 10, *offsets* 10, *scales* 10, *seeds* 3. [*ANC.*

L. Dalhansoni (comm.) is a hybrid between L. Hansoni and L. Martagon, and has long stems carrying widely-spaced drooping flowers of mahogany-red, spotted and speckled with yellow, and should be planted three to four inches deep in a light loamy lime-free soil.
*4-ft. Aug.–Sept. B. 1-ft. Sq. Bulblets* 10, *offsets* 10, *scales* 10, *seeds* 3. *N.*

L. daURICUM (From Dahuria), Siberia, is known as the Candlestick Lily, and has bright orange-red flowers spotted with purple-black, held erect. It thrives best in a soil which is rich in lime, in a sunny place.
*2-ft. June. B. 1-ft. Sq. Bulblets* 10, *offsets* 10, *scales* 10, *seeds* 3. *C.*

L. DAURICUM VAR. GRANDIFLORUM has larger orange-red flowers with red tips.
*2-ft. June. B. 1-ft. Sq. Bulblets* 10, *offsets* 10, *scales* 10, *seeds* 3. *C.*

L. DAURICUM VAR. INCOMPARABILE has flowers of crimson.
*2-ft. June. B. 1-ft. Sq. Bulblets* 10, *offsets* 10, *scales* 10, *seeds* 3. *C.*

L. DAURICUM VAR. VENUSTUM has apricot flowers without spots.
*2-ft. June. B. 1-ft. Sq. Bulblets* 10, *offsets* 10, *scales* 10, *seeds* 3. *C.*

L. Davidii (comm.), China, is a stem-rooting Lily with nodding flowers of about three inches in length, cinnabar-red spotted with black. It is variable in height, approximating to six feet, is stem-rooting, and should be planted at least eight inches deep in sandy loam with some leaf-mould added, in a position where it gets some sun or is partially shaded.
*6-ft. July–Aug. B. 1-ft. Sq. Bulblets* 10, *offsets* 10, *scales* 10, *seeds* 3. *N.*

L. Duchartrei (comm.), W. China, is a stem-rooting Lily with nodding reflexed-petalled flowers of white tinged with rose. Thriving in ordinary garden soil, lightened with sand, in a partially shaded place, it runs with freedom in a suitable spot. L. Duchartrei var. Farreri has white flowers spotted with purple and seems to prefer soil which contains some lime.
*2-ft. June–July. B. 1-ft. Sq. Bulblets* 10, *offsets* 10, *scales* 10, *seeds* 3. *N.*

L. ELEGANS (Graceful), Japan, sometimes known as *L. Thunbergianum*, grows to two feet in height and has erect orange-red flowers speckled with purple-black. It is available in a large number of forms, the chief of which are:—

ALUTACEUM, which is very dwarf, between nine inches and one foot in height, and apricot-orange in colour.

AURANTIACUM has salmon flowers tipped with red.

FULGENS is deep red.

Horsmannii, rich crimson.

MACULATUM, orange, with scarlet towards the edges.

*2-ft. June–July. B. 1-ft. Sq. Offsets* 10, *scales* 10, *seeds* 3. *N.*

L. GIGANTEUM (Giant), Himalayas, thrives best in open woodland and produces a long spire of large white flowers, tinged with green outside and striped with purplish red within, and fragrant and slightly hanging. It requires a light, lime-free soil which is rich, and should be planted just below the surface.
10-*ft. July. B.* 2-*ft. Sq. Bulblets* 10, *offsets* 10, *scales* 10, *seeds* 3. *N.*

L. GRAYI (comm.), Virginia, has rather small, funnel-shaped flowers of red, tinged with yellow and spotted with purple-bronze, from two to four on a stem, held in a horizontal or drooping position. It is not stem-rooting, and should be planted just below the surface of the soil in sandy, leafy soil, in some shade.
3-*ft. July. B.* ¾-*ft. Sq. Bulblets* 10, *offsets* 10, *scales* 10, *seeds* 3. *N.*

L. HANSONI (comm.), Japan, grows to five feet in height and bears small orange-yellow flowers spotted with purple-brown, drooping from large clusters. It is fragrant, and thrives in lime-free soil. It is stem-rooting and should be planted about nine inches deep in partial shade.
5-*ft. June–July. B.* 1-*ft. Sq. Bulblets* 10, *offsets* 10, *scales* 10, *seeds* 3. *N.*

L. HENRYI (comm.), China, bears spires of from ten to twenty large, orange, reflexed flowers, spotted with bronze, upon stems of nine feet, in height. It is stem-rooting and should be planted deeply in limy, leafy loam in a sunny position.
9-*ft. Aug. B.* 2-*ft. Sq. Bulblets* 10, *offsets* 10, *scales* 10, *seeds* 3. *C. Pl.* 50.

L. HUMBOLDTII (comm.), California, has still larger reddish-orange flowers spotted with purple-brown, with the petals much turned back, and hanging slightly in the clusters. It grows well in sandy, leafy loam and is not stem-rooting. It requires a certain amount of shade at the root. L. HUMBOLDTII VAR. MAGNIFICUM is still larger.
6-*ft. July. B.* 1½-*ft. Sq. Bulblets* 10, *offsets* 10, *scales* 10, *seeds* 3. *N.*

L. JAPONICUM (Japanese), Japan, is also known as *L. Krameri*, grows to three feet in height, and has pink trumpet-shaped flowers borne in groups of from two to five, held horizontally. The flowers are sweetly scented, and the plant is stem-rooting, requiring to be grown deeply in sandy, leafy soil in some shade.
3-*ft. June–July. B.* 1-*ft. Sq. Bulblets* 10, *offsets* 10, *scales* 10, *seeds* 3. *N.*

L. KELLOGGII (comm.), California, has pale-pink reflexed flowers up to 2½ inches in length, and held erect, spotted with purplish-black and deepening in colour with age. This Lily is base-rooting, and the bulb requires to be planted four inches deep in light, leafy soil in a partly shaded site.
3-*ft. June–July. B.* 1-*ft. Sq. Bulblets* 9, *offsets* 9, *scales* 9, *seeds* 3. *N.*

L. LONGIFLORUM (Long-flowered), Japan, is the White Trumpet Lily, seldom grown in the garden, being mainly forced under glass for early decoration. It is stem-rooting and grows in a compost of light, leafy loam, though in the garden it is apt to be shortlived and require constant renewal. The flowers, which are about six inches in length, are pure white, trumpet-shaped and held horizontally. It is available in a large number of variable forms.

*3-ft. July–Aug. B. 1½-ft Sq. Bulblets* 10, *offsets* 10, *scales* 10, *seeds* 3. *N.*

L. MARTAGON (Turk's-cap Lily), W. Asia, has tall, slender spikes of pink or purplish-rose flowers, spotted with purplish-black, held drooping, with the petals reflexed. It is base-rooting, thrives best in a light, leafy loam, with some lime, and may be grown in either sun or shade. L. MARTAGON VAR. ALBUM has white flowers and VAR. DALMATICUM has very dark crimson flowers.

*4-ft–5-ft. June–July. B. 1-ft. Sq. Bulblets* 9, *offsets* 9, *scales* 9, [*seeds* 3. *C.*

L. MEDEOLOIDES (Resembling Medeola), the Wheel Lily from Japan, grows to two feet in height, has orange-red reflexed and drooping flowers spotted with black, and requires to be grown in a lime-free, leafy soil in a shaded position.

*2½-ft. June–July. B. 1-ft. Sq. Bulblets* 10, *offsets* 10, *scales* 10, [*seeds* 3. *N.*

L. MONADELPHUM (Having the filaments of the stamens united), Persia, is a base-rooting Lily with large, trumpet-shaped, reflexed flowers of golden-yellow, held drooping, in sprays of from five to twenty. It prefers a rich, light loam in a partially shaded site.

*6-ft. June–July. B. 1½-ft. Sq. Bulblets* 10, *offsets* 10, *scales* 10, [*seeds* 3. *N.*

L. MONADELPHUM SZOVITZIANUM has sulphur-yellow flowers but is otherwise similar.

L. PARDALINUM (Spotted like a panther), California, is the Leopard or Panther Lily, is base-rooting, and produces large, open clusters of orange-red flowers spotted with purple, yellow at the base, with the petals turned back and the flowers held drooping. It thrives best in a shaded site in a leafy, lime-free loam, and is probably best in a moist soil. L. PARDALINUM CALIFORNICUM has smaller leaves but the compensation of larger flowers.

*6-ft.–8-ft. July–August. B. 1½-ft. Sq. Bulblets* 10, *offsets* 10, *scales* 10, [*seeds* 3. *N.*

L. PHILADELPHICUM (From Philadelphia), N. America, is the Orange-cup Lily, and has orange-red flowers spotted with purple, held erect, and carrying claws on the petals. It is stem-rooting and should be planted deeply in a sunny place in sandy and leafy soil.

*2-ft.–3-ft. June–July. B. 1-ft. Sq. Bulblets* 10, *offsets* 10, *scales* 10, [*seeds* 3. *N.*

L. PHILIPPINENSE, Philippine Islands, has long, tubular flowers of creamy-white tinged with green, held horizontally, and tinged with brown outside. It should be grown in deep lime-free soil in semi-shade.

*4-ft. August–September. B. 1½-ft. Sq. Bulblets* 10, *offsets* 10, *scales* 10, [*seeds* 3. *N.*

L. POMPONIUM (Pompous or splendid), S. France, has drooping scarlet flowers with much-reflexed petals, and is malodorous. The flowers are borne upon long stems in diffuse sprays in June. It should be planted shallowly in limy loam, in a sunny place, neither too close to the house nor to the nose!
*3-ft. June–July. B. 1-ft. Sq. Bulblets* 10, *offsets* 10, *scales* 10, *seeds* 3. *C.*

L. PYRENAICUM (Pyrenees) is known as the Yellow Turk's-cap Lily, and has waxy lemon-yellow flowers spotted with purple-black, about two inches in diameter, borne nodding. It is base-rooting, thrives in ordinary garden soil, and is probably one of the earliest of the Lilies to flower, making its appearance first in May.
*3-ft. May–June. B. 1-ft. Sq. Bulblets* 9, *offsets* 9, *scales* 9, *seeds* 9. *N.*

L. REGALE (Royal), W. China, is probably the most popular of all the white Lilies, being quite indifferent to the type of soil in which it will grow. The funnel-shaped flowers are borne in groups of from five to twenty, lilac or purple without, white within, shaded to yellow at the base, borne horizontally, and sweetly scented. It is a stem-rooting Lily, and therefore requires deep planting.
*4-ft.–6-ft. July. B. 1¼-ft. Sq. Bulblets* 10, *offsets* 10, *scales* 10, *seeds* 3. [*ANC.*

L. RUBELLUM (Shining red), Japan, grows well in leafy, sandy soil to which some loam has been added, and produces trumpet-shaped flowers of attractive rose-pink, held horizontally. It is stem-rooting and requires to be deeply planted.
*1½-ft. June. B. 1-ft. Sq. Bulblets* 10, *offsets* 10, *scales* 10, *seeds* 10. *N.*

L. SARGENTIAE (comm.), China, has large, white, funnel-shaped flowers, of rose-purple outside, held horizontally, borne upon stout stems of some four to five feet in height. It is sweetly scented and is stem-rooting, and should be deeply planted in rich loamy soil.
*4-ft.–6-ft. Aug. B. 1½-ft. Sq. Bulblets* 10, *offsets* 10, *scales* 10, *seeds* 3. *N.*

L. SPECIOSUM (Showy), Japan, is stem-rooting and requires a rich, sandy, loamy soil. The flowers are of white flushed with rose and spotted with rose-red, drooping and reflexed. It is fragrant, and is available in a large number of forms. L. SPECIOSUM VAR. ALBUM has white flowers, VAR. KRAETZERI has white flowers tinged with green, VAR. MAGNIFICUM has red-flushed flowers spotted with pink, VAR. MELPOMENE is crimson margined with white, and VAR. RUBRUM has flowers of carmine-pink. They should be planted six to eight inches deep.
*4½-ft. August–September. B. 1½-ft. Sq. Bulblets* 10, *offsets* 10, *scales* 10, [*seeds* 3. *N.*

L. SUPERBUM (Magnificent), N. America, is the American Swamp Lily, and is best suited to moist, shady borders in light, lime-free loam. The flowers have their petals reflexed and are of bright orange-scarlet spotted with purple. The bulbs should be planted five inches deep.
*5-ft.–6-ft. July–August. B. 1½-ft. Sq. Bulblets* 10, *offsets* 10, *scales* 10, [*seeds* 3. *N.* 48.

L. TENUIFOLIUM (With slender leaves), Siberia, has bright-scarlet reflexed flowers borne two to four on a stem in May or June. It thrives best in a partly shaded site in lime-free soil, consisting of leaf-mould and sandy loam.

2-*ft.* *May–June.* *B.* $\frac{3}{4}$-*ft.* *Sq.* *Bulblets* 10, *offsets* 10, *scales* 10, [*seeds* 3. *N.*

L. TESTACEUM (Shell-like), garden origin, has drooping, fragrant flowers of pale apricot, sometimes flushed with pink, borne upon strong stems in attractive open clusters.

6-*ft.* *June–July.* *B.* 1½-*ft.* *Sq.* *Bulblets* 10, *offsets* 10, *scales* 10, [*seeds* 3. *N.*

L. TIGRINUM (Tiger Lily), Japan, is probably one of the oldest Lilies in cultivation. The drooping, reflexed flowers, which are up to five inches across, are of orange-red, spotted with purple-black, and borne upon strong stems of four to five feet in height. The bulbs are stem-rooting and should be planted about eight inches deep in ordinary garden soil in full sun. It is best propagated from the bulblets which it produces from the leaf axils. It is available in a large number of varieties, including VAR. FLORE PLENO which has double flowers, and a giant variety called FORTUNEI.

5-*ft.* *August–September.* *B.* 2-*ft.* *Sq.* *Bulblets* 10, *offsets* 10, *scales* 10, [*seeds* 3. *N.*

L. WARDII (comm.), Tibet, resembles a Martagon Lily with flowers of purplish-pink. It thrives best in ordinary light garden soil in a sunny position.

4-*ft.* *August–September.* *B.* 1-*ft.* *Sq.* *Bulblets* 10, *offsets* 10, *scales* 10, [*seeds* 10. *N.*

L. WASHINGTONIANUM (comm.), California, grows to six feet in height and has long, fragrant, white flowers, sometimes spotted with purple, borne horizontally. It thrives in leafy mould and sand in a partially shaded site.

6-*ft.* *June–July.* *B.* 1½-*ft.* *Sq.* *Bulblets* 10, *offsets* 10, *scales* 10, *seeds* 3. *N.*

L. WILLMOTTIAE (comm.), China, has orange-red flowers spotted with brown, with turned-back petals, held drooping in open clusters, somewhat resembling the Tiger Lily. It is best grown in ordinary loamy soil in a sunny position and, being stem-rooting, should be planted deeply.

4-*ft.* *July–August.* *B.* 1-*ft.* *Sq.* *Bulblets* 10, *offsets* 10, *scales* 10, *seeds* 3. [*ANC.*

**LIMONIUM** (*see* STATICE).

**LINARIA** (Scrophulariaceae), from G. linon—flax, which some of the species resemble in appearance.

L. DALMATICA (From Dalmatia), S.E. Europe, has grey-green foliage neatly encircling its rising stems and bears large, golden, Antirrhinum-like flowers, each with a straight spur. It is easily cultivated in any garden soil and is sufficiently invasive to become a plant which one may not give to one's neighbours without thought of the morrow. 2-*ft*. *May–September*. *H*. 2-*ft*. *Sq*. *D*3. *N*.

L. GENISTIFOLIA (With foliage like Broom), Europe, has narrow-pointed green leaves and bears sprays of light-yellow flowers touched with orange at the lips. 2½-*ft*. *May–September*. *H*. 2-*ft*. *Sq*. *D*3. *N*.

L. MACEDONICA (From Macedonia) has greyish-green oval leaves and bears long sprays of bright-yellow flowers marked with orange on the lip. L. MACEDONICA SPECIOSA has still larger and brighter flowers. 3-*ft*. *July–September*. *H*. 2-*ft*. *Sq*. *D*3. *N*.

L. PURPUREA (Purple), S. Europe, grows from two to three feet in height and carries slender spires of purple-blue flowers touched with white upon the palate. It is particularly easy to grow from seed, and has a long flowering period.
3-*ft*. *July–September*. *H*. 1-*ft*. *Sq*. *Sd*2. *ANC*. *Pl*. 5.

L. PURPUREA CANON WENT has particularly pretty spires of flowers of bright pink touched upon the lip with orange.
2-*ft*. *July–September*. *H*. 1-*ft*. *Sq*. *Sd*2. *ANC*. *Pl*. 5.

L. TRIORNITHOPHORA (Resembling three birds), Spain, grows to two feet in height and has large flowers of pale violet with an orange palate. 2-*ft*. *July–September*. *H*. 1-*ft*. *Sq*. *Sd*2. *N*.

**LINDELOFIA** (Boraginaceae), named in honour of von Lindelof, a German botanist.

The one species is easily grown from seed in a well-drained sunny soil.

L. LONGIFLORA (Bearing long flowers), Himalayas, is the *L. spectabilis* of catalogues, and makes a tuft of rough, long, lanceolate leaves and bears curled-up sprays of pink buds which open to deep-blue tubular flowers of great beauty.
1½-*ft*. *May–August*. *H*. 1-*ft*. *Sq*. *Sd*2. *N*.

**LINUM** (Linaceae), a name derived from G. linon: named after the flax which is provided by one of the species, L. usitatissimum.

Propagation is most easily effected from seed.

L. FLAVUM (Pure yellow), Europe, has large golden five-petalled flowers borne upon herbaceous growth and rounded bright-green leaves. It is of easy cultivation in any good garden soil.
1-*ft*. *June–September*. *H*. 1-*ft*. *Sq*. *Sd*2. *N*. 3/1.

L. NARBONNENSE (From Narbonne), France, has slender arching stems with narrow green leaves and large terminal flowers of bright azure-blue, and is one of the few plants which the gardener should be

Pentstemon barbatus ABCDEFHJKMOQSU
Astilbe hybrida "Fanal" BCDFGHKLMOPQTU
Campanula barbata JKLMNOPST

Physostegia virginiana "Vivid"

persuaded to obtain by any means; a few pence will, of course, buy it, and it will provide seeds for ever.

*2-ft. June–September. H. 2-ft. Sq. Sd2. N.* 37/1.

L. PERENNE (Perennial), Europe, is even more slender in its growth, with narrower, somewhat softer leaves and clouds of large flowers of butterfly-blue. It is extremely easy to produce from seed and is invaluable for a position in the front of the border.

*2-ft. June–September. H. 1½-ft. Sq. Sd2. C.*

L. VISCOSUM (Sticky), S. Europe, is another uncommon plant sending up a large number of erect stems with sticky, notched, green leaves topped with rose-pink flowers, each with a blue eye.

*1½-ft. June–August. H. 1-ft. Sq. Sd2. N.*

**LOBELIA** (Campanulaceae), named in commemoration of Matthew Lobel, physician to King James I.

Tall herbaceous Lobelias are not so well known as they merit to be. They are extremely decorative and bear bright-green or dark-red leaves, and flower late in the year when colour is difficult to obtain. The large number of horticultural varieties are derived from the hybridisation of L. cardinalis, L. fulgens and L. syphilitica. They thrive upon rich soil and plenty of moisture and respond in most marked degree to feeding.

L. CARDINALIS (Deep scarlet), N. America, grows to three feet in height, with smooth, polished, dark-green leaves and terminal spires of bright-scarlet flowers in August–October.

*3-ft. August–October. H. 1-ft. Sq. D10. N.*

L. FULGENS (Shining red), Mexico, grows to three feet in height, has bronze foliage and bears terminal spires and deep-red flowers late in the year, similar in shape to the flowers of the bedding Lobelias, but much enlarged. *3-ft. July–September. H. 1-ft. Sq. D10. N.*

L. HYBRIDA (Hybrid) is a group comprising garden hybrids between the various species, of which the following are probably most outstanding:—

ARTHUR HUMBERT, which is a bright scarlet.

CHARMING, which is of even brighter scarlet.

JACK MACMASTERS is violet-blue with dark-purple foliage.

JEAN is reddish-purple, dark-bronzy foliage.

KING ALFRED has bronze foliage and scarlet flowers, borne in branching spires.

RIVERSIDE: Petunia-purple flowers are borne above bronzy foliage.

SILVER QUEEN is a most attractive light-blue shade.

THE TEST has brilliant-scarlet outstanding flowers.

*3-ft.–4-ft. August–September. H. 1½-ft. Sq. D10. N.*

L. SYPHILITICA (referring to the medicinal use of the plant), N. America, has smooth, green, oval leaves and bears deep-blue flowers in long terminal racemes.

2-*ft.* *July–August.* *H.* 1-*ft. Sq.* *D*10. *A.* 40/2.

L. TUPA (native name), Chile, has oval, toothed, wrinkled leaves and extremely large blood-red flowers borne in long sprays upon plants which, under good cultivation, will reach a height of eight feet.

8-*ft.* *August–September.* *H.* 3-*ft. Sq.* *Cg*6. *N.*

**LUPINUS** (Leguminosae), from L. lupus—wolf; said to be so named because of the deep-rooting character of certain of the species, which it was claimed impoverished the soil.

The herbaceous perennial Lupins are great favourites, wonderfully improved in recent years by means of cross breeding and selection, to such an extent that they now provide a range of colouring exceeded by no other plant. Cultivation is comparatively easy, as Lupins will thrive in any soil which has been deeply dug and well manured. They flourish with equal vigour in either sunny sites or partial shade, and develop into plants of approximately three feet in diameter, carrying numerous stately spikes of colourful flowers. The best times for planting are in October or November, February or March. They cannot be said to be long-lived, and should be replaced from stock when deterioration is noticed.

The only disadvantage they bring to the herbaceous border is in the fact that after June they become untidy and lack colour, but if they are set toward the rear of the border this fact can be concealed. They lend themselves, however, very readily to treatment in borders composed entirely of Lupins and can create under these circumstances such a blaze of colour that it will remain in the memory throughout the months when the Lupin no longer is in flower. In recent years the advent of the wonderful Russell Lupins produced by the skill, patience and genius of Mr. George Russell has added much to the beauty and the stature of the Lupin, and too much in praise of this wonderful development cannot be said.

Before considering the various types of Lupinus polyphyllus we will consider the species from which they have sprung; these are:—

L. NOOTKATENSIS (From Nutka), W. N. America, has hairy foliage and produces long spires of blue flowers, sometimes tipped with red or golden-yellow. 3-*ft.* *May–July.* *H.* 3-*ft. Sq.* *Sd*2. *N.*

L. PERENNIS (Perennial), Maine, has downy foliage and produces shorter spikes of blue flowers in open spires; it also can be found with flowers either pink or white in colour.

2-*ft.* *May–June.* *H.* 2-*ft. Sq.* *Sd*2. *N.*

L. POLYPHYLLUS (Many-leaved), N. America, has green leaves made up of many leaflets, and long spires of variable blue flowers followed by woolly pods. 4-*ft.* *May–June.* *H.* 3-*ft. Sq.* *Sd*2. *N.*

L. POLYPHYLLUS VAR. ALBUS has white flowers; VAR. BICOLOR has blue and white flowers, and VAR. ROSEUS has rose-coloured flowers.

It is from these species that the modern Lupin has sprung by the process of cross fertilisation and selection. The varieties which follow are named varieties of outstanding merit which are the best of their kind:— *Pl.* 52 & 53.

ADA is chrome-yellow, with stout, bold spikes. *3-ft.–5-ft. May–June.*

APRICOT is apricot-orange. *3-ft.–5-ft. May–June.*

BETTY OF YORK opens pale lavender, changing with age to deep violet, standards cream, changing to rosy-violet. *3-ft.–3½-ft.*

BISHOPGATE is a fine cerise-pink self-coloured variety. *3-ft.–3½-ft.*

BONINGALE BELLE has pink bells with cerise standards. *3-ft.–3½-ft.*

BONINGALE BUTTERFLY is carmine-rose with standards of cerise and gold. *3-ft.–3½-ft.*

BONINGALE CHARM is peach-pink with standards of lemon-yellow. *3-ft.–3½-ft.*

BONINGALE LAD is deep blue with standards of mauve and white. *3-ft.–3½-ft.*

BONINGALE LASS has yellow standards with rose-pink bells. *3-ft.–3½-ft.*

BONINGALE MAID is pale apricot with orange standards. *3-ft.–3½-ft.*

BONINGALE SPLENDOUR is deep blue with white standards. *3-ft.–3½-ft.*

BRENDA PRICHARD has flowers of deep orange of even tone. *3-ft.–4-ft.*

BRONZE QUEEN has golden-bronze flowers. *3-ft.–5-ft. May–June.*

CAM is azure blue with standards of pale yellow. *3-ft.–3½-ft.*

CATHERINE OF YORK is pale salmon-pink with standards of yellow. *3-ft.–3½-ft.*

CHARMING is soft rose. *3-ft.–5-ft. May–June.*

CHOCOLATE SOLDIER is dark chocolate with yellow standards. *3-ft.–5-ft. May–June.*

CHRISTINE OF YORK has rosy-mauve bells with white standards. *3-ft.–3½-ft.*

CITY OF YORK has bright-red, full spikes. *3-ft.–3½-ft.*

CLIBRAN'S RED is deep red. *3-ft.–5-ft. May–June.*

CLYDE opens pale salmon, changing to cerise-pink. *3-ft.–3½-ft.*

C. M. PRICHARD is apricot. *3-ft.–5-ft. May–June.*

COCQUELICOT is salmon-pink. *3-ft.–5-ft. May–June.*

COUNTESS OF MARCH opens white, deepening to mauve-purple. *3-ft.–5-ft. May–June.*

DEE has salmon-pink bells with standards of yellow. *3-ft.–3½-ft.*

DOWNER'S DELIGHT has flowers of even crimson tone. *3-ft.–4-ft.*

EILEEN is cherry-rose. 3-*ft.*–5-*ft.* *May–June.*

ELAINE HANMER has bright-cerise bells with yellow standards. 3-*ft.*–3½-*ft.*

ELIZABETH ARDEN is tan, suffused with yellow. 3-*ft.*–5-*ft.* *May–June.*

EMPEROR is of good deep pink. 3-*ft.*–5-*ft.* *May–June.*

FASCINATION is rosy-violet, veined with purple. 3-*ft.*–5-*ft.* *May–June.*

FELICITY OF YORK has violet-mauve bells with white standards. 3-*ft.*–3½-*ft.*

FIREFLY is rose-red. 3-*ft.*–5-*ft.* *May–June.*

FLORENCE OF YORK is salmon-orange. 3-*ft*–3½-*ft.*

FOXII is blue and white. 3-*ft.*–5-*ft.* *May–June.*

GENERAL HOLDITCH has violet-blue bells and standards touched with crimson. 3-*ft.* *May–June.* *Pl.* 55.

GEORGE RUSSELL has coral-pink bells turning to pure pink, with standards of citron-yellow turning to cream, with pink edge. 3-*ft.*–3½-*ft.*

GERTRUDE OF YORK is lilac-mauve with white standards. 3-*ft.*–3½-*ft.*

GLADYS COOPER is slate-blue, with standards pinkish-mauve marked with blue. 3-*ft.*–3½-*ft.*

GOLD CREST is gold with a bronze shading. 3-*ft.*–5-*ft.* *May–June.*

GOLDEN THOUGHTS is fawn shaded with rose. 3-*ft.*–5-*ft.* *May–June.*

GOODWOOD is deep pink. 3-*ft.*–5-*ft.* *May–June.*

GRENADIER has fine orange-scarlet spikes. 3-*ft.*–5-*ft.* *May–June.*

HAPPINESS is still one of the best purples. 3-*ft.*–5-*ft.* *May–June.*

HELEN OF YORK is deep rosy-violet with standards of bright yellow. 3-*ft.*–3½-*ft.*

HIGHLANDER is a clear-pink self-coloured variety. 3-*ft.*–5-*ft.* *May–June.*

IOLANTHE is white flushed with blue. 3-*ft.*–5-*ft.* *May–June.*

ISABEL OF YORK has pale buff bells and red and gold standards. 3-*ft.*–3½-*ft.*

ISIS is navy-blue with standards of lemon-yellow. 3-*ft.*–3½-*ft.*

JANET OF YORK combines bright-mauve bells with standards of white. 3-*ft.*–3½-*ft.*

JENNIFER OF YORK is pale biscuit-yellow with standards of creamy-yellow tipped with gold. 3-*ft.*–3½-*ft.*

JOAN OF YORK is bright cerise with white standards edged cerise marked with pale blue. 3-*ft.*–3½-*ft.*

JOSEPHINE is slaty-blue, with clear lemon-yellow standards. 3-*ft.*–3½-*ft.*

JUDITH OF YORK is coral-salmon and has standards with centres of yellow, crimson and purple. 3-*ft.*–3½-*ft.*

Knavesmire has salmon-orange bells with standards edged with yellow. *3-ft.–3½-ft.*

Lady Beatrix Stanley is deep rose-pink. *3-ft.–3½-ft.*

Lady Terry is pale red with standards of deep red marked with orange. *3-ft.–3½-ft.*

Lady Wilfred Thompson is pale pink and has standards of pale yellow turning to white and edged with pink. *3-ft.–3½-ft.*

Lavender Bee is pale lavender turning deeper with age. *3-ft.–5-ft. May–June.*

Madeline of York combines violet with pale yellow. *3-ft.–3½-ft.*

Mary of York is smoky-blue with standards of pale gold. *3-ft.–3½-ft.*

Maud Tippets is orange-red, with burgundy-red standards. *3-ft.–3½-ft. Pl.* 55.

May Princess is deep purple. *3-ft.–5-ft. May–June.*

May Queen is royal purple. *3-ft.–5-ft. May–June.*

May Robinson combines apricot and fawn. *3-ft.–5-ft. May–June.*

Moerheimii is variable pink. *3-ft.–5-ft. May–June.*

Monkgate is deep blue with white standards. *3-ft.–3½-ft.*

Mount Everest has white, solid spikes. *3-ft.–5-ft. May–June.*

Mrs. D. Mathieson is a fine lavender-blue. *3-ft.–5-ft. May–June.*

Mrs. Garnet Botfield is the best deep yellow. *3-ft.–3½-ft.*

Mrs. Mickletwaite has salmon-pink bells with standards of pale gold. *3-ft.–3½-ft.*

Mrs. Noel Terry is blush-pink with standards of creamy-white. *3-ft.–3½-ft.*

Mrs. Penry Williams has cerise standards and deep salmon-pink bells. *3-ft. May–June. Pl.* 54.

Nellie B. Allan has deep-salmon bells with similar standards with yellow markings at the base. *3-ft.–3½-ft.*

Opal has fine, clear, opal-blue spikes. *3-ft.–5-ft. May–June.*

Orwell is salmon-apricot, with standards of bright yellow. *3-ft.–3½-ft.*

Painted Lady is peach-pink. *3-ft.–3½-ft.*

Patricia of York is a very fine yellow self. *3-ft.–3½-ft.*

Pearly Blue is sky-blue tinged with mauve. *3-ft.–3½-ft.*

Princess Elizabeth has rose-pink standards with salmon-pink bells. *3-ft.–4-ft. May–June. Pl.* 54.

Prudence of York is of deep pink with white standards. *3-ft.–3½-ft.*

Queen of the West is pale mauve. *3-ft.–5-ft. May–June.*

Rapture has deep-pink bells and red standards. *3-ft. May–June. Pl.* 55.

Red Star is brilliant reddish-purple. *3-ft.–5-ft. May–June.*

Riverslea is rosy-crimson. *3-ft.–5-ft. May–June.*

ROBIN HOOD has deep slate-blue bells with standards of buttercup-yellow. *3-ft.–3½-ft.*

ROSALIND is a rich-pink self-coloured variety. *3-ft.–5-ft. May–June.*

RUBY KING is carmine-purple. *3-ft.–5-ft. May–June.*

SAXE BLUE has clear saxe-blue flowers. *3-ft.–5-ft. May–June.*

SHANNON is bright pink with standards of white. *3-ft.–3½-ft.*

SONNY is bright cerise. *3-ft.–3½-ft.*

SULPHUR GEM has sulphur-yellow spikes. *3-ft.–5-ft. May–June.*

SUNSET is yellow, turning bronze with age. *3-ft.–5-ft. May–June.*

SUNSHINE is yellow, shaded with old gold. *3-ft.–5-ft. May–June.*

SUSAN OF YORK has terracotta-pink bells with standards of yellow. *3-ft.–3½-ft.*

TESSA OF YORK is salmon-pink deepening to rose, with standards of rose-pink deepening to crimson. *3-ft.–3½-ft.*

TRENT is coral-pink with standards of primrose-yellow. *3-ft.–3½-ft.*

TWEED is bright pink, shading to pale orange, with golden-yellow standards. *3-ft.–3½-ft.*

21ST LANCERS combines lavender, rose, and yellow. *3-ft.–5-ft. May–June.*

WEBER has flowers of soft salmon-pink. *3-ft.–4-ft.*

WISTARIA is forget-me-not blue. *3-ft.–5-ft. May–June.*

WYE has deep salmon-pink bells with gold standards crimson-edged. *3-ft.–3½-ft.*

YELLOW CLOUD is pale yellow with amber standards. *3-ft.–5-ft. May–June.*

YORK CASTLE is rosy-mauve with standards of mauve and white. *3-ft.–3½-ft.*

YORK MINSTER has pale salmon bells with standards of pink flushed creamy-yellow.

**LYCHNIS** (Caryophyllaceae), from G. lychnos—lamp, referring to the brightness of the flowers.

L. ARKWRIGHTII (comm.), garden origin, is a hybrid of L. Haageana and L. chalcedonica, grows to about eighteen inches in height, and bears large flowers with cleft petals varying in colour from orange to crimson. It thrives best in a soil which is retentive of moisture.
*1½-ft. July–August. H. 1½-ft. Sq. Sd2. N.*

L. CHALCEDONICA (From Chalcedonia), Asia Minor, grows to about two and a half feet in height, and has tight terminal clusters of bright-scarlet flowers. The foliage clasps the stems and is rough in texture. There are variable colour forms, from white to salmon and even dark red. An exceptionally fine form is L. CHALCEDONICA RUBRA PLENA with double flowers of crimson-scarlet.
*2½-ft. June–July. H. 2-ft. Sq. Sd2. D3. N. Pl. 56.*

L. Coronaria (Resembling Coronaria), S. Europe, is the Rose Campion, with wide, densely white, woolly leaves and large crimson flowers borne singly upon branching stems, and flourishing in dry, chalky soil. *3-ft. June–July. H. 2-ft. Sq. Sd2. C.*

L. Flos-cuculi (Cuckoo flower) is a slender-stemmed perennial with narrow, spear-shaped leaves, slightly hairy below and sticky above, bearing in loose and open sprays ragged-petalled flowers varying from pink to red. *2-ft. May–August. H. 2-ft. Sq. Sd2. C.*

L. Flos-Jovis (Flower of Jove) has white, hairy, pointed, wide leaves and bears large flowers of deep rose-pink.
*1½-ft. June–July. H. 1½-ft. Sq. Sd2. N.*

L. Haageana (comm.), garden origin, is a hybrid of L. fulgens and L. coronata, and has exceptionally large flowers of orange-red, scarlet or even crimson. *1-ft. June–July. H. 1-ft. Sq. Sd2. N.*

L. Viscaria (Sticky), Europe, is the German Catch-fly, growing to one and a half feet in height. The leaves are long and narrow, and the red or purple flowers are borne in loose clusters with sticky patches, from which the plant gets its name, below the flowers. Of all the garden varieties worth a place in the garden the variety flore pleno is probably the best, as its ragged double flowers persist for an exceptionally long time. It makes an admirable plant for the front of the flower border. The flowers, which are freely borne, are rose-red in colour and last equally well on the plant or when they are cut.
*1½-ft. May–July. H. 1½-ft. Sq. Sd2. N.*

**LYSIMACHIA** (Primulaceae), probably from G. lysis—abatement, and mache—strife; from which Loosestrife. It is, however, possible that the genus is named after Lysimachus, a King of Thrace, for whom it is claimed that he discovered the soothing properties of the plant.

L. barystachys (Heavy-spiked), Japan, has attractive spires of bell-shaped five-petalled flowers of clear white, borne tightly together. This plant is suitable, as a rule, for a moist situation.
*2-ft. July. H. 1½-ft. Sq. D3. N.*

L. clethroides (Resembling Alder), China, has similar one-sided hairy sprays of pure-white flowers above foliage which colours attractively in autumn. *2-ft. June–July. H. 1½-ft. Sq. D3. N.*

L. pseudo-Henryi (Sham Henryi), China, has large, pointed hairy leaves and bears sprays of large five-petalled starry yellow flowers.
*1-ft. June–July. H. 1½-ft. Sq. D3. N.*

**LYTHRUM** (Lythraceae), from G. lythron—blood, with reference to the colour of the flowers.

The Purple Loosestrife is suitable for growth either by the waterside or the herbaceous border, preferring as a rule a soil which is moderately moist.

L. SALICARIA (Resembling the Willow) is native to the British Isles, and carries long leafy spikes of purple flowers about three-quarters of an inch in diameter. The variety ROSEUM SUPERBUM has large rose-pink flowers, and LADY SACKVILLE flowers of bright rose. ROSE QUEEN has flowers of clear rose. L. SUPERBUM PROLIFIC is a variety which thrives in a wet soil, and produces with great freedom flower-spikes of bright purple-rose. L. SUPERBUM THE BEACON is slightly taller, with flowers of rose-red.

*3-ft. June–September. H. 1½-ft. Sq. D3. N. Pl.* 68.

L. VIRGATUM (Twiggy), Europe, is very similar in appearance but has narrow leaves and smaller flowers in more open spires.

*2-ft. July–September. H. 2-ft. Sq. D3. N. Pl.* 68.

**MACLEAYA** (*see* BOCCONIA).

**MALVA** (Malvaceae), from G. malakos—soothing; probably with reference to the emollient made from the seeds.

M. ALCEA (old name) makes a large clump of wiry stems with five-parted, narrowly cut leaves, and bears in open, loose sprays deep-rose flowers reminiscent of the Hollyhock.

*4-ft. July–September. H. 3-ft. Sq. D3. N. Pl.* 77.

M. MOSCHATA (Musky), Europe, is the Musk Mallow, the leaves of which are slightly scented; has five-parted, narrow leaves with the lobes again cut into divisions, and bears similar flowers of reddish-purple. The variety M. MOSCHATA ALBA is an exceptionally attractive plant, worthy of a place in any border.

*2-ft. June–July. H. 2-ft. Sq. Sd2. N. Pl.* 72.

**MALVASTRUM** (Malvaceae), derived from Malva and L. astrum—star.

The plants are allied to the Mallows and are attractive in well-drained sandy soil.

M. COCCINEUM (Scarlet), N. America, has a persistent running root becoming thick and woody, and silvery-grey-green foliage, and bears its brick-red flowers in terminal clusters and in the leaf axils. It is perfectly hardy in good light soil.

*1-ft. June–August. H. 1½-ft. Sq. D3. N. Pl.* 67.

**MECONOPSIS** (Papaveraceae), from G. mekon—poppy, and opsis—resemblance.

The species are widely distributed throughout the world, but mainly confined to the Himalayas. All the species prefer a loose, well-drained but moist leafy soil, and will not tolerate a hot, dry, sunny position. They are best planted in a site where they are partially shaded, and the surface dressed with grit and leaf-mould, in equal parts, annually. All the species propagate quite freely from seed, except M. quintuplinervia. M. betonicaefolia, M. cambrica, M. grandis and M. quintuplinervia are true perennials; the remainder are monocarpic.

Echinops Ritro ABCDEFGHJK
Platycodon grandiflorum album FGKLOPST
Platycodon grandiflorum GHLMPQRSU

66

Potentilla nepalensis Willmottiae

M. BETONICAEFOLIA VAR. BAILEYI (Betony-leaved; comm.), Yunnan, throws up stems of about three feet in height, and bears in loose sprays at the top a number of sky-blue silken-petalled flowers of about three inches in diameter, centred with a tuft of golden anthers. M. betonicaefolia is probably better known as *M. Baileyi* and produces itself freely from seed. If the seedlings are allowed to flower before they have formed more than a single rosette they will die after flowering, but if the flowering stems are picked out to prevent this, the plant may be grown as a good and persistent perennial. It requires the normal cultivation of the species.

*3-ft. July. H. 1-ft. Sq. Sd2. A.*

M. CAMBRICA (Welsh), Europe, is a perennial with grey-green leaves and single, solitary, pale-yellow flowers. The double-flowered variety with orange-yellow flowers is particularly attractive. It seems to thrive equally well in any soil and in either a sunny or shady site.

*1½-ft. June–September. H. 1-ft. Sq. Sd2. ANC.*

M. DHWOJII (comm.), Nepal, makes a most attractive rosette of fine, ferny foliage, densely covered with golden-bronze hair, and touched with morning dew has probably the most beautiful foliage to be found in the whole of the garden. It bears, when it flowers, a cone-shaped spire of pale-yellow flowers, and dies after these have been produced. It should not on this account be omitted from the garden, as it can be freely produced from seed.

*2-ft. June–July. E. 1-ft. Sq. Sd2. N.*

M. GRANDIS (Splendid), Himalayas, makes a rosette of oval, roughly-toothed, hairy leaves and produces two-foot stems carrying deep-blue flowers of about five inches in diameter. The colour is extremely variable, but at its best an amazing deep blue, centred with pale-yellow stamens, and at its worst a dingy purple-blue unworthy of much attention. A good form is breath-taking in its beauty.

*2-ft. May–June. H. 2-ft. Sq. Sd2. N.*

M. INTEGRIFOLIA (Leaves with a smooth edge), Tibet, is the Lamp-shade or Yellow Chinese Poppy, has smooth-edged, large, pale-green leaves, and bears an eighteen-inch spire of very pale-yellow flowers up to six inches in diameter. This, too, expires when it has flowered, but, again, accommodates with much seed.

*1½-ft. July. E. 1-ft. Sq. Sd2. N.*

M. QUINTUPLINERVIA (With five-nerved leaves), Tibet, makes basal rosettes of rough, hairy leaves, which increase by means of underground runners and bear, one upon a stem, large hanging flowers of lavender-blue which deepen to purple at the base, and are centred with large clusters of cream stamens.

*1½-ft. May–June. H. 1-ft. Sq. D8. A.* 636/3.

M. REGIA (Royal), Nepal, stuns the observer with the magnificence of its pale-green leaves covered with silvery hairs, the individual rosettes sometimes reaching five feet in diameter. It eventually bears—sometimes in four or five years—a pyramidal spire, some six feet in height, of large yellow flowers, and passes, to remain a fascinating memory. 5-*ft.*-6-*ft.* *June.* *E.* 5-*ft. Sq.* *Sd*2. *A.* 601/1.

M. SUPERBA (Superb), Himalayas, is of similar appearance but seldom as large, with clear-white flowers similarly produced. It, too, dies after flowering. 4-*ft.* *June.* *E.* 3-*ft. Sq.* *Sd*2. *A.*

M. WALLICHII (comm.), Nepal, is also monocarpic, and again has much-cut leaves covered with bronze hair. The flowering spire, which may be as tall as six feet, carries pale-blue flowers about two inches in diameter, centred with clusters of yellow stamens. It is a variable plant, and care should be taken to see that the seed from which it is raised is produced from a variety which has a good colour. 6-*ft.* *June–July.* *E.* 3-*ft. Sq.* *Sd*2. *N.*

**MELITTIS** (Labiatae), from G. melissa—bee, referring to the honey-producing qualities of the flowers.

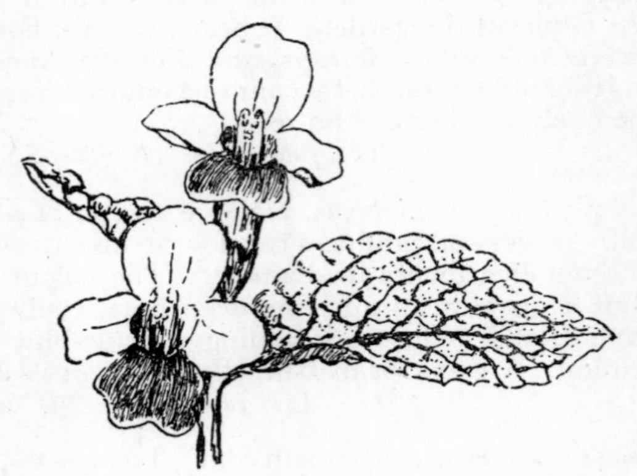

MELITTIS MELISSOPHYLLUM

M. MELISSOPHYLLUM (With leaves like Melissa), S. Europe, is a fascinating aromatic plant with stout, stiff stems and rough, green leaves, and with musk-scented flowers of white with wine-purple bands, freely borne in the leaf axils. It grows well in any good garden soil and propagates readily from seed. 1-*ft.* *May–June.* *H.* 1-*ft. Sq.* *Sd*3. *N.*

**MERTENSIA** (Boraginaceae) is named after F. C. Mertens, a German botanist.

M. CILIATA (Fringed), Rocky Mountains, generally masquerades as *M. sibirica,* and has large blue-green leaves, and long diffuse sprays of hanging blue flowers following the pink buds. It is easy to grow and reproduces itself with freedom from seed.

2-*ft.* *May–June.* *H.* 2-*ft. Sq.* *Sd*2. *N.*

M. VIRGINICA, Virginia, which has pride of place in the herbaceous border, produces, in good open soil, wide and waving strands of blue and pink, in large nodding clusters, amply set off by its grey-green shiny foliage. 2-*ft.* *May.* *H.* 1-*ft. Sq.* *Sd*2. *N.*

**MICHAUXIA** (Campanulaceae); the name is commemorative of A. Michaux, a French botanist.

Though monocarpic, M. campanuloides is so beautiful that it should not be missed. It thrives in rich but well-drained soil with plenty of lime.

M. CAMPANULOIDES (Campanula-like), Asia Minor, grows to three feet in height and produces loose sprays of lily-like flowers with long protruding stamens. 3-*ft.* *June–July.* *H.* 2-*ft. Sq.* *Sd*2. *N.*

**MIMULUS** (Scrophulariaceae), from L. mimus—mimic, the flowers being supposed to resemble a mask or a monkey's face.

A group of plants which are of doubtful hardiness, but are best fitted by a rich moist soil, and give an astonishing display of bright colour under these conditions for a long and protracted period.

M. CARDINALIS (Deep scarlet), N. America, is a tall plant with bright-scarlet flowers with pinched-back petals and outstanding yellow throat, delighting in a sunny, moist site. A number of hybrids are now available in colours which vary considerably, from white to deep crimson. 2-*ft.* *June–July.* *H.* 1-*ft. Sq.* *Sd*2. *N.* 14.

M. CUPREUS (Copper-coloured), Chile, is a close-growing plant approximating to half a foot in height, with flowers of coppery-orange. It has given rise to a number of varieties, all of which are of great beauty.

| | |
|---|---|
| Bees' Dazzler | blood-red, 719 |
| Bismarck | cherry-red |
| Chelsea Pensioner | crimson-scarlet |
| Plymtree | cherry-pink. *Pl.* 57 |
| R. C. Leslie | speckled bronze |
| Whitcroft's Scarlet | scarlet |

Where it is desired to keep the variety true to colour it is necessary that stock should be prepared from cuttings, which will root with the greatest of freedom. For safety's sake these plants should be kept with some protection during the winter. All are admirable in locations at the front of moist borders, or similar positions in shady places.

¾-*ft.* *June–September.* *H.* 1-*ft. Sq.* *Sd*2. *Cg*9. *N.*

M. LUTEUS (Yellow), Chile, has naturalised itself in the streams and pools in this country, but will grow perfectly well in damp positions. It has given rise to M. LUTEUS MACULATUS, which is similar but has large flowers spotted with red, and M. LUTEUS MERSTHAM HOSE IN HOSE, the hardiest species of all, with apricot-yellow double flowers.

*1-ft. May–August. E. 1-ft. Sq. D4. N.*

MIMULUS CARDINALIS

M. RINGENS (Open), E. N. America, is also hardy, making an upright-growing narrow plant with thin green leaves and branching heads of deep-lavender flowers.

*2-ft. June–August. H. 1-ft. Sq. Sd3. A.*

**MONARDA** (Labiatae), named after N. Monardez, a Spanish botanist.

Monardas are of easy cultivation in any good garden soil and easily propagated by division in the spring.

M. DIDYMA (Double), E. N. America, is known as the Oswego Tea or Bee-balm. It grows to two feet in height and has aromatic foliage and bears its flowers in circular groups in the leaf axils and at the ends of the stems. The colour is variable, generally red, but also occasionally white, pink or violet. The outstanding garden hybrid is undoubtedly that called CAMBRIDGE SCARLET.

*2½-ft. July–August. H. 3-ft. Sq. D3. N. Pl. 71.*

**MORINA** (Dipsaceae) is named after L. Morin, a French botanist, and is commonly called the Whorl-flower, because its flowers are produced in rings.

M. LONGIFOLIA (Long-leaved), Himalayas, forms basal tufts of ornamental thistle-like leaves and has deadnettle flowers, which are first white but change with age to pink and then to crimson. It is best grown in a sheltered position in good, well-dug, rich soil.

**MULGEDIUM** (*see* LACTUCA).

**MUSCARI** (Liliaceae), from G. moschos—musk, some of the species having the typical odour of the musk.

These are the Grape Hyacinths, useful in the garden in any soil in a sunny position. The species generally found to be of use in the herbaceous border are:—

M. CONICUM (Conical), S. Europe, has closely-packed spires of rounded blue flowers. The variety M. CONICUM HEAVENLY BLUE has similar flowers of clear but bright blue.
¾-*ft.* *March–April.* *B.* ¼-*ft. Sq.* *D*6. *N.* 639/1.

M. PLUMOSUM (Plumed), Asia Minor, has its flowers curiously tasselled and appears to be a Grape Hyacinth which has become fluffy and glamorised. ⅔-*ft.* *April–May.* ⅓-*ft. Sq.* *D*6. *N.* 34/2.

**MYOSOTIDIUM** (Boraginaceae), from G. mys—mouse, otes—ears, and eidos—appearance; that is, of forget-me-not-like appearance.

The one species, M. NOBILE, which is a native of the Chatham Islands, thrives best in a moist border in good soil. It should not be attempted except in the South of England. It has large, shiny leaves, reaching one foot in length, and bears sprays of small blue flowers, darker in the centre, in tight sprays sometimes six inches in diameter.
2-*ft.* *April–June.* *H.* 2-*ft. Sq.* *Sd*3. *N.*

**MYOSOTIS** (Boraginaceae), from G. mys—mouse, and otes—ears, from the shape of the leaves. This name was not applied originally to the Forget-me-not.

M. ALPESTRIS (Alpine), S. Europe, is a dwarf plant with a short but dense mass of large flowers of soft azure-blue, with eyes of bright yellow, admirably suited to the front of the border. It is a perennial and may be produced by division of the root in September.
½-*ft.* *April–May.* *E.* ⅔-*ft. Sq.* *D*9. *Sd*7. *N.* 642/1.

M. AZORICA (From the Azores) grows to about one foot in height and has similar flowers of violet-purple. It is best grown in a light soil in a sunny site, where it waxes with vigour.
1-*ft.* *June–July.* *E.* ½-*ft. Sq.* *Sd*7. *N.* 43–39.

**NARCISSUS** (Amaryllidaceae), from G. narkissos, derived from narkao —to be stupefied; some of the bulbs having the power to induce stupefaction.

Narcissus is the botanical name of the genus comprising both the Narcissus and the Daffodil. "Daffodil" is more properly applied to flowers which have trumpets, and "Narcissus" to those which have cups or crowns. A brief summary of some of the divisions of Narcissi would appear to be necessary in order that the types may be clearly distinguished.

(*a*) The Trumpet Daffodils are those in which the trumpet is as long as, or longer than, the perianth segments. Examples of these are: King Alfred, W. P. Milner, and Empress.

(*b*) The incomparabilis section. Here the cup is more than one-third but less than the full length of the perianth segments. An example of this is:—Sir Watkin.

(*c*) The Barrii section. The cup or crown is less than one-third of the length of the perianth segments. An example of this is:—Red Emperor.

(*d*) The Leedsii section. The perianth is white and the cup or crown white, cream or lemon. Example:—White Lady.

(*e*) The triandrus hybrids. Examples:—N. triandrus albus, Johnstonii, Queen of Spain.

(*f*) The cyclaminius hybrids. Example:—February Gold.

(*g*) The Jonquilla hybrids. Example:—Buttercup.

(*h*) The Tazetta varieties are the bunch-flowered Narcissi which bear large bunches of small flowers, typified by the variety known as Paper White.

(*i*) The poeticus varieties are typified by the variety known as Pheasant's Eye.

(*j*) The double-flowered varieties, of which Van Sion and Oranges and Lemons are typical.

(*k*) The last section comprises the miniature-flowered Daffodils, of which Narcissus Bulbocodium, N. juncifolius and N. minimus may be said to be representative. (*See* "Alpines in Colour and Cultivation.")

Daffodils may be widely used for filling both flower beds and borders, either alone or in association with other spring-flowering plants. They are best grown in well-drained loamy soil, but as a rule fail to give of their best in light soils. The best artificial manure to use for them is a dressing of bone-meal at the rate of two ounces per square yard, before the bulbs are planted in September or October. The larger bulbs should be planted about six inches deep and the smaller ones about three inches deep. They may be left alone for many years until they become so crowded that they fail to flower freely, but as a rule it will be found that they must be lifted at the end of four years. On the whole, the best practice is to lift and replant them annually as soon as the leaves have died down. For the herbaceous border Narcissi should be planted in colonies of from 25 to 100, and spaced according to the size of the bulb, room being left for their development. They may, after flowering, be dug out and transferred to the reserve border, where they may be left to ripen. The selection of the better varieties now follows:—

TRUMPET VARIETIES:

- CORINTHIAN has a trumpet of deep yellow and perianth of primrose-yellow.
- EMPEROR has a golden-yellow trumpet and deep primrose perianth.
- EMPRESS has a golden-yellow trumpet and broad white perianth.
- GOLDEN SPUR has large flowers with golden-yellow trumpets.
- KING ALFRED is golden-yellow with a deeply frilled mouth.
- MADAME DE GRAFF has flowers of pure white.
- MRS. E. H. KRELAGE has creamy-white flowers of perfect form.
- PRINCEPS MAXIMUS has yellow flowers with sulphur-white perianth.
- VAN WAVERIN'S GIANT is a double flower with bright-yellow trumpet and primrose-yellow perianth.
- WHITE EMPEROR is pure white.

INCOMPARABILIS VARIETIES:

- CROESUS has a large primrose perianth and deep-red cup.
- HELIOS is of canary-yellow with deeper cup.
- IDEAL is of clear yellow.
- LUCIFER has large flowers with white perianth and orange-red cup.
- SIR WATKIN has a primrose perianth with a deep-golden cup.
- WILL SCARLET has a creamy-white perianth and the cup rimmed with fiery-orange.

BARRII VARIETIES:

- ARTUS has a yellow cup edged with red and a cream perianth.
- BARRII CONSPICUUS has a soft-yellow flower with the cup edged with orange-scarlet.
- BATH'S FLAME is of deep yellow, with cup edged with orange-red.
- EARLY SURPRISE has a perianth of ivory-white, with a lemon-yellow cup edged with scarlet.
- FIREBRAND has flowers of creamy-white with a fiery-red cup.
- RED BEACON has an ivory-white perianth with fluted brilliant orange-scarlet cup.

LEEDSII VARIETIES:

- EMPIRE has deep-cream flowers with overlapping petals.
- QUEEN OF THE NORTH is of pure white with a lemon-yellow perianth.
- SOUTHERN GEM has a large, pure white perianth and a pale citron crown.
- WHITE LADY has a crumpled cup of canary-yellow with a pure white perianth.

**NARCISSUS (continued)**

TRIANDRUS:

QUEEN OF SPAIN has flowers of soft canary-yellow with long sulphur trumpet.

SILVER CHIMES is a white-flowered variety.

TRIANDRUS ALBUS has globular drooping flowers of creamy-white, with a reflexed perianth.

VENETIA is pure white, slightly green in the centre.

CYCLAMINEUS:

BERYL is of clear yellow with bright-orange cup.

JONQUILS AND JONQUIL HYBRIDS:

AMBER has sweetly scented flowers of deep yellow.

BUTTERCUP has deep-yellow, sweetly scented flowers.

CAMPERNELLE REGULOSUS has pure-yellow flowers, borne two on a stem, and is very sweetly scented.

TAZETTA:

ADMIRATION is of deep yellow with a red eye.

ELVIRA has flowers of pure white with a yellow eye.

LAURENS KOSTER has a pure-white perianth with an orange cup.

POLYANTHUS:

PAPER WHITE has flowers of pure white, borne in large clusters.

GLORIOSA is a white-flowered variety with an orange cup.

SOLEIL D'OR is deep yellow with an orange cup.

POETICUS VARIETIES:

GLORY OF LISSE has large flowers of pure white margined with vivid red.

HORACE has flowers of silvery-white with the cup edged scarlet.

ORNATUS MAXIMUS has a white perianth with an orange crown edged scarlet.

QUEEN OF ENGLAND has white flowers with yellow eye and margined with crimson.

RED RIM is of pure white with deep scarlet rim.

RUPERT BROOKE is a late variety with flat petals.

DOUBLE VARIETIES:

ALBA PLENA has double, very sweetly scented, white flowers.

MARY COPELAND has a thick white perianth with orange-scarlet cup.

ORANGE PHOENIX has double rose-shaped flowers of white with reddish-orange segments.

TWINK has flowers of primrose-yellow with vivid orange segments.

VAN SION is of deep golden-yellow.

Malvastrum coccineum BCHEKLOP
Gentiana asclepiadea FGHM
Potentilla argyrophylla var. atrosanguinea OPMQ
Potentilla argyrophylla "Gibson's Scarlet" NPRTU

Poterium obtusum ABCDEFGHJL
Lythrum virgatum JKNORS

Lythrum Salicaria var. roseum LMPQTU

**NEPETA** (Labiatae), probably derived from Nepete, an Etrurian city.

Nepetas are extremely useful for obtaining large masses of colour for the front of the border.

N. Mussini (comm.), Caucasus, makes a rounded loose tuft of grey-green foliage comprising many wiry stems, each of which carries a long, loose spray of lavender flowers.
*1-ft. May–October. H.* 1½*-ft. Sq. Cg4. N.* 8.

N. nervosa (Having veins), Himalayas, has green, pointed foliage and carries tight heads of somewhat small, pale-blue flowers, unattractive individually but of striking appearance when borne in the large masses which are characteristic of the plant.
1¼*-ft. May–July. H.* 1*-ft. Sq. Sd9. N.*

N. ucranica (Ukrainian), S. Russia, is more often known as *N. grandiflora*, and bears large, loose sprays of bright-blue flowers somewhat similar to those of N. Mussini.
1½*-ft. May–June. H.* 1½*-ft. Sq. Cg7. N.* 40/1.

**NERINE** (Amaryllidaceae) is named after a Princess of Grecian mythology.

Nerine can only be grown out of doors in the Southern districts in sheltered spots. The best place for this purpose is in a sunny well-drained border against a south wall. The bulbs should be planted in August in light, sandy loam which is well drained. The best variety for the purpose is:—

N. Bowdeni (comm.), which has lily-like flowers of tender pink, borne in umbels at the top of a long, strong stem.
1½*-ft. August–September. B.* 1*-ft. Sq. D8. N. Pl.* 51.

**NOMOCHARIS** (Liliaceae), from G. nomos—an air, and charieis—beautiful; i.e. having a lovely air.

A group of hardy bulbs of recent introduction, generally hailing from China, which bear open, lily-like flowers without tubes upon slender stems, and require cultural conditions similar to those of the Lilies. As a rule they love a certain amount of root shade and are best planted with some kind of stem covering. The best situation, as a rule, appears to be in beds of the miniature Rhododendrons, which require identical conditions.

N. Mairei (comm.), Yunnan, has six-petalled, open, white flowers, with deckled-edged petals heavily spotted with dark orchid-purple, on long slender stems, but in cultivation is liable to be basically pink unless propagated only from scales.
2*-ft. June. B.* ½*-ft. Sq. Scales* 2. *N.*

N. PARDANTHINA (Spotted), Yunnan, has similarly shaped flowers, a little less overlapping in the petals, which are pale rose, or pale purple lightly speckled with crimson-maroon towards the centre.

*2-ft. June. B.* $\frac{1}{2}$*-ft. Sq. Scales* 2. *N.*

N. PARDANTHINA VAR. FARRERI (comm.), Yunnan, has narrower foliage, is less frilled and paler in colour, but bears its flowers in somewhat larger sprays. *2-ft. June. B.* $\frac{1}{2}$*-ft. Sq. Scales* 2. *N.*

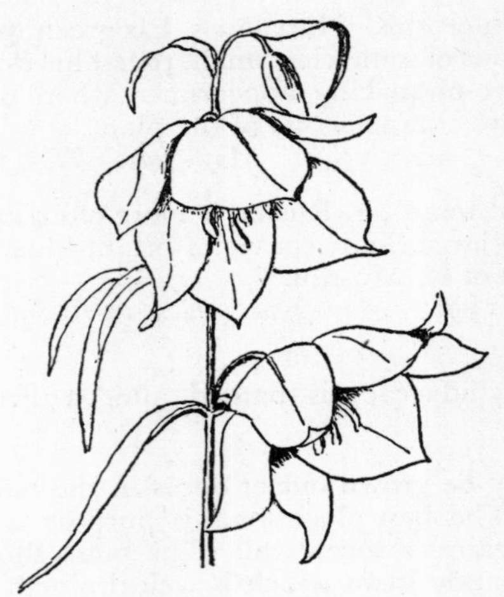

NOMOCHARIS PARDANTHINA

**OENOTHERA** (Onagraceae), from G. oinos—wine, and thera—taste; the root of Oenothera biennis being said to encourage a taste for wine.

These plants are lovers of the sun and are of moderately easy cultivation, asking generally only for a place in the sun.

O. FRUTICOSA (Shrubby), N. America, is also known as *O. serotina* and has reddish stems, shiny handsome leaves, and bears large, bright-yellow, open flowers. The variety YOUNGEI has larger leaves and is very free-flowering, and WILLIAM CUTHBERTSON has buds of bright red. *2-ft. June–August. H. 2-ft. Sq. D*3. *N.*

O. FRYVERKII (comm.), N. America, is similar but bears larger clusters of somewhat smaller flowers.

*2-ft. June–August. H. 2-ft. Sq. D*3. *N. Pl.* 36.

O. GLAUCA (Sea-green), E. N. America, is also very like O. fruticosa but has shiny and somewhat grey-green foliage. Variety FRASERI differs only botanically and may to all intents and purposes be regarded as identical.

*2-ft. June–September. H. 2-ft. Sq. D3. N.*

O. SPECIOSA (Showy), Montana, spreads by means of running underground roots, has grey-green serrated leaves, and bears at the tops of its long stems large clear-white flowers blending into cream, with attractive pale-green centres.

*1½-ft. July–September. H. 1-ft. Sq. Sd2. N. Pl.* 75.

OENOTHERA FRUTICOSA

O. SPECIOSA ROSEA (Showy; rose), garden origin, is most probably a seedling of the above, but is more dwarf and has flowers which open to pale pink but fade with age to deep rose.

*1-ft. July–September. H. 2-ft. Sq. D4. N.* 637/3.

**OMPHALODES** (Boraginaceae) is derived from G. omphalos—navel, and eidos—appearance, referring to the shape of the seed.

Two dwarf-growing representatives are eminently suited to shady positions in the front of the border and are therefore included. They are easy to cultivate in any leafy garden soil.

O. CAPPADOCICA (From Cappadocia), Asia Minor, has dark-green unpolished leaves and bears tight sprays of large, deep forget-me-not-blue flowers. *1-ft. May–June. H. 1½-ft. Sq. D3. N.* 41/1.

O. VERNA (Spring-flowering), S. Europe, is commonly called Blue-eyed Mary, and runs and roots, producing rather brighter blue flowers than those of O. cappadocica, with clear-white eyes. It is best grown in a shady place and given plenty of room in which to run.

*¾-ft. March–May. H. 1-ft. Sq. D9. N.*

**ORIGANUM** (Labiatae), from G. oros—mountain, and ganos—beauty.

All the plants making up this genus (which is also known as AMARACUS, and the Marjoram) are sweetly aromatic and bear hanging, hop-like heads of flowers subtended by papery bracts. They prefer, need and appreciate hot, dry, sunny spots, if any there be, and repay these kind attentions with a display of late summer colour. The only species completely suitable to the herbaceous border is O. pulchrum.

O. PULCHRUM (Beautiful), Greece, is a dainty aromatic plant with green, netted leaves and deep-pink flowers enshrouded with purple bracts, giving generously its graceful sprays in late summer.
*¾-ft. August–September. E. ¾-ft. Sq. Cg4. N.* 003/1.

**OXALIS** (Geraniaceae), from G. oxos—sour wine; from the sour taste of the leaves.

A group of herbaceous and bulbous-rooted plants numbering among them O. corniculata purpurea, sometimes called tropaeoloides, and the even smaller but equally devastating O. repens, which, though not required in one's own garden, should never be given to friends, since, like all good actions of this kind, they are likely to reward the donor after many days. O. corniculata throws its seeds with the vicious precision of a machine-gun, and anchors itself to the ground with a tenacity that defies the nimblest and strongest of fingers; its name is mentioned merely as a warning. Of the genus Oxalis only a few species at present in cultivation are fitted for the herbaceous border.

O. FLORIBUNDA (Abundantly flowered), South America, is very often found in the cottage garden, but produces its heads of clear rose-pink flowers for such a long period that it is quite at home at the front of the herbaceous border.
*1-ft. May–September. B. 1-ft. Sq. D3. N.*

O. VALDIVIENSIS (From Valdivia), Chile, is another bulbous-rooted Oxalis with clover-like leaves, and is just as useful in its way as O. floribunda, producing its large heads in abundance and requiring a sheltered spot in light leafy soil.
*1-ft. August–September. B. 1-ft. Sq. D10. N.*

**PAEONIA** (Ranunculaceae), named after a physician of ancient Greece, Paeon, who used the plant medicinally.

Very few of the species of Paeonies are widely grown, and a large number of hybrids with either single or double flowers have been produced by the horticulturist, with constant additions from year to year. Paeonies thrive in a sunny or partially shaded site in well-dug, deep and rich soil. They should not be planted in a site having an eastern aspect, or in any position where the soil is likely to dry out in summer.

Paeonies are vigorous, leafy plants which take up a considerable amount of room, and as they have finished flowering by the end of June they add little to the beauty of the border after that date. They should therefore be placed with considerable care so that large barren, colourless patches are not too obtrusive. As a rule, they require about two and a half feet square in which to develop; they are best planted from October to March, to such a depth that the crowns are covered by two to three inches of soil.

P. ALBIFLORA (White-flowered), Japan, has long tuberous roots, leaves divided into six parts usually veined with red, and single white or pink flowers up to six inches in diameter. It is probably one of the parents of many of the garden forms.
*2½-ft. May–June. H. 2-ft. Sq. D10. Sd10. N.*

P. CORALLINA (Colour of coral), S. Europe, is red-purple, and has large seed-pods containing black and coral-red seeds which are particularly attractive when open in the summer and early autumn.
*2-ft. May–June. H. 2-ft. Sq. Sd10. N.*

P. LOBATA (Lobed), Spain, has salmon-scarlet single flowers and is the only Paeony of this colour.
*2½-ft. May–June. H. 2½-ft. Sq. Sd10. N.*

P. OBOVATA (Egg-shaped), Japan, has large, white or pink, single flowers of great beauty, centred with golden stamens and followed by the typical black and red seeds of the species.
*1½-ft. May–June. H. 1½-ft. Sq. Sd10. N.*

P. OFFICINALIS (Of the shop), Europe, is the old double-flowered Paeonia with large-petalled flowers of dark crimson. Its variety ALBO-PLENA has double white flowers; VAR. ROSEO-PLENA has carmine-rose flowers, and RUBRO-PLENA double crimson flowers.
*2-ft. May–June. H. 1½-ft. Sq. Sd10. N.*

P. SINENSIS OR CHINENSIS (Chinese), is probably derived from P. albiflora and has large, double, crimson flowers. It gave rise to many of the garden types, of which the following are good examples:—

SINGLE-FLOWERED VARIETIES:

AMORETTA is dwarf and produces its single pink flowers with freedom.

CHERRY RIPE is tall-growing and has flowers of deep cherry-rose.

COUNTY GIRL has flowers of apple-blossom-pink.

EVA has flowers of deep salmon-pink with narrow golden foliage.

GERTRUDE has large pink flowers with golden centres.

IVANHOE has striking cherry-red flowers.

JEWEL is an attractive lavender-pink.

LETITIA is dwarf, early, and has flowers of soft light rose.

NERO has attractive large flowers of bright pink.

NYMPH has large flesh-pink flowers.

PRIDE OF SOMERSET is rich ruby-red.

PURE LOVE is white like a Giant Water-lily.

THE MOOR is maroon-crimson.

DOUBLE-FLOWERED VARIETIES:

ALBERT CROUSSE has rounded flowers of shell-pink, deepening in colour in the centre.

AUGUSTE DESSERT is rose-red, each petal being edged with silver.

BARONESS SCHROEDER has huge white flowers with fleshy-pink shadings.

BRITISH BEAUTY has sweetly scented flowers of rose-pink with silvered edges.

DELIA is white with a creamy-yellow centre.

DUCHESSE DE NEMOURS has creamy-white, sweetly scented flowers.

EDULIS SUPERBA flowers early, is deep pink and very fragrant.

EMPEROR OF RUSSIA is deep crimson-purple.

FÉLIX CROUSSE has deep rose-red flowers.

FESTIVA MAXIMA has large flowers of white with central crimson markings.

FRANCES WILLARD is blush-white with carmine touches, changing to pure white with age.

KARL ROSENFELD is of vigorous growth, with large red flowers.

KELWAY'S GLORIOUS has fragrant white flowers.

KELWAY'S QUEEN has large pinkish-mauve flowers, flecked in the centre with crimson.

LADY ALEXANDRA DUFF has immense flowers of pale blush-pink, with yellow stamens.

LADY BERESFORD has large flowers of lavender-pink and cream.

LE CYGNE produces very large, creamy-white flowers with a touch of green in the centre.

LONGFELLOW has bright-crimson flowers.

LOUIS VAN HOUTTE has large violet-crimson flowers.

MARGUERITE GERARD is pale pink, with a centre of sulphur-yellow.

MARIE CROUSSE has salmon-pink flowers, beautifully formed.

MARTHA BULLOCH has huge blossoms of silvery shell-pink, deepening to rose-pink in the centre.

MARY BEST has centre petals of salmon-pink, with deeper guard petals.

MARY BRAND has flowers of a distinctive red.

MONSIEUR JULES ELIE has silvery-pink flowers.

Monsieur Martin Cahuzac has medium-sized, dark purple-garnet flowers with black reflexes.

Norfolk has moderate-size flowers of lavender edged with silver.

Philippe Rivoire has rich-crimson flowers, beautifully formed.

Philomele has bright-pink guard petals, with paler-pink centre with orange filaments.

Portia has very large, beautiful, clear-white flowers.

President Roosevelt is a brilliant variety with blooms in early mid-season.

Primevère has guard petals of deep creamy-yellow, with centre petals of sulphur-yellow.

Reine des Roses is soft rose in colour and of fine shape.

Reine Hortense is hydrangea-pink with crimson markings on guard and centre petals.

Richard Carvel has red flowers.

Sainfoin has large flowers of unshaded rose.

Sarah Bernhardt has perfectly formed flowers of apple-blossom pink.

Solange has flowers of delicate waxy-white, deepening centrally to orange and golden-brown.

Therese produces violet-rose flowers changing to lilac-white.

Walter Faxon has delicate rose-coloured flowers.

*2-ft.–3-ft. June–July. H. 2½-ft. Sq. D3. N. Pl.* 58.

**PAPAVER** (Papaveraceae), probably from G. papa—thick milk, with reference to the thick juice of the plant which exudes when the stem is cut.

The Poppy most useful for the border, and the only one for this purpose which is truly perennial, is P. orientale, which is available in a huge number of attractive shades of colour.

P. orientale (Eastern), E. Europe, has large, deeply-cut, hairy, green leaves and bears huge flowers of brilliant colours in May and June. It hates a root disturbance, and as a rule establishes but slowly, and should therefore remain in the border without interference from year to year. It should not be planted in large groups in the mixed herbaceous border, but kept out of prominence, since its flowering period is short and it has little ornamental value after that. It is propagated by means of root cuttings, where it is desired to keep the progeny true to colour and form. The roots are lifted as soon as the foliage has died down, and cut into pieces two to three inches in length, placed lying horizontally in a box of sandy soil, covered with an inch or so of the same soil, and kept in this manner in a cold frame during the winter, with an occasional watering so that the soil does not become dust-dry; the roots will be found to have become plants by the spring. Some of the best varieties are:—

**PAPAVER (continued)**

Australia—ox-blood or spectrum-red
Barr's White—white
Beauty of Livermere—crimson
Cavalier—scarlet-red
Crimson Pompon—blood-red
Enchantress—rose-pink
Gold of Ophir—golden-orange
Helen Elizabeth—pink
Henri Cayeux Improved—old-rose
Indian Chief—mahogany
Jeanne Mawson—geranium-pink
Joyce—red
Lord Lambourne—orange-scarlet
May Queen—red-salmon
May Sadler—salmon-pink
Mrs. Harkness—salmon-rose
Mrs. Perry—orange-apricot
Mrs. Stobart—salmon-pink
Nancy—rose-red
Princess Ena—orange-salmon
Purity—pink
Salmon Glow—salmon-orange
Sass Pink—pink
Snowflame—white and flame-orange
Toreador—carmine-red
Watermelon—deep cerise
Wunderkind—cerise
Wurtembergia—rose-red

*3-ft. June–July. H. 2½-ft. Sq. Cr11. N. Pl.* 59.

P. ORIENTALE PETER PAN has cerise-scarlet flowers but is very dwarf, seldom exceeding one foot in height.

*1-ft. June–July. H. 2-ft. Sq. Cr11. N.*

**PATRINIA** (Valerianaceae) is named after M. Patrin, a Russian traveller.

P. PALMATA (Shaped like a hand), Japan, has green finely-cut foliage and bears flat heads of golden-yellow flowers in rather loose sprays for a long period. It is a good plant in light soils in a sunny position at the front of the border.

*1-ft. July–September. H. 1-ft. Sq. D4. N.*

**PENTSTEMON** or PENSTEMON (Scrophulariaceae), from G. pente—five, and stemon—stamen; that is, having five stamens.

There is a great deal of confusion with regard to the names of the species, and the following descriptions take into account the latest amendments brought about by the most recent American information. Pentstemons may be either herbaceous perennials or shrubs; the division is not particularly clearly marked. The hybrids generally found in the herbaceous border are given the name of P. gloxinoides and are descended from P. Hartwegii and P. Cobaea. In most mild districts they will winter successfully, and they may be kept going in more severe parts by cuttings placed in boxes of sandy soil, in a cold frame, in September. All Pentstemons need full sun and may be propagated from cuttings, or from seeds sown in February.

P. BARBATUS (Bearded), Mexico, sometimes known as *Chelone barbata*, grows to three feet in height and bears sprays of hanging scarlet two-lobed flowers on long, wiry, branching stems.

*3-ft. June–September. H. 1½-ft. Sq. Sd2. N. Pl.* 63.

Rudbeckia Golden Glow ABCDFGHKL
Centaurea macrocephala EJLMPQ
Centaurea ruthenica JKNO

Eryngium planum ABCDFGHJKL
Salvia azurea NORS

Salvia farinacea PQTU

P. CAMPANULATUS ROSEUS (Flowers resembling bells), Mexico, has slender, toothed foliage of paler green, and grows upright, and produces long sprays of pale lilac-pink flowers with white throats.
1½-*ft.* *June–August.* *H.* 1-*ft. Sq.* *Cg*8. *N.* *Pl.* 11.

P. EATONI (comm.), Utah, has rather larger and wider green leaves than most of the species, and bears long spires of large, bright-red, two-lipped flowers. 1½-*ft.* *June–July.* *H.* 1-*ft. Sq.* *Sd*3. *N.*

P. GLOXINOIDES (Resembling Gloxinia), garden origin, is the garden type already mentioned. Varieties of these are:—

ALICE HINDLEY, with pale-blue flowers shaded with rose.
DAY DREAM, with pink flowers with a white throat.
KING GEORGE V, with bright-crimson flowers.
MAJESTIC, with purple-violet flowers.
NEWBURY GEM has brilliant-scarlet flowers.
TWEED has dark-rose flowers.
WHITE BEDDER has flowers of clear white.

2-*ft.* *July–September.* *E.* 1¼-*ft. Sq.* *Cg*9. *N.*

P. GLABER (Smooth), Wyoming, has close tufts of large, oval, evergreen leaves and bears sprays of bright-blue flowers. P. GLABER ROSEUS is similar but has flowers of delicate pink and is every bit as charming, and just as accommodating.
1½-*ft.* *June–July.* *E.* 1-*ft. Sq.* *D*3. *N.*

P. HIRSUTUS (Hairy), Wisconsin, is also known as *P. pubescens* and has dark-green, rather hairy foliage and an exceedingly large number of rather short sprays of lavender-blue flowers, deepening in places to purple. 1½-*ft.* *June–July.* *E.* 1½-*ft. Sq.* *D*3. *N.*

P. ISOPHYLLUS (With equal number of leaves), Mexico, has shiny green, lanceolate leaves and bears long sprays of large scarlet flowers with hairy white throats.
2-*ft.* *June–August.* *H.* 1½-*ft. Sq.* *Cg*4. *N.* 20/1.

P. RICHARDSONII (comm.), British Columbia, has long, notched, spear-shaped, green leaves and long, slender sprays of thin wine-red flowers, the sterile stamens being bearded.
1½-*ft.* *June–August.* *H.* 1-*ft. Sq.* *Cg*4. *N.*

P. SPECIOSUS (Showy), California, has the wide, oval green leaves of P. glaber, combined with attractive tubular flowers of purple-blue.
1½-*ft.* *June–August.* *H.* 1½-*ft. Sq.* *D*3. *N.*

**PEROWSKIA** (Labiatae) is commemorative of M. Perowsky, a Russian botanist.

P. ATRIPLICIFOLIA (Atriplex-leaved) is more correctly a shrub, but is eminently suited for growth at the back of the herbaceous border. The grey-green foliage seems heavily felted, and is strongly aromatic, the long, open sprays of blue to lavender-blue flowers being reminiscent of those of a giant Catmint. It will grow well in any good garden soil in a sunny place.

*5-ft. August–September. D. 3-ft. Sq. Ch9. N.*

**PETASITES** (Compositae), from G. petasos—a wide hat or sunshade: a reference to the large leaf.

Is a relative of the Coltsfoot (Tussilago Farfara), and at times as invasive and difficult to eradicate. It should have no place other than a wild spot, though its beauty and fragrance are undeniable.

P. FRAGRANS (Sweetly scented), Mediterranean region, is the Winter Heliotrope, or Sweet Coltsfoot, and has rounded leaves shaped like a colt's foot, green above and silky-white below, bearing in January and February delightful scented, pale- and deep-lilac, daisy-like flowers. Every piece of root will grow, and it can become such a pest that neither work nor prayer will eradicate it. It will thus be found to be occasionally advertised for sale!

*1-ft. January–February. H. 6-ft. Sq. Cr1–12. ANC.*

**PHLOMIS** (Labiatae), from G. phlomes—the Verbascum, a woolly plant which these are supposed to resemble.

The bulk of the species are suitable for the back of the border and are easily grown in any soil.

P. CASHMERIANA (Cashmir), Himalayas, has very wide, woolly foliage and bears pale-purple flowers in whorls.

*3-ft. July–September. H. 3-ft. Sq. D3. N.*

P. SAMIA (old name), Greece, has hairy, woolly leaves, very wrinkled, and small whorls of purple flowers with very tiny bracts.

*3-ft. August–September. H. 3-ft. Sq. D3. N.*

P. VISCOSA (Sticky), Asia Minor, also known as *P. Russelliana*, has hairy leaves, densely white beneath, sticky above, and bears yellow nettle-like flowers in whorled clusters.

*3-ft. June–August. H. 3-ft. Sq. Cg4. N.*

**PHLOX** (Polemoniaceae), from G. phlego—to burn, or G. phlox—flame; probably in relation to the brilliant colouring of the flowers.

The herbaceous perennial Phloxes, which provide such a feast of colour in August and September, are descended from Phlox decussata, or, more correctly, P. paniculata, the native American Phlox. The name generally given to these hybrids is P. decussata, and so they are dealt with under that name. Originally those Phloxes which were descended from P. suffruticosa were kept separately, but they have now been grouped together, as the descendants have become almost indistinguishable.

The Phlox requires good fertile soil and is never really a success in soil which is light or which dries out during the summer. It is surface-rooting and therefore must be kept moist, and where the soil is light it should be given a somewhat shady site. It is subject to a large number of pests, including Phlox Eelworm, and plants which exhibit signs of twisted, brittle leaves or swollen new growth, or become stunted or poor, should be suspected at once, and lifted and burnt. The ground in which they were grown should be kept clear of similar plants for at least three years.

Phloxes are easily propagated from cuttings or by divisions of the old root. Cuttings are generally taken of the current year's growth as early in the year as possible, non-flowering shoots being chosen where they are available.

P. DECUSSATA (Cross-leaved), garden origin, comprises the hybrids mentioned above, for which cultural conditions have been fully noted. The following named varieties are among the best of their kind:—

A. E. AMOS has soft-scarlet flowers in large, outstanding trusses *3-ft.*

AFRICA has well-shaped flower-heads of brilliant carmine-red with blood-red centre. *3-ft.*

ANTONIN MERCIER is free-flowering and of medium height, with lilac-blue flowers. *3-ft.*

APOLLO has fine branching spikes of purple flowers. *3-ft.*

ATLANTA has immense flowers of white, shaded pale blue. *2½-ft.–3-ft.*

AURORE sets off its large salmon-scarlet flowers with a bright purple eye. *3-ft.*

AVIATOR bears very large heads of Parma-violet, lightening in the centre. *3-ft.*

BARON VON DEDEM is bright crimson-scarlet. *2-ft.*

B. COMTE produces large heads of bright-purple flowers, and is a tall-growing variety. *4-ft.*

BLUE BOY is the nearest to a Blue Phlox yet produced; is of medium height and a good grower. *3-ft.*

BORDER BEACON is a fine variety with salmon-scarlet flowers. *3-ft.*

CAROLINE VANDENBERG has attractive flowers of deep lavender-blue. *3-ft.* 36/1. *Pl.* 61.

CHARLES CURTIS has been described by the raiser as being sunset-red, and is probably one of the finest Phloxes in existence. *2½-ft.–3-ft.*

CHEERFULNESS is of vigorous growth, and has flowers of salmon-orange. 3-*ft.*

COQUELIQUOT has large orange-scarlet flowers. 3-*ft.*

COUNT ZEPPELIN (*see* Graf Zeppelin).

DAILY SKETCH is rose-pink with a deeper eye, and has the largest flowers of all. 3-*ft.* 527/2 *to* 527. *Pl.* 61.

D. M. MCKINNON has salmon-pink flowers paling towards the centre. 3-*ft.*

EMINENCE is taller and has flowers of purple with a distinct crimson eye. 4-*ft.*

ETHEL PRITCHARD is Parma-violet with deeper eye. 3-*ft.* 36/2. *Pl.* 61.

ETNA has the most brilliant orange-scarlet flowers. 3½-*ft.*

EUROPA has snow-white flowers, each with a central carmine zone. 3-*ft.*–3½-*ft.*

EVANGELINE is attractive with its unshaded salmon-pink flowers. 3-*ft.*

EXCELSA has white-centred flowers of soft pink. 2½-*ft.*

FIRETAIL is another free-flowering variety with blooms of carmine-red centred with blood-red. 3-*ft.*

G. A. STROHLEIN has brilliant orange-scarlet flowers with carmine eye. 3½-*ft.*

GENERAL VON HEUTZ is salmon-scarlet with a white eye. 3½-*ft.*

GEORGE STIPP is a new variety, producing salmon-coloured flowers, paling towards the centre. 3-*ft.*

GRAF ZEPPELIN is a free-flowering type which produces blooms of pure white with a red centre. 3-*ft.* *Eye* 29. *Pl.* 62.

JESSIE FORBES has flowers of pale rose with a bright-carmine eye. 3½-*ft.*

JULES SANDEAU is somewhat dwarf in habit, but has large heads of bright-pink flowers, produced with great freedom and for a longer period than with most Phloxes. 2-*ft.*

KARL FOERSTER has large orange-red flowers. 3-*ft.*

LE MAHDI is taller and bears large clustered flowers of violet-blue. 3½-*ft.* 34. *Pl.* 62.

LEO SCHLAGETER is carmine-scarlet deepening towards the centre. 3-*ft.* 22–822/1. *Pl.* 60.

LORD BEARSTED has violet-purple flowers with neat carmine centre. 3½-*ft.*

MARY LOUISE is the whitest of all Phloxes, with the largest flowers of all. 2-*ft.*

MIA RUYS is the best and largest-flowered dwarf white. 2-*ft.* *Pl.* 1.

MORGENROOD has rose flowers deepening towards the centre. 2½-*ft.*

Mrs. Askew has rose-pink flowers deepening to carmine at the centre. 23/1. *Pl.* 60.

Mrs. Jenkins is a fast-growing, late-flowering variety with pure-white blossoms. 3-*ft.*

Newbird has flowers of crimson. 3-*ft.* 727. *Pl.* 62.

Olympia is probably the most vigorous variety of all, growing to three to five feet in height, with flowers of clear white, shading to bright red in the centre. 3-*ft.*–5-*ft.*

Rheinlander has large flower-heads of salmon-pink. 3-*ft.*

Rosalie Ingram adds to its fine form large colourful salmon-pink flowers. 3½-*ft.*

Saladin has orange-scarlet flowers with crimson eyes. 3-*ft.*

Salmon Beauty produces salmon-pink flowers with a white eye. 3-*ft.*

Sam Pope has salmon-pink flowers with a crimson-scarlet eye. 20/1, *eye* 822/1. *Pl.* 60.

Sweetheart has white-centred rose-coloured flowers. 2½-*ft.*

Widar has violet flowers with a clear-white eye, and is of medium height. 3-*ft.*

William Ramsay has large trusses of deep-violet flowers. 4-*ft.*

P. divaricata (Spreading), Quebec, also known as *P. canadensis*, has upright stems with oval green leaves and bears large heads of pale violet-blue flowers. It is much loved by slugs, but fortunately grows well in any good garden soil.

1-*ft.* *May–June.* *H.* 1-*ft. Sq.* *Cg*5. *N.* 642/3.

P. divaricata Laphamii (comm.), N. America, has thinner and longer leaves, and flowers of slightly deeper colour.

1½-*ft.* *May–June.* *H.* 1-*ft. Sq.* *Cg*5. *N.* 642/2.

P. ovata (Egg-shaped), Carolina, is also known as *P. Carolina*, and has oval leaves and large purplish-pink flowers, in somewhat smaller clusters than those of the garden Phloxes, in the late summer.

1½-*ft.* *August–September.* *H.* 1-*ft. Sq.* *D*3. *N.*

P. pilosa (Hairy), Ontario, has very thin, wiry leaves, and pale-purple flowers in small clusters. It does best in light, dry soil.

1½-*ft.* *June–July.* *H.* 1-*ft. Sq.* *Cg*4. *N.*

**PHORMIUM** (Liliaceae), from G. phormos—basket, the leaves having been used for basket-making.

P. tenax (Tough), New Zealand, is a tall, stately plant, with tough, massive, sword-like leaves, hardy only in sheltered positions in most soils, suitable for the pond-side. Its leathery, green leaves are edged with red and split at the top, and the pale-red flowers are produced in long spikes. 8-*ft.* *August–October.* *E.* 6-*ft. Sq.* *D*3. *N.*

**PHYSALIS** (Solanaceae), from G. physa—bladder; from the inflated calyx of most of the species.

These are the Chinese Lantern plants so often used for winter decoration.

P. Alkekengi (comm.), Japan, is probably also *P. Bunyardi* and *P. Francheti*, and forms a diffuse plant with long underground stems producing small whitish flowers, followed by large Chinese-Lantern-like bladders of orange and blood-red, up to two inches or so in length.

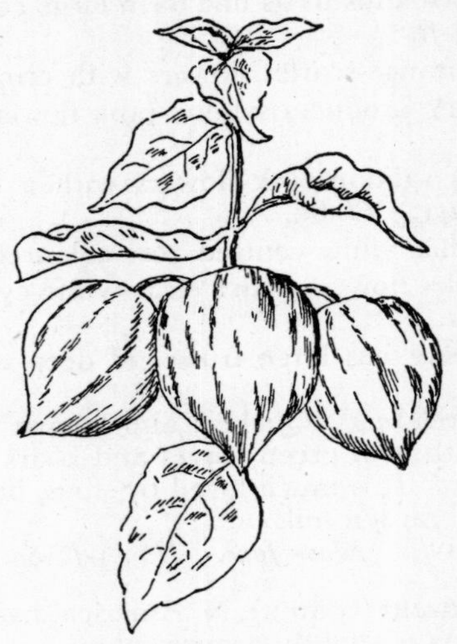

PHYSALIS ALKEKENGI

It is perfectly hardy in a well-drained sunny soil which is not too heavy. It can be propagated by the division of roots in March. Though the same species, P. Alkekengi usually listed by nurserymen has smaller and less inflated calyces.

*2½-ft. September–October. H. 3-ft. Sq. D3. N.*

**PHYSOSTEGIA** (Labiatae), from G. physa—bladder, and stege—a covering: a reference to the build of the calyx.

P. virginiana is an extremely useful plant in the garden, since it produces some very large masses of colour late in the year. It is of easy cultivation in any soil and is propagated by division, which will encourage it to flourish anew.

P. virginiana (Virginian), Virginia, has lance-shaped leaves, with strong, square spikes of rose-purple to rose-pink flowers in branching spires up to a foot in length. The flowers are produced in spires which seem to be four-sided, and the individual flowers are so fixed to the stems that they may be placed in any position; for this reason it has been called the "Obedient Plant." P. VIRGINIANA ALBA has white flowers; P. VIRGINIANA VIVID has bright-pink flowers, and both are better plants than the original.

*3-ft. September–November. H. 2-ft. Sq. D3. N. Pl.* 51 *&* 64.

**PHYTEUMA** (Campanulaceae), from G. phyton—plant.

Though generally grown in the rock garden, one species at least is more at home in the herbaceous border, thriving in any good garden soil, and is easily propagated from the seed which it produces with some freedom.

P. LOBELIOIDES (Resembling Lobelia), Asia Minor, has narrow, wavy-edged, grass-like leaves and blue, open, thin-petalled, starry flowers borne in long graceful spires.

*2-ft. June–July. H. 1-ft. Sq. Sd2. N.*

**PHYTOLACCA** (Phytolaccaceae), from G. phyton—plant, and lacca—varnish, from the brilliant colouring of the juice of the fruit.

P. AMERICANA (American), Maine to Mexico, is also known as *P. decandra* and the Pokeberry, and is grown for the ornamental value of the berries which follow the white, green or pink flowers which are borne in tight terminal clusters. It is easy to grow in any good garden soil in a somewhat sheltered site.

*5-ft. May–October. 5-ft. Sq. H. Sd2. N.*

**PLATYCODON** (Campanulaceae), from G. platys—broad, and kodon—bell: the flower being of wide bell shape.

This is the Balloon-flower or Chinese Bell-flower, with a root like a parsnip, which can be dug up, dried and replanted without seeming hindrance to the growth of the plant. It flourishes well in a sunny position in any light sandy soil.

P. GRANDIFLORUM (Large-flowered), China, throws up stems of about two feet in height, bearing large balloon-like buds opening to large powder-blue flowers with deeper veins, in substantial sprays.

*2-ft. August–September. H. 1-ft. Sq. Sd2. N.* 37. *Pl.* 65.

P. GRANDIFLORUM ALBUM (Large-flowered; white), garden origin, is similar in every way except that it has white flowers, generally with bright-blue veining.

*2-ft. August–September. H. 1-ft. Sq. Sd2. N. Pl.* 65.

P. GRANDIFLORUM SEMI-PLENUM has similar flowers which are partly double. *2-ft. August–September. H. 1-ft. Sq. Sd2. N.*

**POLEMONIUM** (Polemoniaceae), from G. polemos—war; the discovery of this plant was said by Pliny to have led to war.

A group of hardy perennial plants with attractive pinnate foliage, thriving in good garden loam and easily produced by division or from the seed which is freely given.

P. CAERULEUM (Sky-blue), Europe, is the Jacob's Ladder, with tufts of pinnate leaves divided into 11–21 segments, with sprays of bright-blue flowers setting off its yellow stamens. P. CAERULEUM ALBUM is similar with white flowers; P. CAERULEUM VAR. HIMALAYANUM has much larger blue flowers.
2-*ft.* *June–August.* *H.* 1½-*ft. Sq.* *D*3. *Sd*2. *N.*

P. CARNEUM (Flesh-coloured), California, has similar dissected leaves made up of from 5–17 leaflets of pale sea-green. The large open flowers are at first of pale salmon-pink and fade to purple.
1-*ft.* *May–June.* *H.* 1-*ft. Sq.* *D*9. *Sd*2. *N.*

P. FLAVUM (Pure yellow), New Mexico, has similar attractive foliage with orange flowers about an inch or so in diameter, the interior being of pale yellow. 2-*ft.* *June–August.* *H.* 1-*ft. Sq.* *D*3. *Sd*2. *N.*

P. HUMILE (Lowly), N. America, is sometimes known as *P. Richardsonii* and closely resembles P. caeruleum, but is more condensed and has sky-blue flowers. 1-*ft.* *June–August.* *H.* 1-*ft. Sq.* *D*3. *Sd*2. *N.*

**POLYGONATUM** (Liliaceae), from G. polys—many, and gony—joint; so called because of the knotted joints of the root.

This is the Solomon's Seal, thriving in shady positions in good soil, where the creeping roots will run and throw up their graceful flowering stems.

P. MULTIFLORUM (Many-flowered), Europe, grows to two and a half feet in height and produces small, hanging, lily-of-the-valley-like flowers of cream and green. Extracts from the roots are much used for curing swellings and bruises due to hard knocks.
2-*ft.* *May–June.* *H.* 1-*ft. Sq.* *D*3. *ANC.*

**POLYGONUM** (Polygonaceae), from G. polys—many, and gony—joint, referring to the many joints of the stems of the species.

A group of plants with knotted stems, of easy cultivation in average soil and propagated easily from cuttings or divisions.

P. AFFINE (Related to), Himalayas, the *P. Brunonis* of catalogues, forms tufts of wide-pointed oval leaves and bears countless spikes of closely packed clear-pink flowers. The foliage in winter turns brownish-yellow and is equally attractive.
1-*ft.* *August–October.* *H.* 1½-*ft. Sq.* *D*3. *ANC.*

Monarda didyma CDFGHLM
Salvia fulva EFJK
Monarda didyma "Cambridge Scarlet" NOPQRSTU

Dahlia Merckii BCDGHJKNO
Scabiosa macedonica FMPQTU
Malva moschata LPRS

P. AMPLEXICAULE (Stem-clasping), Himalayas, has long, green, lanceolate leaves on long trailing stems and bears tightly packed spires of rose-red flowers. P. AMPLEXICAULE VAR. ATROSANGUINEUM has still darker red flowers (721/3).

*3-ft. August–October. H. 3-ft. Sq. D3. ANC. Pl.* 73.

P. BISTORTA (Twice turned—twisted root), Europe, grows to some two feet in height and bears above its attractive netted foliage dense spikes of appealing pink flowers like those of the Lily of the Valley.

*2½-ft. May–August. H. 2-ft. Sq. N. Pl.* 6.

P. CAPITATUM (With heads of composite flowers), Himalayas, is a trailing plant with elliptical, pointed foliage touched with red, and bears rounded heads of deep-pink flowers. Once this has flowered it will reproduce itself freely from seed, but will never prove a pest.

*1-ft. June–August. H. 1½-ft. Sq. Sd3. N.*

**POTENTILLA** (Rosaceae), from L. potens—powerful; from its attributed medicinal characteristics.

The hardy herbaceous Potentillas are of easy growth, thriving in ordinary well-dug garden soil, preferably in a fully sunny exposure. They reproduce freely from seed, though seldom keeping their true colours. The double-flowered varieties may be reproduced from division. The shrubby Potentillas are outside the scope of this book.

P. ARGENTEA VAR. CALABRA (Silvery-leaved), from Calabria, Italy, has five-lobed silvery-grey leaves and bears upon spires sulphur-yellow flowers most attractively disposed.

*1-ft. May–June. H. 1½-ft. Sq. Sd3. N.*

P. ARGYROPHYLLA (Silvery-leaved), Himalayas, has leaves divided into three parts, grey-green above and silvery below, and flowers of bright yellow borne in loose clusters. It is an extremely variable form, sometimes being found with red-eyed yellow flowers, and is responsible in part for many of the garden forms, of which—

ATROSANGUINEA has single flowers of deep crimson. 819. *Pl.* 67.

BRUNETTE has double, ochre-yellow flowers.

GIBSON'S SCARLET has attractive crimson-scarlet flowers. *Pl.* 67.

GLOIRE DE NANCY has deep-yellow double flowers.

HAMLET has dark-crimson double flowers.

VICTOR LEMOINE has vermilion flowers touched with yellow.

*2-ft. June–August. H. 1½-ft. Sq. Sd2. D3. N.*

P. NEPALENSIS (From Nepal), also known as *P. formosa*, has green, hairy leaves divided into five parts, and forking spires of red flowers one inch across. P. NEPALENSIS MISS WILLMOTT (WILLMOTTIAE) is particularly attractive with red-eyed deep-pink flowers, and P. NEPALENSIS ROXANA has flowers of orange-rose lined with red.

$1\frac{1}{2}$-*ft.* *June–September.* *H.* $1\frac{1}{2}$-*ft. Sq.* *Sd2.* *D3.* *N.* *Pl.* 66.

**POTERIUM** (Rosaceae), from G. poterion—a drinking cup; from the shape of the calyx of the flower.

One species is easy of cultivation in ordinary garden soil, preferably in a moist spot. It can be propagated easily by division of the root.

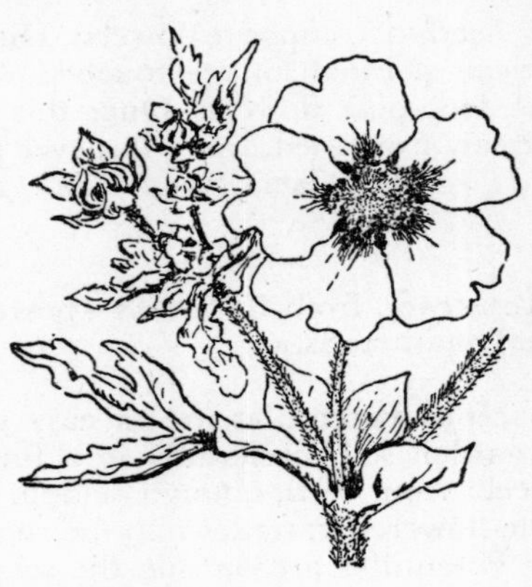

POTENTILLA NEPALENSIS

P. OBTUSUM (Blunt, or rounded), Japan, also known as *Sanguisorba obtusa*, grows to about two and a half feet in height and has pinnately divided leaves made up of 11–15 leaflets of attractive appearance. The typical bottlebrush flowers are of deep rose-pink, nodding at the tips. $2\frac{1}{2}$-*ft.* *July–September.* *H.* $2\frac{1}{2}$-*ft. Sq.* *D3.* *N.* *Pl.* 68.

P. OBTUSUM ALBUM (White) is similar but has flowers of clear white.

$2\frac{1}{2}$-*ft.* *July–September.* *H.* $2\frac{1}{2}$-*ft. Sq.* *D3.* *N.*

**PRIMULA** (Primulaceae), from L. primus—first: that is, the first of the flowers to greet the spring.

The Primulas are so vast in their scope that the task of selection cannot be an easy one, so that plants not in extensive cultivation have had to be excluded. The fact that many Primulas figure in the following list should not delude the gardener into the belief that all the varieties may with safety be grown in any herbaceous border; such is not the case. Many of the so-called bog and woodland Primulas may be grown without difficulty in a moist and partially shaded border, provided that the soil is retentive of moisture, or the soil is rich in humus. It is fatal, however, to assume that the bog Primulas may successfully be grown in light dry soils in sunny positions. On the other hand, the rock Primulas, of which P. Auricula may be said to be representative, are eminently satisfactory plants in the average garden, growing with alacrity and flowering with freedom in the largest of towns without difficulty. The species have not been divided into moisture-loving and rock types, but full notes on the cultivation of each variety have been given under its appropriate name.

PRIMULA ALPICOLA

P. ALPICOLA (Growing in the mountains) has long, green, serrated-edged leaves, and bears, upon stems of upwards of a foot in height, hanging creamy-yellow bell flowers, white within the bell. It is sweetly scented and thrives in a moist but well-drained soil. A variety P. ALPICOLA VIOLACEA and a number of other coloured forms now exist which are equally beautiful. It is admirable in the front of a shady border in comparatively rich but not light soil.

*1½-ft. June–July. H. 1-ft. Sq. Sd2. N.*

P. AURICULA (Ear-shaped), Europe, is one of the species thriving in dry soils, where depth will secure the moisture the surface denies. It has given rise to the border or garden Auriculas often known as P. pubescens, which will be dealt with under that name. P. Auricula has golden-yellow flowers freely borne upon stout mealy stems, and can be grown without difficulty under the same conditions as the Auricula hybrids. *½-ft. April–May. E. ½-ft. Sq. D8. C.*

P. BEESIANA (comm.), Yunnan, is one of the moisture-loving Primulas with tiers of flowers of bright magenta. It is difficult to place, but admirable in a wild green surrounding. If used in the border it should be planted in a position where it gets plenty of sun and moisture. *2-ft. May–June. H. 1½-ft. Sq. Sd2. N.*

P. BULLESIANA, garden origin, is a hybrid between P. Beesiana and P. Bulleyana. It grows to two and a half feet in height and produces tiers of flowers variable in colour, shading from cream to rose, mauve and purple, and claret to red. It may also be grown in moist borders and is fully at home around pools or in the bog garden. When grown in the moist border, the site should be partially shaded.
*2½-ft. May–June. H. 1½-ft. Sq. Sd2. N.*

P. BULLEYANA (comm.), China, is another moisture-loving Primula with large tufts of stiff, notched leaves, with thick stems bearing rings of red flower buds which open to large golden-yellow flowers. It is best suited to a moist site in a sunny position.
*2½-ft. May–June. H. 1½-ft. Sq. Sd2. N.*

P. CHUNGENSIS (From Tibet) is another moisture-loving Primula with tiers of flowers smaller than those of P. Bulleyana, but with a very strong constitution, thriving in similar spots.
*2-ft. May–June. H. 1½-ft. Sq. Sd2. N.*

P. CORTUSOIDES (Resembling Cortusa), Siberia, has very shapely, hairy, green foliage and produces many sprays of rose-coloured flowers. It should be planted in a leafy soil in a shady position.
*1-ft. May–June. H. 1-ft. Sq. D3. A.*

P. DENTICULATA (Toothed), Himalayas, has large, wide, toothed leaves, and produces, before the leaves are fully grown, globular heads of lilac-coloured flowers. It is suitable to grow in shady corners in the borders, or in the sun where it is damp. Innumerable colours exist, beginning with P. DENTICULATA ALBA, which has white flowers; HAY'S VAR., with tight heads of almost violet flowers; ROSEA, with pink flowers; RUBRA, with magenta-red flowers; SYLVIA WATSON, with flowers of violet-blue.

It propagates most easily from seed, which germinates with the utmost readiness. If, however, coloured forms are to be kept, it should be propagated by means of root cuttings which should be taken during the time when the head of the plant is dormant, that is to say, during the winter months.
*1-ft. March–April. H. 1-ft. Sq. Cr12. D9. N.*

P. ELATIOR (Taller), the Oxslip, Europe, is like the Cowslip but has taller spires of flowers of paler yellow, and is suitable for cool corners in some shade, where as a rule it will speedily naturalise itself.
*1-ft. April–May. H. 1-ft. Sq. D9. N.*

P. FLORINDAE (comm.), Tibet, is one of the tallest of the species, with gigantic stems of sweetly scented sulphur-yellow hanging bells. In a dry soil it is a complete disappointment; nevertheless, it is easy to grow in any place where it does not become completely sun-dried, though it gets attenuated. In a moist, rich soil, however, it is the crown of the gardener's achievement to behold its luscious, sweetly scented, ample heads on stout, inflexible stems.

*3-ft. June–July. H. 1½-ft. Sq. Sd2. N.* 2/1–1/3.

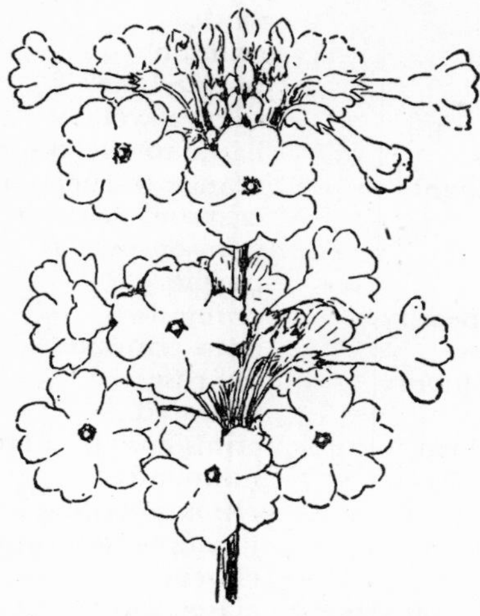

PRIMULA HELODOXA

P. GARRYARDE (comm.), garden origin, is a group of hybrid primroses of Irish origin, with large, wrinkled, green or red-bronze leaves and huge heads of delicately coloured and sometimes frilled flowers. The type is a great improvement upon the Juliana hybrids, the flower-heads often being six to eight inches in diameter. The best varieties are:—

ENID is of deep rose-pink with an orange eye.

GALAHAD has immense clusters of frilled white flowers.

GRAIL has flowers of deep purple-red.

GUINEVERE has flowers of soft pink with a yellow eye.

VICTORY has flowers of regal purple.

*⅔-ft. March–June. H. 1-ft. Sq. D7. N.*

P. HELODOXA (Glory of the marsh), Yunnan, is a Primula thriving upon moist soils, bearing exceptionally tall stems with many tiers of rich deep yellow flowers. It should not be attempted in any but moist soil. *2-ft. June–July. H. 1-ft. Sq. Sd9. D9. N.*

P. JULIAE (comm.), Caucasus, makes a mat of rounded heart-shaped leaves with winged leaf-stalks, and bears almost stemless purple flowers in large clusters down among them. It is a useful plant for edgings in loamy soils in somewhat shady sites.

*⅓-ft. March–April. E. 1-ft. Sq. D9. N.*

P. × JULIANA (comm.), garden origin, groups together the hybrids descended from P. Juliae, which are taller in habit but brighter in colour, and may be used for precisely the same purpose. The varieties in general cultivation are:—

| | |
|---|---|
| alba | white |
| Betty Green | crimson |
| Bunty | purple-blue |
| Dorothy | sulphur-yellow |
| E. R. Janes | flame to cherry-red |
| Garden Delight | orange to cherry-red |
| Gloria | crimson, gold eye |
| Jewel | crimson-purple |
| Jill | purple |
| Lingwood Beauty | crimson-red |
| Miss Massey | deep crimson |
| Mrs. McGillivray | old rose |
| Mrs. Neave | wine-red |
| Morton hybrid | crimson with a large yellow eye |
| Pam | maroon-red |
| Pilgrim | crimson with orange and scarlet eye |
| Sparkler | flame, hose-in-hose flowers |
| Wanda | claret |
| Wanda Hose-in-Hose | claret, hose-in-hose flowers |

P. LICHIANGENSIS (From Lichiang), Yunnan, has lobed leaves of most attractive shape, and sweetly scented magenta-rose flowers with green eyes, borne in loose but fascinating clusters.

*1-ft. May–June. H. ¾-ft. Sq. Sd2. N.* 31.

P. NUTANS (Nodding), Yunnan, has green, hairy, lanceolate leaves, and bears strong, stiff stems which carry huge, hanging, sweetly scented bells of lavender-violet, powdered with meal. It grows best in a neutral soil, well drained at the surface, preferably facing north, and appreciates plenty of moisture during the growing period.

*1½-ft. June–July. H. 1-ft. Sq. Sd2. N.*

P. POISSONI (comm.), Yunnan, has smooth, green leaves with pale ribs and long stems, bearing whorls of flaming-magenta flowers. It is best suited by a moist rich soil and is propagated with comparative ease from seed. *3-ft. June–July. H. 1-ft. Sq. Sd2. N.*

P. POLYANTHA (Many-flowered), garden origin, is a hybrid group of parentage P. veris, P. elatior and P. vulgaris, and comprises the Polyanthus of gardens, with leaves similar to those of the primrose, and clustered heads of flowers of variable colour. It is of exceptional hardiness, is a good perennial, and can be propagated by division in late July or early August, when the divided plants should be given a shady reserve bed before being transferred to more permanent quarters later in the year. The outstanding example of P. polyantha is the variety called BARROWBY GEM, which has large, sweetly scented flowers of golden-orange.

*⅔-ft. March–April. E. 1-ft. Sq. D7. N.*

P. PUBESCENS (Downy), Europe, is a group of hybrids of the parentage P. Auricula and P. hirsuta, and includes the Auriculas of gardens with broad leaves and large heads of sweetly scented flowers freely borne in April and May. They are easily grown in any soil which is not too light, and can be propagated by division after flowering. They may be freely produced from seed. The colour range is wide: white, mauve, purple, red and yellow are the shades abounding.

*½-ft. April–May. E. ⅔-ft. Sq. D7. C.*

P. PULVERULENTA (Powdered with meal), China, has long, rough, green leaves, often reaching a foot in length, and throws up strong flowering stems heavily powdered with white meal, and has tiered flowers of bright purple with brown eyes. It is best grown in a moist, rich soil containing plenty of humus, in a sunny or partially shaded site, and is propagated from seed or division. P. PULVERULENTA BARTLEY STRAIN is a selected strain with similar flowers of pink and salmon-pink, much better than the type which, by reason of its enchanting range of colours, it has supplanted in the garden. It has also helped to produce, with the aid of P. Cockburniana, a range of fine hybrids of bright red shade, of which RED HUGH and MILLER'S CRIMSON are typical and require similar conditions.

*3-ft. June–July. H. 1½-ft. Sq. Sd2. D8. N.*

P. SIKKIMENSIS (From Sikkim), Himalayas, has oval, wrinkled, serrated leaves of shiny green, and carries upon its flowering stems terminal clusters of sweetly scented, pale-yellow, hanging cowslip-like flowers powdered with white meal inside. It can be easily grown in any damp soil and is produced from seed.

*2-ft. July–August. H. 1⅓-ft. Sq. Sd2. N.*

P. VULGARIS (Common), Europe, is also known as *P. acaulis* and the Primrose. A number of garden varieties are particularly attractive in leafy or moist soils in shady sites. The Blue-flowered Primrose, P. VULGARIS CAERULEA, the colour of which is variable, can be particularly attractive. The double-flowered forms are somewhat more difficult to grow. They should be given the benefit of leafy, lime-free soils and some shade. They appear to require almost yearly division or repropagation, which should be done after they flower.

*½-ft. March–April. E. ⅔-ft. Sq. D9. N.*

**PRUNELLA** (Labiatae) is a corruption of Brunella, from German die Bräune—quinsy, which this herb was once supposed to cure.

Prunellas are of easy cultivation in any good soil in a somewhat shady site, and are of dwarf growth and suitable for the front of the border.

P. GRANDIFLORA (Large-flowered), Austria, grows to about nine inches in height and bears dense spikes of purple flowers on low-growing tufted plants. P. GRANDIFLORA VAR. ALBA is similar, with white flowers; VAR. CARMINEA has carmine flowers, and VAR. RUBRA red flowers. *¾-ft. June–July. E. 1-ft. Sq. D8. N.*

**PULMONARIA** (Boraginaceae), from L. pulmo—lung, the herb having been used medically to treat diseases of the lungs.

Pulmonarias are very useful plants, flowering early in the year and growing in shady sites where other plants will be found difficult to grow. All are strikingly beautiful in early spring, and grow well in any good garden soil.

P. ANGUSTIFOLIA (Narrow-leaved), Europe, has rough, wide, pointed, green leaves and bears crooks of funnel-shaped flowers of purplish-blue in low-growing masses.
*1-ft. March–April. E. 1⅓-ft. Sq. E. D9. ANC.*

P. ANGUSTIFOLIA VAR. AZUREA (Sky-blue), Europe, is similar in general characteristics, but has flowers of exceptionally pure gentian-blue.
*1-ft. March–April. E. 1⅔-ft. Sq. D9. N.* 4/11.

P. MONTANA (Of the mountains), Europe, is also called *P. mollis* and *P. rubra.* It has wider leaves and is of the same habit, and has most attractive flowers of bright salmon-red.
*1⅓-ft. March–April. E. 1⅓-ft. Sq. D9. N.*

P. OFFICINALIS (Of the shop), Europe, also known as *P. maculata*, has wide, rough, pointed leaves spotted with white, and bears sprays of red flowers which fade to violet.
*1-ft. March–April. E. 1⅓-ft. Sq. D9. N.*

P. SACCHARATA (Sugared), Europe, is the Bethlehem Sage, with rough green leaves spotted with white, and bears pink funnel-shaped flowers which change to blue as they age.
*1⅓-ft. March–April. E. 1⅓-ft. Sq. D9. N.*

**PYRETHRUM** (Compositae), from G. pyr—fire, because of the acrid or biting taste of the root.

Pyrethrums are classed by the botanist in the genus CHRYSANTHEMUM but are here retained under this name, since they will still be found to be so listed by the horticulturists. They thrive on well-drained soil in sunny places, and are seldom happy on very heavy land which is wet in winter. The best time to plant is in early autumn, so that a certain amount of root growth is made before the winter intervenes. Failing this, planting should be done in early March. No plant gives a greater display of colour than the Pyrethrum when well grown. It may be cut

Liatris pycnostachya ABDEFGHMQ
Polygonum amplexicaule var. atrosanguineum JKNOP
Sidalcea malvaeflora "Sussex Queen" GLMNPQRSTU

Solidago Leraft ABEFJ

Euphorbia polychroma CDH
Stokesia cyanea praecox GJKLNOP

back after its first flowering has been completed, and if well manured will produce a second but perhaps less outstanding display of colour later in the year. It is propagated by division of the root, preferably in mid or late March. Some of the outstanding varieties are:—

SINGLE-FLOWERED:

A. M. KELWAY, with flowers of bright rose.

COUNTESS ONSLOW, with large flowers of flesh-pink.

CRIMSON VELVET has large crimson-scarlet flowers.

EILEEN KELWAY is a heavily-petalled variety with large, rich-pink flowers.

EILEEN MAY ROBINSON has attractive flowers of shell-pink.

KELWAY'S GLORIOUS has large scarlet flowers and is the earliest of all to flower.

MARGERY ROBINSON is deep rose.

PRIMROSE DAME has deep-cream flowers.

SCARLET GLOW has crimson-scarlet flowers; and

SNOWFLAKE is, naturally, pure white.

DOUBLE-FLOWERED PYRETHRUMS have flowers domed in the centre, with closely packed but smaller ray florets surrounded by rather larger ones.

APHRODITE is pure white.

CARL VOGT is the earliest variety, with white flowers.

DIOMEDE is silvery-pink.

KING OSCAR is crimson-scarlet.

LADY KILDARE is buff-yellow, tinged with flesh-pink.

LORD ROSEBERY has deep-crimson flowers.

MADELEINE is salmon-pink.

MELTON has deep-crimson flowers.

QUEEN MARY has salmon-pink flowers of undeniable beauty.

YVONNE CAYEUX, with primrose flowers shading to buff, presents the most unusual picture.

*1½-ft.–2-ft. April–June. H. 1½-ft. Sq. D3. N.*

**RANUNCULUS** (Ranunculaceae), from L. rana—a frog, some of the species being found in damp places inhabited by frogs.

The Buttercup or Crowfoot is a perennial, and is of wide distribution throughout the world. As a general rule it may be said to appreciate a moist soil. Among the attractive border plants in the genus are:—

R. ACONITIFOLIUS (With leaves like Aconite), Europe, has handsome, broadly toothed, shiny leaves, tuberous roots, and bears many clear-white flowers in loose sprays in great quantity. It is known as Fair Maids of France. *2½-ft. May–June. H. 2-ft. Sq. D3. N.*

R. ACONITIFOLIUS FLORE PLENO, with double, white flowers, known as the White Bachelor's Button, is similar in all its characteristics, but has many-petalled rounded flowers of clear white.

*2½-ft. May–June. H. 2-ft. Sq. D3. N.*

R. ACRIS FLORE PLENO (Bitter; double-flowered), Europe, is commonly known as Yellow Bachelor's Button, and makes a much-branching plant on a fibrous root, bearing many double, golden-yellow, button-like flowers. *2-ft. June–August. H. 2-ft. Sq. D3. N.*

R. ASIATICUS (From Asia), S.E. Europe and Asia, is, in its horticultural forms, remarkably double, and is known as the Turban or Persian Ranunculus. The root is a claw-like tuber, which is generally planted in February, with the tips of the claws downward, the growing part being at a point where the claws join. It thrives best in well-drained soil in a sunny place, and is available in a very large range of colours. After flowering, and when the leaves begin to die down, the tubers are dug up and allowed to become sun-dried before being replanted the following February. *1-ft. May–June. B. ⅓-ft. Sq. Sd2. N.*

R. FICARIA (Fig-like—from the shape of the leaves), Europe, has fleshy roots and heart-shaped leaves, and produces upon short stems large golden-yellow flowers with eight or nine petals.

*½-ft. May–June. H. 1-ft. Sq. Sd2. N.*

**REHMANNIA** (Scrophulariaceae), named after J. Rehmann, a Russian doctor.

Rehmannia is of easy cultivation, either in the cool greenhouse or in the sheltered border, in light soil. The variety most generally grown is:

R. ALATA (Winged), China, which grows to about two feet in height. It has lance-shaped leaves, much notched and irregular in outline, winged round the stems, and bears in the leaf axils rosy-purple flowers reminiscent of those of the Foxglove, but with the calyx divided into five distinct segments. The throat of the flowers is yellow and heavily speckled.

*2-ft. May–August. H. 1½-ft. Sq. Cr3. N. Pl. 32.*

**RHEUM** (Polygonaceae), from Rha, the old name of the River Volga, on whose banks certain of the kinds grow wild; or, more probably, from G. rheo—to flow, a reference to the medicinal value of some species.

The wild Rhubarbs are not suited to small herbaceous borders, as they grow quickly and assume such large dimensions. They are suitable only for the largest of gardens. They have bold and striking foliage, and though the individual flowers are small they can be particularly striking in appearance, as they are borne in long, curious and attractive spikes.

R. COLLINIANUM (comm.), China, has very broad much-cut leaves of attractive appearance, and spikes of red flowers.

*6-ft. June–July. H. 8-ft. Sq. D3. N.*

R. EMODI (comm.), Himalayas, grows up to ten feet in height and has heart-shaped leaves of bronze-green, and bears purple flowers in densely packed spires.

*6-ft.–10-ft. June–July. H. 10-ft. Sq. D3. N.*

R. PALMATUM (Hand-shaped), N.E. Asia, has leaves divided into five parts and deeply lobed, and bears upon six-foot stems its spires of creamy-white flowers. *6-ft. June–July. H. 8-ft. Sq. D3. N.*

**RODGERSIA** (Saxifragaceae) is named after Commodore Rodgers, of the United States Navy, who commanded the expedition in which R. podophylla was discovered.

A group of perennial plants which resemble the Astilbe and bear fluffy Spiraea-like flowers in attractive spikes. Cultural conditions are similar to that for Astilbe: moist soil and some shade.

R. AESCULIFOLIA (Leaves resembling those of the Horse-Chestnut), China, has large chestnut-like leaves, and bears flat sprays of fluffy white flowers, like wind-borne cotton.

*3-ft. June–August. H. 2-ft. Sq. D3. N.*

R. PODOPHYLLA (Leaves with a foot-stalk) has heavily-netted leaves, divided into five parts, and attractive sprays of creamy-white flowers of about a foot in length. The foliage takes on fascinating colouring in the autumn. It should be grown in a spot where it does not become too sun-parched.

*4-ft. June–August. H. 3-ft. Sq. D3. N.*

**ROMNEYA** (Papaveraceae), named after T. Romney Robinson, an astronomer.

Two species differing only botanically, which run freely underground and are propagated by suckers or division with some difficulty. They can be propagated by means of root cuttings, which should be between three and four inches in length, taken in March, covered with soil to a depth of about half an inch, and kept in a cold frame until growth takes place.

R. COULTERI (comm.), California, is the Californian Tree-Poppy, which grows to a height of from four to six feet, according to its place, and requires a sheltered position in sandy loam. The shapely foliage is sea-green or grey, and the large poppy-like heads suitably contain the large clusters of golden stamens.

*4-ft. July–September. E. 6-ft. Sq. Cr3. N.*

R. TRICHOCALYX (With hairy calyx), California, differs only botanically, and shares not only the characteristics but the delicious scent of the foregoing. By some it is held to be easier to cultivate, but this is a matter which requires some confirmation, though a single plant nursed with care in 1935 now occupies over 100 square feet.
*3-ft. July–September. E. 6-ft. Sq. Cr3. N.*

**ROSCOEA** (Zingiberaceae), named after Roscoe, the founder of the Liverpool Botanic Society.

Exceptionally lovely dwarf perennial plants, perfectly hardy in sheltered, light, rich soils, and thriving to advantage in shady sites. They have tuberous roots and stemless, Iris-like leaves of bright green, and bright flowers in short spikes, reminiscent of certain of the orchids.

R. CAUTLEOIDES (Resembling Cautleya), W. China, has short spikes of delightful primrose-yellow flowers, freely produced under the right conditions. It should be kept moist during the summer months.
*1-ft. June–July. H. 1-ft. Sq. D3. A.*

R. PURPUREA (Purple), W. China, is similar in appearance and habit of growth, but has flowers of attractive pale purple.
*1-ft. June–July. H. 1-ft. Sq. D3. A.*

**RUDBECKIA** (Compositae); the name commemorates Olaf Rudbeck, a Swedish professor of botany.

The Cone-flowers resemble in some part the Sunflower, and are in their way equally attractive. They thrive in almost any soil or situation, are easily propagated by division, and have a range of height which makes them available for either the front or the back of the border.

R. CALIFORNICA (Californian), Oregon, has golden-yellow single flowers with high brown central discs, borne singly upon graceful stems.
*5-ft. July–September. H. 2½-ft. Sq. D3. ANC.*

R. LACINIATA (Laciniated, cut), E. N. America, has large golden-yellow flowers with conical green discs, produced in the utmost profusion, upon plants with fascinatingly cut green foliage.
*5-ft. August–September. H. 3-ft. Sq. D3. ANC.*

R. LACINIATA FLORE PLENO, sometimes known as *R. Golden Glow*, has very attractive double flowers of golden-yellow, and may be regarded as one of the maids-of-all-work of the garden.
*5-ft. August–September. H. 3-ft. Sq. D3. ANC. Pl. 69.*

R. NITIDA (Shining), N. America, has rounded lance-shaped leaves and large pure-yellow flowers with tall green cones, and is sometimes known as *R. nitida hirta* or *R. laevigata Autumn Glory*.
*6-ft. August–October. H. 3-ft. Sq. D3. ANC.*

R. SPECIOSA (Showy), N. America, is also known as *R. Newmanii*, and has striking golden-yellow flowers, frequently orange at the base, with high central discs of purple-brown or black, and is of dwarf growth with narrow and unobtrusive foliage. It is one of the most attractive plants for the flower border and probably one of the most outstanding in the late summer or early autumn.

*2-ft. July–October. H. 2½-ft. Sq. D3. ANC.*

R. SUBTOMENTOSA (Somewhat downy), N. America, has long, grey, somewhat rough, toothed leaves, and bears large golden-yellow flowers with a small dull-purple disc.

*3-ft. August–September. H. 2½-ft. Sq. D3. ANC.*

**SALVIA** (Labiatae), from L. salveo—to be well; from the medicinal properties ascribed to certain of the plants.

The Sages comprise a group of herbaceous plants and shrubs, requiring diverse treatment which is detailed under the various names. Only the herbaceous varieties or the varieties generally to be found in the border are dealt with here.

S. AZUREA (Sky-blue), N. America, also known as *S. caerulea*, has grey, hairy foliage, with straight, short leaves, and spikes of bright-blue flowers borne in many-headed spires. It should be grown in well-drained soil in a sunny but sheltered site.

*4-ft. August–September. H. 3-ft. Sq. Sd2. N. Pl. 70.*

S. BULLEYANA (comm.), Himalayas, has attractive large leaves heavily netted, and bears short spikes of yellow nettle-like flowers with purple markings, and is a plant which will intrigue your friends before all others! It requires a good soil in a sunny site.

*2-ft. June–July. H. 1½-ft. Sq. Sd2. N.*

S. DICHROA (Two-coloured), N. Africa, has long, straight sprays of deep-blue flowers with a white spot on the lower lip, borne upon strong stems, clad with long, toothed leaves, and requiring to be grown in moderately light soil in some sun.

*3-ft. July–September. H. 2½-ft. Sq. D3. N.*

S. FARINACEA (Mealy), Texas, has hairy, narrowly oval, aromatic foliage and bears long, narrow sprays of violet-blue sage flowers with mealy calyces. *3-ft. July–August. H. 2½-ft. Sq. Sd2. N. Pl. 70.*

S. FULVA (Tawny), Mexico, has green leaves and large, hairy, tawny-red flowers, and is best suited by a sheltered position.

*2½-ft. July–August. H. 2-ft. Sq. Sd3. N. Pl. 71.*

S. GLUTINOSA (Sticky), S. Europe, has rather large, sticky, toothed leaves and bears sprays of large pale-yellow sage flowers. It cannot be said to be too easy to grow, but is worth trying in a good rich soil in a sheltered site. *2½-ft. July–August. H. 2½-ft. Sq. Sd2. N.*

S. NEMOROSA (Of the glades), Europe, also known as *S. virgata nemorosa*, is the Violet Sage. It forms a much-branching bush with wrinkled, toothed leaves, and bears long sprays of violet-blue flowers of sombre, sober magnificence.

*3-ft. July–September. H. 3-ft. Sq. Sd2. ANC. Pl.* 79.

S. PRATENSIS (Of the meadows), Europe, has wrinkled, rounded leaves, sometimes spotted with red, and bears long sprays of bright-blue flowers. S. PRATENSIS VAR. ALBA has white flowers, S. PRATENSIS BAUMGARTENI has violet flowers, S. PRATENSIS RUBICUNDA has rose-red flowers, and S. PRATENSIS TENORII has blue flowers.

*2-ft. June–August. H. 2-ft. Sq. Sd2. N.*

S. TURKESTANICA (From Turkestan), S.E. Europe, grows from three to six feet in height, with large, broad, hairy, toothed leaves, and bears long sprays of pale-blue flowers set off by large bracts of deep pink, passing to purple. It is apt to prove monocarpic, and a number of the plants should have their flowering tips removed each year in order that the succession may be fully assured.

*3-ft.–6-ft. July–September. H. 3-ft. Sq. Sd2. N. Pl.* 79.

S. ULIGINOSA (Growing in swamps), S. America, has rounded, toothed, lance-shaped leaves and bears long, undivided sprays of Cambridge-blue flowers upon its six-foot leafy stems. This should be grown in a soil which is retentive of moisture.

*6-ft. August–September. H. 3-ft. Sq. D3. N.*

**SAPONARIA** (Caryophyllaceae), from L. sapo—soap, the bruised leaves of S. officinalis making a lather resembling soap.

These plants are of easy cultivation in any garden soil, preferring a place in the sun.

S. OFFICINALIS (Of the shop), W. Asia, sometimes known as *Silene Saponaria* or Bouncing Bet, has five-petalled flowers in tight terminal clusters, generally of glowing pink. The most popular garden form is undoubtedly that known as S. OFFICINALIS FLORE PLENO, which has double flowers of salmon-pink.

*1½-ft. June–August. H. 1½-ft. Sq. Sd2. N.*

S. OFFICINALIS ALBA FLORE PLENO is similar but has white flowers slightly tinted with rose. *1½-ft. June–August. H. 1½-ft. Sq. Sd2. N.*

**SCABIOSA** (Dipsaceae), from scabies—the itch; from the plant's medicinal use as a cure.

Scabious are easily grown in good garden soil, are exceptionally free-flowering and very good as cut flowers. Few of the species have given rise to really good garden plants other than those mentioned below. Without a doubt, S. caucasica, together with its garden derivatives, is the most popular. It may be propagated freely from division in the early spring.

S. CAUCASICA (Caucasian), from the Caucasus, has grey undivided basal leaves of long lance shape, with the stem leaves divided into three or five segments. The large pincushion-like flowers, surrounded by flat and large florets, are of light lavender-blue, and are freely produced from June to September. The following garden varieties are exceptionally good:—

ALBA, which is pure white.

CLIVE GRAVES, which is rich mauve.

DIAMOND is very dark blue.

GOLDINGENSIS, which is lavender-blue, is tall and very hardy.

ISAAC HOUSE is deep blue.

PERFECTA is pale blue and larger than the type.

2-*ft*. *June–September*. *H*. 2-*ft*. *Sq*. *Sd*2. *D*3. *N*.

S. COLUMBARIA (Pigeon-coloured), Europe, has grey-green toothed leaves pinnately cut into segments and bears typical scabious heads of pale blue with great freedom. It grows well in any good garden soil. 1½-*ft*. *May–July*. *E*. 1½-*ft*. *Sq*. *Sd*9. *N*. 636/2.

S. COLUMBARIA ROSEA is similar but has flowers of rosy-mauve, fitting the foliage with deft artistry.

2-*ft*. *May–July*. *E*. 1½-*ft*. *Sq*. *Sd*9. *N*.

S. OCHROLEUCA (Yellowish-white), Europe, has much-branching stems and bears attractive flowers of sulphur-yellow.

2-*ft*. *July–September*. *H*. 1½-*ft*. *Sq*. *Sd*9. *N*.

S. TATARICA (From Tartary), Russia, is also known as *Cephalaria tatarica*, and closely resembles S. caucasica except that it grows a great deal taller and has flowers of creamy-white or pale yellow, which, if you are partial to such tints, will conjure visions of pale moonbeams.

4-*ft*. *June–August*. *H*. 1½-*ft*. *Sq*. *Sd*9. *N*.

**SCHIZOSTYLIS** (Iridaceae), from G. schizo—cut, and stylos—style; the style being deeply divided.

Schizostylis is the Kaffir Lily or Crimson Flag, and is a plant with a fleshy root, Iris-like leaves and sprays of flowers resembling those of the Crocus but borne in large sprays. It is hardy in all but the severest districts and grows well in any light loamy soil.

S. COCCINEA (Scarlet), S. Africa, grows to two feet in height, with long, grass-like leaves, and bears deep-crimson crocus-like flowers in short sprays. The variety MRS. HEGGARTY is similar but has flowers of salmon-pink and produces them a little later than S. coccinea.

2-*ft.* *October–November.* *H.* ½-*ft. Sq.* *D*6. *N.*

**SCILLA** (Liliaceae), either from G. skyllo—to injure, the bulbs being said to be injurious (which, in view of their prolific production, is a great pity!), or alternatively from G. skilla—a sea onion.

These are excellent bulbous plants planted under the shade of trees, where they will, during the month of May, provide an outstandingly bright show of colour. The best of the varieties to use for this purpose are:—

S. HISPANICA (Spanish), Spain and Portugal, is sometimes known as *S. campanulata.* It has flowers rather larger than those of the wild Bluebell, of variable blue, sometimes sky-blue, sometimes clouded by mists, and even tinted by the sunset.

1⅓-*ft.* *May.* *B.* ⅓-*ft. Sq.* *D*9. *ANC.*

S. NONSCRIPTA (Undescribed), Europe, is also known as *S. festalis* and *S. nutans*, and, in spite of its many names, is just the wild Bluebell, very useful for growing under trees, naturalising in grass and occupying those places in which it is difficult to provide colour in the month of May.

1-*ft.* *May.* *B.* ¼-*ft. Sq.* *D*9. *ANC.*

S. SIBIRICA (Siberian), W. Asia, has hanging wheel-shaped flowers of electric blue, borne in groups of three or more, and is undoubtedly the most startling colour of all, and flowers considerably earlier. It is one of those things you always forget to buy, since you see it in flower six months (at least) before you can plant it.

½-*ft.* *February–March.* *B.* ⅓-*ft. Sq.* *D*6. *N.* 45/1.

**SCUTELLARIA** (Labiatae), from L. scutella—a small salver; from the shape of the calyx.

Is commonly known as the Skull-cap, and is of comparatively easy growth in reasonably light soil.

S. BAICALENSIS (From Lake Baikal), Russia, is also known as *S. macrantha* and is an upright plant with lanceolate leaves and short but attractive sprays of two-lipped sky-blue flowers reminiscent of the Pentstemon. It is perfectly hardy and grows well in any soil which is not too heavy, and ranks high among my personal favourites.

1⅓-*ft.* *July–August.* *H.* 1-*ft. Sq.* *Sd*2. *N.* 37/1.

S. LATERIFLORA (Flowers to one side), N. America, has rounded oval leaves and bears slender arching spires of pale blue flowers.

1½-*ft.* *July.* *H.* 1-*ft. Sq.* *Sd*2. *N.*

Sparaxis pulcherrima ABEF
Astilbe hybrida rosea BCDFGH
Oenothera speciosa KLMOP

Thalictrum dipterocarpum ABCDFGHKLMOPQ
Delphinium paniculatum EFGNOST
Gypsophila repens rosea plena EJNPQRSTU

**SEDUM** (Crassulaceae), from L. sedeo—to sit; from their habit, which the only example here fails to obey.

S. SPECTABILE (Showy), Central China, stands up and looks around with its large, grey, flat, notched leaves and large, flat heads of pink flowers, sometimes reaching as much as one foot in diameter. Bees and butterflies seem to adore them, and nothing could be better for them except the varied brilliance which adds to their other charms a deep rose-pink complexion.

*1¼-ft. August–October. H. 1½-ft. Sq. Cg5. N.*

**SENECIO** (Compositae), from L. senex—an old man: by analogy, the bare seed receptacles being compared to a bald head.

The Groundsels are a vast race of both herbaceous plants and shrubs, but few of the herbaceous varieties have yet become as popular as they deserve to be in the garden. They are of easy culture; the herbaceous types may be freely propagated from seed, from cuttings and by division.

S. ADONIDIFOLIUS (Adonis-leaved), S. Europe, is called *S. abrotanifolius* (the name of a completely different plant) in most catalogues. It has very finely cut, pinnately divided leaves, and clusters of small brilliant-orange flowers, freely borne.

*1⅓-ft. May–June. E. 1½-ft. Sq. Cg4. Sd9. A.*

S. CLIVORUM (Of the hills), Japan, is also known as *Ligularia clivorum*, and has large, rounded leaves, sharply toothed, and often exceeding a foot in diameter. The branching flower-stems, with ragged orange-yellow daisy flowers, are centred with dark-brown discs. The variety called OTHELLO has purplish foliage and rich orange-yellow flowers.

*4-ft. August–September. H. 3-ft. Sq. D3. N.*

S. DORONICUM (Resembling Doronicum), Europe, makes a mat of round oval leaves and bears its golden-yellow daisy flowers upon stems of a foot or so in the early summer. A pleasant plant, which will never let the gardener down.

*1-ft. June–July. E. 2-ft. Sq. D3. ANC.*

S. MACROPHYLLUS (Long-leaved), Europe, also known as *Jacobaea macrophylla*, has long, grey leaves, exceeding a foot in length, and bears spreading clusters of yellow flowers in late summer.

*5-ft. July–September. H. 3½-ft. Sq. D3. ANC.*

S. PULCHER (Beautiful), S. America, has long, lobed, silvery leaves, and bears small heads of reddish-purple flowers with yellow centres, and is just as good as it sounds.

*2-ft. August–October. H. 2-ft. Sq. Sd2. D3. N.*

S. TANGUTICUS (From Siberia) has cut foliage and bears loose clusters of yellow flowers in large multiple terminal sprays, which translated means that it is a good yellow Ragwort!

*5-ft. September–October. H. 3½-ft. Sq. D3. N.*

S. VEITCHIANUS (comm.), China, also known as *Ligularia Veitchiana*, has very large, long, sharply-toothed leaves, and bears strong spikes of yellow daisy flowers in late summer.

*4-ft. August–September. H. 3-ft. Sq. D3. N.*

**SIDALCEA** (Malvaceae), from G. side—a name for Malva, and alkea —healing; probably for some curative virtue.

The Sidalceas have become in recent years among the most attractive of hardy flowering plants, many horticultural varieties of great charm having been added. The general characteristics are a height of four feet and flowers which are borne in sprays, resembling those of a small Hollyhock, in shades of white, pink, rose and red. Sidalceas may be planted in ordinary cultivated garden soil in autumn or early spring, and should be left undisturbed as far as possible in order that the maximum display shall be obtained.

S. CANDIDA (White), W. N. America, has its basal leaves broad and almost heart-shaped, bearing five- or seven-parted leaves upon the uprising stems. The modest white hollyhock flowers are borne in long spikes freely produced.

*3½-ft. June–August. H. 2-ft. Sq. D3. Sd2. N.*

S. MALVAEFLORA (Mallow-flowered), California, is similar in its characteristics but has larger flowers of rose, freely borne in slender spires. The following hybrids of S. malvaeflora are particularly attractive:—

CRIMSON KING has crimson-pink flowers borne in compact spikes.

ELSIE HEUGH has large silvery-pink flowers, attractively fringed. *3-ft.*

KATHLEEN BUNYARD has deep-crimson flowers. *2-ft.*

LISTERI has large spikes of satin-pink flowers very freely produced. *3½-ft.*

MONARCH has large, wide, open flowers of deep rose-pink. *4-ft.*

MRS. BERKELEY is a double-flowered variety with dark-rose flowers borne in tapering spikes. 28/1.

MRS. BORRADAILE is a dwarf variety with crimson flowers. *2½-ft.*

ROSE QUEEN is a tall variety with rose-pink flowers.

RUBY has ruby-red flowers freely produced.

SCARLET BEAUTY is similar, with flowers of the deepest rose-pink.

SUSSEX QUEEN has flowers of satin-pink and is one of the best. *3½-ft. Pl.* 73.

WENSLEYDALE is a fine shade of rose-red. *3-ft.*

*Variable. July–August. H. 2-ft. Sq. D3. Sd2. N.*

**SILENE** (Caryophyllaceae), from G. sialon—saliva; the sticky excretion from the leaves of some of the species is said to catch flies, hence the common name Catchfly.

Most of the species are very dwarf in habit and eminently suited for growth in the rock garden. The following species are suitable for growing in the herbaceous border, where normal cultivation in sunny sites is the most appropriate treatment.

S. Asterias (Star-fish), S.E. Europe, has oblong, pointed leaves, produced in neat rosettes, and bears tight clusters of rose-red flowers at the tips of the flowering stems, from which it would appear to be aptly named, as indeed it is.

3-*ft.* *June–September.* *E.* 1½-*ft. Sq.* *Sd*2. *N.*

S. compacta (Compact), Asia Minor, is also known as *S. orientalis*, and has clustered heads of deep-pink flowers borne on long stems above grey-green rosettes of foliage, and though it is as diffuse as the last, its growth is, without doubt, neat.

2-*ft.* *July.* *E.* 1½-*ft. Sq.* *Sd*2. *N.*

**SISYRINCHIUM** (Iridaceae), from G. sys—pig, and rynchos—snout; pigs being said to dig and devour its roots.

Known as the Blue-eyed Grass, Sisyrinchiums are fit for growth in either rock gardens or the front of the herbaceous border. All thrive in good garden soil and may be propagated from division, but will do so without let or hindrance from the seed which they will produce and distribute with equal diligence.

S. angustifolium (Narrow-leaved), N. America, is also known as *S. anceps*, and makes a tuft of thin, green, sword-shaped leaves and stems, which seem to bear their violet-blue flowers bursting out from the tips. 1-*ft.* *June–September.* *E.* 1-*ft. Sq.* *D*3. *N.*

S. bermudianum (From Bermuda), is of the same habit, but has longer, thinner-petalled flowers of violet-blue with a yellow base, and loses all its sombre gloom when the sun shines upon it.

1-*ft.* *June–September.* *E.* 1-*ft. Sq.* *D*3. *N.*

S. convolutum (Rolled round—a reference to the appearance of the flowers when dying), California, known also as *S. californicum* and *Hydastylus californicus*, has wider leaves of paler green, and bears larger flowers with overlapping petals of clear golden-yellow, and is, without doubt, the best of its type.

1-*ft.* *June–October.* *E.* 1-*ft. Sq.* *Sd*2. *N.* 41/1.

S. Douglasii (comm.), British Columbia, is also *S. grandiflorum.* It has rounded rush-like leaves and bears in the early spring hanging bells of reddish-purple so large that one looks at them in some amazement,

their production appearing so impossible. S. Douglasii album, white, is similar but produces flowers of clearest and purest white.
1-*ft.* *February–March.* *H.* ½-*ft. Sq.* *D*6. *N.*

S. striatum (With grooved leaves), Argentina, looks like a paler-leaved Iris germanica, centred by flowering stems upon which are borne sprays of lemon-yellow six-petalled flowers in tight clusters. This inherits the ability of the genus to reproduce from seed, to a degree even more marked than in its relations.
2½-*ft.* *May–July.* *E.* 2-*ft. Sq.* *Sd*2. *N.*

**SOLIDAGO** (Compositae), from L. solidare—to unite; from its use in medicine.

The genus Solidago is typified by the Goldenrod, and produces compound panicles of tiny daisy flowers, particularly attractive in the mass. They grow well in ordinary garden soil in full sun and, if anything, are a little brighter and more compact in a soil which is poor, a little rationing being conducive to better health and behaviour.

S. altissima (The tallest), E. N. America, forms basal tufts of long-toothed, lance-shaped leaves, green and slightly hairy, and bears curving one-sided sprays of golden-yellow flowers in dense pyramid-shaped heads. 5-*ft.* *August–September.* *H.* 3½-*ft. Sq.* *D*3. *ANC.*

S. Ballardii (comm.), N. America, is similar in outline but does not exceed three and a half feet in height.
3½-*ft.* *August–September.* *H.* 3½-*ft. Sq.* *D*3. *ANC.*

S. canadensis (Canadian), N. America, is another variety varying little in appearance from S. altissima, the only difference being a botanical one. 3½-*ft.* *August–September.* *H.* 3½-*ft. Sq.* *D*3. *ANC.*

S. hybrida comprises the hybrid Goldenrods of garden origin, of which the best are:—

Gold Elf, of similar appearance. Two to three feet in height.

Golden Wings, with large feathery heads of bright yellow produced late in the year. 5-*ft.* *September–October.*

Gold Strahl, with feathery spikes of deep golden-yellow. 2½-*ft.* *August–September.*

Leraft, of compact bushy growth, with the sprays of golden yellow flowers, is reminiscent of Mimosa, and useful for the same purpose. 2-*ft.* *Pl.* 74.

**SPARAXIS** (*see* DIERAMA).

**SPIRAEA** (Rosaceae), from G. speira—wreath, a reference to the manner in which the fruits are borne.

The Spiraeas are a large genus consisting of both shrubs and herbaceous plants, all of which have attractive feathery flowers borne either in flat corymbs or in loose feather-like sprays. The herbaceous Spiraeas are eminently suited to the flower border in soils which are not hot and dry, and can be best grown by incorporating plenty of humus in the soil.

S. ARUNCUS (old name for the Goat's-beard), Siberia, has long, lanceolate leaves, much toothed, and bears long and impressive feathery plumes of white flowers. *4-ft. June–July. H. 3-ft. Sq. D3. N.*

S. ARUNCUS VAR. KNEIFFII (comm.) has ferny foliage and similar flowers borne on shorter stems. *3-ft. June–July. H. 3-ft. Sq. D3. N.*

S. FILIPENDULA (Hanging on threads), Europe, is also known as *Filipendula hexapetala*, is the Dropwort, and has a tuberous root-stock, fern-like leaves, and creamy-white, sweetly scented flowers. The variety S. FILIPENDULA FL. PL. is similar, but has attractive double white flowers. *2-ft. June–July. H. 2-ft. Sq. D3. N.*

S. LOBATA (Lobed), N. America, is also known as *Filipendula rubra*, and has large palmate leaves and feathery flowers of peach-blossom-pink; VAR. VENUSTA has flowers of deeper pink, and MAGNIFICA adds a foot or so to its height and has flowers of still deeper pink, which should be a twofold justification for its name.
*3-ft. July–August. H. 2½-ft. Sq. D3. N.*

S. PALMATA (Palm-shaped), Japan, has hand-shaped leaves and bears spreading plumes of deep purplish-pink; is also known as *Filipendula purpurea*. S. PALMATA VAR. ALBA has white flowers but is otherwise similar. *3-ft. July–August. H. 2½-ft. Sq. D3. N.*

S. ULMARIA (Elm-leaved), Europe, is the Meadowsweet, with creamy-white, sweetly scented flowers borne in long feathery plumes. The variety S. ULMARIA FL. PL. has double flowers and is probably even more attractive; VAR. AUREA has foliage variegated with gold, and VARIEGATA has foliage tinted green and white.
*3-ft. July–August. H. 2-ft. Sq. D3. N.*

**STACHYS** (Labiatae), from G. stachys—a spike.

S. COCCINEA (Scarlet), N. America, has pointed oval leaves, heavily reticulated, and bears in the leaf axils attractive nettle-like flowers of coral-red, and is so unlike any other plant that it might be regarded as a "collector's piece."
*1-ft. June–August. H. 1½-ft. Sq. Sd2. N.*

S. GRANDIFLORA (Large-flowered), E. Europe, has hairy, rounded leaves and bears sprays of violet or rosy-purple flowers in profusion.
*1½-ft. June–August. H. 1½-ft. Sq. Sd2. N.*

S. LANATA (Woolly), E. Europe, has white woolly leaves and is commonly called Lamb's Ears. The silvery foliage is a particularly attractive contrast to other plants. The flowers are purple but insignificant; it is a plant that the expert despises but the children love.
*2-ft. August. E. 2-ft. Sq. D3. ANC.*

**STATICE** (Plumbaginaceae), from G. statizo—to stop; from the medical use of some of the species for their astringent properties.

The genus Statice has recently been divided into three genera: Armeria, Acantholimon and Limonium. For the sake of simplicity the following, which fall into the group now covered by Limonium, are retained under the better-known name, with cross references to the present name. The general characteristics of the species are the loose branching spikes and widely distributed small flowers resembling in distribution those of the Gypsophila.

S. EXIMIA (Of rare beauty), Central Asia, is also known as *Limonium eximium*, has wavy-edged oblong leaves with widely distributed lilac-rose flowers. *2-ft. July–September. E. 3-ft. Sq. Sd2. N.*

S. GMELINII (comm.), Siberia, also known as *Limonium Gmelinii*, forms basal rosettes of bluntly oval leaves, and bears diffuse but bushy heads of purplish-blue small flowers.
*2-ft. July–September. E. 2½-ft. Sq. Sd2. N.*

S. INCANA (Grey, as with age), S.E. Europe, is very dwarf, seldom exceeding a foot in height, and has extremely large heads of pinkish-white flowers. It is known as *Limonium tataricum*, but this does not prevent its use at the front of the border.
*1-ft. July–September. E. 1½-ft. Sq. Sd2. N.*

S. LATIFOLIA (Wide-leaved), E. Europe, also known as *Limonium latifolium*, has long elliptical leaves and bears huge heads of blue and white flowers produced with the utmost freedom. S. LATIFOLIA ALBA has white flowers, ROSEA is similar but has pink flowers, and VIOLETTA has flowers of dark lilac.
*2-ft. July–September. H. 2½-ft. Sq. Sd2. N.*

**STERNBERGIA** (Liliaceae), named after Count Sternberg, a German botanist.

Sternbergia is a bulbous-rooted plant requiring warm exposure and deep planting in good leafy soil. It is one of the many plants reputed to be the biblical Lily of the Field. Two varieties are particularly good for autumn flowering in the warm sunny border; they are:—

S. LUTEA (Yellow), Asia Minor, which has green, channelled, strap-like leaves and bears its graceful golden-yellow crocus-like flowers before the leaves appear in the autumn.

*½-ft. September–October. B. ⅓-ft. Sq. D6. N.*

S. MACRANTHA (Large-flowered), Asia Minor, is similar in appearance but has larger flowers and is generally of taller growth, but with that loses much of the grace of line which endears S. lutea to one's heart.

*1-ft. September–October. B. ⅓-ft. Sq. D6. N.*

**STOKESIA** (Compositae); the name commemorates Dr. Stokes, an English botanist.

Stokesias are autumn-flowering plants requiring a sheltered position in the warm sunny border, with flowers reminiscent of those of the Sweet Sultan—glamorised a little perhaps: but, then, consider its habitat.

S. CYANEA (Azure), U.S.A., is also known as *S. laevis*, and makes a short basal growth of somewhat long, rough, grey-green leaves, and bears Sweet-Sultan-like flowers of lavender-blue. The variety S. CYANEA ALBA has white flowers, and S. CYANEA LUTEA creamy-white flowers; VAR. PRAECOX flowers about a month earlier than the type; VAR. ROSEA has pink flowers, and VAR. SUPERBA is deeper in colour and taller in height.

*2-ft. September–October. H. 1½-ft. Sq. D3. ANC. Pl. 74.*

**STYLOPHORUM** (Papaveraceae), from G. stylos—style, and phoreo —to bear, the styles being retained upon the seed capsules.

S. DIPHYLLUM (Two-leaved), N. America, is the Celandine Poppy, with two- or three-flowered clusters of deep-yellow poppy-like flowers, borne upon black, wiry stems, best suited by a somewhat shaded site and light, leafy soil. *1½-ft. April–May. H. 1½-ft. Sq. Sd2. N.*

**SYMPHYANDRA** (Campanulaceae), from G. symphyo—unite, and andres—stamens.

These plants resemble Campanulas, are sometimes monocarpic, and bear tubular, hanging flowers of white, cream or blue. They are of easy cultivation in any light garden soil, and are propagated with ease from seed; in fact, once they have flowered, seedlings will always be with you—never, need I add, to worry you.

S. HOFFMANNII (comm.) has white Campanula-like flowers, borne in a spire shaped like a pyramid, and adds grace of contour to neatness of habit. *1½-ft. June–July. H. 1½-ft. Sq. Sd2. N.*

S. PENDULA (Hanging) is similar in appearance but has tubular flowers of creamy-white, hanging downwards, and, if anything, has still greater grace, the pendulous flowers adding the charm of modesty.
*1½-ft. June–July. H. 1½-ft. Sq. Sd2. N.*

**THALICTRUM** (Ranunculaceae), from G. thallo—to flourish; probably referring to the numerous flowers.

A group of hardy herbaceous perennials highly valued for both their ornamental maidenhair-like leaves and the summer flowers. Most varieties are suitable for planting in the herbaceous border and are of easy cultivation in ordinary well-dug garden soil. All propagate with ease from division and may also be raised from seed.

T. ADIANTIFOLIUM (Adiantum-leaved), *see* T. majus.

T. AQUILEGIFOLIUM (Aquilegia-leaved), S.E. Europe, has grey-green leaves similar to those of some of the Aquilegias, and bears rounded clusters of creamy-white flowers made up of white sepals containing pink or purple stamens. It is available in a number of different colours, all of them "jolly" plants. Of these T. AQUILEGIFOLIUM ALBUM has pure-white flowers; PURPUREUM has purple flowers; and ROSEUM has flowers of pale rose.
*3-ft. May–June. H. 2-ft. Sq. D3. N.*

T. DELAVAYI (comm.), E. China, has similar foliage and bears its clusters of purple or lilac flowers with great freedom.
*2-ft. June–July. H. 1½-ft. Sq. D3. N.*

T. DIPTEROCARPUM (With two-winged fruits), W. China, is very variable in height, approximating anything from two to six feet, according to the soil and conditions under which it is grown. It thrives best in a well-drained but moist soil. The loose, conical, nodding sprays of lilac-sepalled flowers are enhanced in beauty by the creamy-yellow stamens. The variety T. DIPTEROCARPUM ALBUM has the sepals of creamy-white, and a recent horticultural form, T. DIPTEROCARPUM HEWITT'S DOUBLE, is a strong-growing, perfectly double-flowered variety, with rose-purple flowers, rather shorter in growth but undeniably hardy.
*2-ft.–6-ft. June–August. H. 1½-ft. Sq. D3. Sd2. N. Pl. 76.*

T. FLAVUM (Yellow), Europe, has similar blue-green foliage and bears rounded clusters of pale-yellow flowers containing bright-yellow stamens—a colour scheme which has to be seen to be emulated.
*4-ft. June–August. H. 2-ft. Sq. D3. N.*

T. MAJUS (Greater), Europe, is usually found in cultivation in the form called *T. adiantifolium,* and has curious greeny-yellow flowers which persist for a while as little brown tassels, when they are even more fascinating. *3-ft. June–August. H. 2-ft. Sq. D3. N.*

Malva Alcea fastigiata BCDFGHKL
Tradescantia "J. C. Weguelin" AEFJN
Tradescantia "Pauline" KOPQ

Tropaeolum speciosum

**THERMOPSIS** (Leguminosae), from G. thermos—Lupin, and opsis—resemblance, are the Sham Lupins.

They are best grown in rich, well-drained soil and require to be well established before giving of their best. The leaves are divided into three finger-like segments, and the flowers are borne in long lupin-like spires from June onwards. The only variety in general cultivation is:—

T. FABACEA (Bean-like), Siberia, which grows to three feet in height and has lupin-like flowers of bright yellow, held upright and produced in branching sprays. *3-ft. June–July. H. 3-ft. Sq. Sd4. N.*

**TIARELLA** (Saxifragaceae), from G. tiara—a turban or diadem; from the shape of the seed capsules.

Tiarellas, of which two only are in common cultivation, are, fortunately, indifferent as to soil.

T. CORDIFOLIA (With heart-shaped leaves), N. America, is best grown in some shade, but is indifferent as to soil. The foliage, which is particularly attractive, is rough, green, and heart-shaped, and rises to five to six inches in height; and the creamy-white flowers, which resemble those of the Spiraea, are produced with great freedom. The plant runs about with great ease and can be propagated by division. *1-ft. May. H. 2-ft. Sq. D9. ANC.*

T. UNIFOLIATA (One-leaved), N. America, grows considerably taller and forms tight clumps rather than running masses. It is particularly attractive and may be relied on to grow in almost any soil in a shady site. *1½-ft. May. H. 2-ft. Sq. D9. ANC.*

**TRADESCANTIA** (Commelinaceae); the name is commemorative of J. Tradescant, gardener to King Charles the First.

The principal kind in use in the herbaceous border is T. virginiana and its derivatives, which are given a number of attractive names such as the Spiderwort, Trinity Flower, and Moses in the Bulrushes. They are best grown in a sunny but moist spot in ordinary garden soil. Propagation is best by means of division.

T. VIRGINIANA (From Virginia), N. America, has long, grass-like leaves and produces in clusters three-petalled flowers of violet-purple. The individual flowers last only for a single day, but are quickly followed by others, so that the plant does not thereby suffer. A number of even better plants have been produced by the gardener's skill. T. VIRGINIANA ALBA has large pure white flowers, VAR. CAERULEA has soft, clear-blue flowers, VAR. DELICATA has pale sky-blue flowers, VAR. J. C. WEGUELIN has very large azure-blue flowers, VAR. MERLIN has large flowers of lavender-pink, and VAR. RUBRA flowers which are almost ruby-red. Pauline has rosy-lavender flowers, while Iris Pritchard produces pure-white flowers faintly tinted with violet. James Stratton has deep-blue flowers, and Purple Dome blossoms of brilliant purple.

*2-ft. June–September. H. 1½-ft. Sq. D3. N. Pl. 77.*

**TRILLIUM** (Liliaceae), from L. trilix—triple, that is, in three parts, the parts of the flower being produced in threes.

The Trilliums are lovers of the shade and appreciate leafy soil; they are suitable only for the front of the shady border and should not be attempted in other situations. The best varieties for this purpose, though not all the varieties in cultivation, are listed below.

T. grandiflorum (Large-flowered), N. America, has the largest flowers of all, made up of three triangular-shaped petals of clear, shining white surrounded by a ruff of polished green triangular-shaped leaves. The flowers as they die change from white to pink, as if to add still more beauty before passing!

*1-ft. May–June. D. ⅔-ft. Sq. D8. AN.*

T. ovatum (Egg-shaped), W. N. America, has rather thinner-petalled flowers of white fading to rose, borne in long, upstanding stems, and is every whit as good if not so usual.

*1-ft. May–June. D. ⅔-ft. Sq. D8. AN.*

T. stylosum (Styled), N. America, is one of the most beautiful of all, with soft, three-petalled, drooping, pink flowers, borne on the top of a stem of a foot in length, circled with three oval, shining green leaves. It has the grace of shy beauty.

*1-ft. May–June. D. ⅔-ft. Sq. D8. AN.*

**TROLLIUS** (Ranunculaceae): the name is possibly derived from L. trollus—a basin, from the shape of the flowers; or from the German trol—a dwarf.

Trollius are best grown in the flower border where the soil is moist and deep or much enriched with some form of humus. They also do well in heavy soils which are not liable to dry out during the summer.

T. asiaticus (From Asia), Siberia, has orange-coloured petals and sepals formed into the shape of an open globe, and attractive butter-cup-like leaves of bronzy-green. It is also known as *T. giganteus.*

*2-ft. May–July. H. 2-ft. Sq. D3. N.*

T. caucasicus (Caucasian), W. Asia, is still taller and has rather less full flowers of orange-yellow, with similar attractive foliage.

*3-ft. May–July. H. 2-ft. Sq. D3. N.*

T. CHINENSIS (Chinese), N. China, is another tall variety with more sepals and petals than the preceding varieties, and with the petals longer than the sepals. *4-ft. May–June. H. 2-ft. Sq. D3. N.*

T. EUROPAEUS (European), Europe, is a native plant abundantly found in the North of England, with large globular lemon-yellow flowers made up of the incurving sepals, the petals being shorter and concealed within. It has similar attractive foliage, and the stems of the plant are curiously greasy to the touch.

*2-ft. May–June. H. 2-ft. Sq. D3. N.*

T. HYBRIDUS (Hybrid) covers all the garden varieties which have been developed from the species, some of the best of which are:—

ABERDONIAN, with clear-yellow semi-double flowers.

CANARY BIRD, large incurving pale-yellow flowers.

FIRE GLOW has immense fiery orange-yellow flowers.

GOLIATH, dark-orange, large, incurving flowers.

HIS MAJESTY, with deep orange-yellow flowers of large size. (3-*ft.*)

*2-ft.–3-ft. May–July. H. 2-ft. Sq. D3. N.*

**TROPAEOLUM** (Tropaeolaceae), from G. tropaion—a trophy.

T. SPECIOSUM (Showy), Chile, is a climbing Nasturtium with pale-green six-parted leaves and hosts of crimson-scarlet flowers followed by attractive bright-blue seeds. It flourishes best in moist soil in a shaded site, with its top growth rambling through bushes in sun.

*12-ft. July–September. H. 1-ft. Sq. Cr3. N. Pl. 78.*

**TULIPA** (Liliaceae) said to be derived from a Turkish word tulbena, or a Persian word, thoulyban or tulipant—turban, which the flowers are supposed to resemble.

The ordinary garden Tulips are said to be derived from T. Gesneriana, a native of Siberia and Asia; certain of the early Tulips are derived from T. suaveolens from South-West Asia. The Darwin Tulips, which are late-flowering, are also derived from T. Gesneriana. Species other than these are generally catalogued as Species Tulips, and they comprise the wild Tulips of other lands. Many of them are particularly attractive in the sunny sheltered border and provide a striking contrast to the more showy and possibly more stereotyped varieties.

Tulips may occupy some parts of the mixed borders but are more generally used to provide spring colour and are later replaced by summer bedding plants. However, the Cottage and Darwin Tulips may be left undisturbed for two years and afterwards be lifted and replanted when the leaves have died down. They require well-drained sandy, loamy soil and should be planted in October or early November, set to a depth of three inches in heavy land and four inches in light soils. They should not be freshly manured, and the best fertiliser to use is bone-meal at the rate of two ounces per square yard.

The early Tulips or April-flowering Tulips, which generally reach a height of twelve inches, are best grown by themselves. Of these, some of the best are:—

| | |
|---|---|
| Cottage Maid | pink and white |
| Couleur Cardinal | orange-scarlet |
| Duchess of Parma | red |
| Keizerskroon | scarlet-red edged with yellow |
| Mon Trésor | bright yellow |
| Pink Beauty | carmine-pink |
| Prince Carnival | yellow flamed with red |
| Vermilion Brilliant | scarlet |
| White Beauty | white |
| Yellow Prince | pure yellow, very sweetly scented |

Late Cottage Tulips are May-flowering Tulips of long-pointed form different in shape from the Darwin Tulips, which are of square cup shape. They are borne on longer stems than the April-flowering Tulips, and when used for bedding purposes, cover in the form of Forget-me-nots is often used. Among some of the better Cottage Tulips (the height of which is given in inches after the name) are:—

| | |
|---|---|
| Albino, 22 | pure white |
| Avis Kennicot, 25 | deep yellow |
| Bouton d'Or, 24 | deep yellow |
| Carrara, 22 | white |
| Dido, 28 | cherry-red, flushed and edged with orange |
| Geisha, 30 | dove-grey |
| Grenadier, 18 | orange-scarlet |
| Inglescombe Yellow, 21 | soft yellow |
| Lady Hillingdon, 28 | orange shaded with buff |
| Le Rêve, 14 | flesh, tinged with buff |
| Moonlight, 24 | pale yellow |
| Perseus, 20 | orange-scarlet |
| Refulgence, 30 | orange |
| Scarlet Glory, 25 | scarlet |
| Yellow Emperor, 24 | golden-yellow |

Darwin Tulips:

| | |
|---|---|
| Baronne de la Tonnaye, 26 | rose |
| Bartigon, 24 | geranium-lake |
| Canada, 24 | white |
| Clara Butt, 22 | rose-pink |
| Dream, 26 | mauve and heliotrope |
| Farncombe Sanders, 28 | cardinal-red |
| Gloria Swanson, 30 | crimson-red |
| Noire, 25 | violet-black |
| Pride of Haarlem, 26 | scarlet-cerise |
| Rev. H. Ewbank, 22 | soft heliotrope-lilac |
| William Copland, 27 | mauve-lilac |
| Yellow Giant, 30 | golden yellow |

Of the species Tulips fitted for growth in the borders the following may be mentioned:—

T. CHRYSANTHA (Golden), Persia, has greyish-green leaves, those on the stem being quite narrow, and bears golden-yellow flowers of sharply pointed outline. The backs of the petals are stained with a cherry-red band. 1-*ft.* *April–May.* *B.* $\frac{1}{4}$-*ft. Sq.* *D7.* *C.* 2/1.

T. CLUSIANA (comm.), Sicily, is the so-called Lady-Tulip and has long, narrow leaves and long white buds with cherry-red bands on the outer petals. The flowers when they open are clear white with a deep purple-blue zone at the centre.
1$\frac{1}{3}$-*ft.* *April.* *B.* $\frac{1}{4}$-*ft. Sq.* *D6.* *C.*

T. EICHLERI (comm.), Asia Minor, has wide, grey-green leaves and bears large, pointed, scarlet buds, striped on the outer petals with silvery-grey, and is a never-ending source of amazement to those who have never seen it before.
1-*ft.* *April.* *B.* 1$\frac{1}{3}$-*ft. Sq.* *D6.* *C.* 19.

T. KAUFMANNIANA (comm.), Central Asia, has short, curled, wide, grey-green leaves, with creamy-white buds, striped with rose upon the back. When open the Tulip is even more beautiful, resembling a fully open Water-lily.
1-*ft.* *February–March.* *B.* $\frac{1}{2}$-*ft. Sq.* *D9.* *C.*

T. PRAESTANS (Excelling), Algeria, is a branching Tulip bearing more than one flower of light scarlet. Sometimes it bears, as if in reproach, but a single flower—when the life of the nurseryman becomes hard; sometimes in celebration it will excel, and I have seen it with seven flowers, when life begins anew.
1-*ft.* *March–April.* *B.* $\frac{1}{2}$-*ft. Sq.* *D7.* *C.* 15.

**UVULARIA** (Liliaceae), from L. uvidus—damp; possibly an allusion to the use of the plant as a cure for diseases of the uvula: hence the common name Throat-wort.

U. GRANDIFLORA (Large-flowered), Quebec, is a plant for the front of the border in light leafy soil in some shade, and has long wiry stems clad with occasional leaves, and bears hanging flowers with three curiously twisted golden-yellow petals.
1-*ft.* *May.* *H.* 1-*ft. Sq.* *D7.* *A.*

**VALERIANA** (Valerianaceae). The name is commemorative of Valerius, who used the plant in medicine; or possibly from L. valeo—to be healthy.

Valerians are best represented by one that is sometimes found listed among them (V. rubra), which will be found dealt with under Centranthus ruber.

V. OFFICINALIS (Of the shop), the Common Valerian or St. George's Herb, is a British native plant often found growing in the damp woods and ditches. It is one of the plants to avoid in the garden, as the roots exert an intense fascination to cats, whose demonstrations of affection the garden is better without. For the sake of the garden no further notes are appended.

**VERBASCUM** (Scrophulariaceae), from L. barbascum—a bearded plant, the stamens of Verbascum being bearded.

Most of the Verbascums are of easy culture in ordinary garden soil in a sunny place. They are easily raised from seed, generally best sown out of doors in May. Some of the varieties are biennial and must be grown annually to ensure succession. The perennial varieties are:—

V. CHAIXII (comm.), has white, heavily felted, large-toothed leaves and bears branching sprays of yellow flowers with purple stamens.
*3-ft. June–August. H. 2-ft. Sq. Sd5. N.*

V. NIGRUM (Black), Europe, has green leaves, very woolly beneath, with clusters of small yellow flowers, borne in spikes, and with the centres touched with violet. *4-ft. July–August. H. 2-ft. Sq. Sd5. N.*

V. NIGRUM ALBUM (White), Europe, varies only in having white flowers similarly touched with violet.
*4-ft. July–August. H. 2-ft. Sq. Sd5. N.*

V. PANNOSUM (Roughly hairy) has felted leaves and bears golden-yellow flowers in tight spires. *6-ft. June–August. H. 3-ft. Sq. Sd5. N.*

V. PHLOMOIDES (Resembling Phlomis), S. Europe, is a white, woolly plant bearing tall sprays of large yellow flowers, opening spasmodically in the spire, and persisting for a very long period.
*5-ft. June–August. H. 2-ft. Sq. Sd5. N.*

V. PHOENICEUM (Phoenician), S. Europe, is rather shorter, with green leaves slightly hairy beneath, and with branching sprays of attractive shades of purple, pink, lilac, rose and violet. The following varieties are of outstanding beauty, and rise to greater heights than that of their parent:—

COTSWOLD BEAUTY, with flowers of pale bronze.

COTSWOLD GEM, with flowers of soft pink.

COTSWOLD QUEEN, with reddish-fawn flowers.

PINK DOMINO, of charming, soft pink. (*4-ft.*)

*1½-ft. June–September. H. 1-ft. Sq. Sd5. N.*

**VERBENA** (Verbenaceae) is said to be derived from the Celtic word ferfain, which eventually led to the English Vervain, the common name for Verbena; but more probably from L. verbenae—sacrificial boughs.

The Verbenas include one or two flowering shrubs, some very pleasant tall-growing varieties of herbaceous plants, a number of almost prostrate bright-flowering carpeting plants, and numerous half-hardy perennials normally used for bedding purposes. The best of the perennial varieties are listed below; they are best suited by light, moderately rich, fertile soil, in a sunny position.

V. BONARIENSIS (From Buenos Aires), S. America, is a tall-growing plant with curious square stems, rough to the touch, and growing in clumps, with its stems as straight as a series of pine trees, bearing at the tips, and upon laterals produced at the leaf axils, small clustered heads of deep-lavender flowers.

*6-ft. July–September. H. 3-ft. Sq. Sd3. N. Pl.* 79.

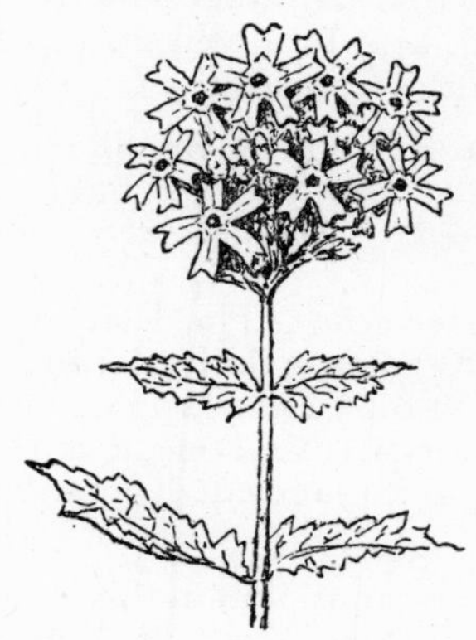

VERBENA CORYMBOSA

V. CHAMAEDRIFOLIA (With leaves like a wild Germander), Central America, is a prostrate garden Verbena, with green leaves, which roots where it touches the ground and produces innumerable heads of bright-scarlet flowers low down upon the ground. It may, however, be grown upright, and here the gardener ties the growing plant to a series of canes, and, under these circumstances, proves it to be one of the most attractive tall-growing plants in the garden. It is of doubtful hardiness in a normal season, and rooted pieces should be potted before the approach of severe weather and kept in a place of greater comfort for the winter.

*3-ft. June–October. 3-ft. Sq. E. Cg7. ANC.* 719/1.

V. CORYMBOSA (Flowering in corymbs), Chile, is the best of all the herbaceous Verbenas. It grows to a height of four feet and runs underground with great freedom, eventually forming a wide, dark-green, rough, leafy bush, which bears innumerable sprays of tight heads like those of the Heliotrope. It is deliciously scented with the same cherry-pie scent, and has survived the past severe winters.

*4-ft. July–September. H. 3½-ft. Sq. Cg8. D3. ANC.*

V. HASTATA (Spear-like), N. America, has spear-shaped leaves serrated at the edges and bears violet-blue flowers in small heads throughout the summer; is hardy, and grows well in any garden soil.
*6-ft. July–September. H. 3-ft. Sq. Sd2. D3. ANC.*

V. TENERA MAHONETI (Slender; comm.), Argentina, is more upright-growing than V. chamaedrifolia, has pale grey-green leaves cut into narrow segments, and bears its composite flower-heads of Parma-violet, striped with white, in great profusion.
*¾-ft. May–October. E. 1-ft. Sq. Cg6. ANC.* 630.

V. VENOSA (Veined), Brazil, is a pleasant plant with exceptionally rough green leaves, rasping to the touch, with somewhat long flower-heads of light violet. It runs underground, and is easily propagated from pieces of the root cut into half-inch lengths and placed in a box of moderately sandy soil, kept in a cold frame during the winter.
*1-ft. June–September. H. 1-ft. Sq. Cr3. N.* 35/2.

V. VENOSA DELICATE LILAC (Veined), Brazil, is a very pleasing variation with flowers of soft lilac and identical habit to that of its parent.
*1-ft. June–September. H. 1-ft. Sq. Cr3. N.*

**VERONICA** (Scrophulariaceae). The derivation of the name is doubtful, but is suggested that it is derived from G. hiera eikon—sacred image; an allusion to St. Veronica's sacred handkerchief. A number of possible derivations exist: one, given by Linnaeus, is a transposition of Vetonica, the ancient Roman name for a province of Spain.

Veronica is a very large genus, and in this country includes the genus Hebe, which consists of New Zealand Veronicas of shrubby and arborescent types. The following list comprises only herbaceous Veronicas; all are of easy cultivation in good garden soil and have an extremely long flowering period.

V. AMETHYSTINA (The colour of amethyst), Central and S. Europe, is a somewhat sprawling plant, behaving in a rather untidy fashion, but it does bedeck itself in June with spires of bright amethyst-blue.
*1-ft.–1½-ft. June. H. 1½-ft. Sq. D3. N.*

V. AMETHYSTINA ROYAL BLUE has flower spikes of gentian-blue.
*1¼-ft. June–July. H. 1½-ft. Sq. D3. N.*

V. AMETHYSTINA BLUE PETER produces an abundance of dark-blue flowers. *1¼-ft.–1½-ft. June. H. 1½-ft. Sq. D3. N.*

V. AMETHYSTINA BLUE SPIRES is a bushy variety with deep-blue flowers.
*2-ft. June. H. 1½-ft. Sq. D3. N.*

V. GENTIANOIDES (Resembling Gentian), S.E. Europe, makes a close mat of shining blue-green gentian-like leaves. Here the resemblance to the Gentian ends, for from these leaves come tall spires of pale milky-blue flowers in almost unending number.
*1½-ft. April–May. E. 2-ft. Sq. D3. ANC.*

Salvia turkestanica ADEHJKMNOPQRSTU
Verbena bonariensis BEFGJKLP
Salvia virgata nemorosa NOPST

Veronica hybrida "Wendy" ABCDE

Geranium Endressii LQPTU

Veronica incana rosea ABEFGJK

Geranium Russell Prichard KLNOPRS

V. GENTIANOIDES VARIEGATA is similar in all its characteristics except that it has variegated foliage.

1½-*ft.* *April–May.* *E.* 2-*ft. Sq.* *D3.* *ANC.*

V. INCANA (Grey with age), Caucasus, is a grey-leaved plant with dwarf habit, bearing many sprays of deep violet-blue flowers which afford a perfect contrast to its leaves. It flowers with alacrity each year and adds both to its size and beauty as the years progress.

1½-*ft.* *June–July.* *E.* 1½-*ft. Sq.* *D3.* *N.*

V. INCANA ROSEA (Rose), garden origin, loses the charm of the ash-grey leaves of its parent, and has similar sprays of flowers which are of deep pink. It is also a little more capricious to grow, but is nevertheless an attractive plant for the front of the border.

1-*ft.* *June–July.* *E.* 1-*ft. Sq.* *D3.* *N.* *Pl.* 80.

V. LONGIFOLIA (With long leaves), Europe, grows upwards of two feet in height and forms a large tuft, bearing long, handsome, somewhat arching sprays of violet-blue flowers, with green, much cut foliage.

3-*ft.* *July–September.* *H.* 2½-*ft. Sq.* *D3.* *N.*

V. LONGIFOLIA VAR. SUBSESSILIS (Almost sessile) bears larger flowers of deeper blue and is one of the finest plants the border may own.

3-*ft.* *July–September.* *H.* 2½-*ft. Sq.* *D3.* *N.*

V. SPICATA (Spiked), Europe, forms a dense mat of oval, notched, green leaves and bears attractive thin sprays of bluish-violet flowers most attractive in the mass. It is of variable colour, the following forms also existing:—

ALBA, with white flowers.

ERIKA, with deep-pink flowers.

ROSEA, with rose-coloured flowers.

× WENDY has rose-coloured flowers. *Pl.* 80.

2-*ft.* *July–September.* *H.* 1½-*ft. Sq.* *D3.* *N.*

V. SPURIA (False), Europe, also known as *V. amethystina* and *V. paniculata*, has hairy linear leaves and bears attractive sprays of sky-blue flowers.

1½-*ft.* *June–July.* *H.* 1¼-*ft. Sq.* *D3.* *N.*

V. TEUCRIUM (old name), Central Europe, has dark-green narrow leaves, borne upon long stems, and bears sprays of lavender-blue flowers on foot-high stems. The following varieties are also highly attractive:

TREHANE has golden-yellow leaves and pale-blue flowers, borne in attractive spikes.

ROYAL BLUE has gentian-blue flowers.

SHIRLEY BLUE has flowers of sky-blue.

These two plants have eminent value for forward positions and are among the most colourful of all herbaceous plants.

1½-*ft.* *June–August.* *H.* 1½-*ft. Sq.* *D3.* *ANC.*

**VIOLA** (Violaceae), from L. viola—a violet.

The bulk of the genus Viola are hardy perennials comprising not only the bedding Violas and the Pansies, and the Sweet Violets, but also the wild Violets of many other lands. The Pansies have been produced largely from the two native wild Pansies V. tricolor and V. lutea. The Sweet Violets have been derived from the wild Violet V. odorata.

The normal type of bedding Violas may be raised from seed or cuttings, but where it is desired to propagate to a colour or type, cuttings are obviously the best method to use. These are obtained in large quantity by cutting back the plants in the late summer, taking the young vigorous basal shoots, and striking them in a box of sandy soil placed in a frame, where they will have rooted in time for planting-out in the spring.

The bedding Violas have a wide range of colour, white, yellow, lavender, violet, and purple predominating. There is also a form which is almost black. Some of the older varieties are particularly attractive, among which one might mention:—

BLUE STONE, with flowers of Cambridge-blue.

HASLEMERE, with lavender-pink flowers.

JACKANAPES, with pricked ears of mahogany-red with the lower half of the flowers of golden-yellow.

Of the other Violas the following are among the best:

V. CORNUTA (Horned), S.W. Europe, forms a close mat of oval toothed leaves and has myriads of flowers like a flight of hovering butterflies, and with narrower petals than those of the flowers of the hybrid types, which adds to the grace and to the beauty of the plant. It may be freely used at the front and edges of the herbaceous border. In the type the flowers are of deep lavender-mauve. V. CORNUTA ALBA has white flowers, and V. CORNUTA PURPUREA flowers of deep purple. Named varieties are:—

ADMIRATION has deep-violet flowers produced in abundance throughout the whole summer.

CATHERINE SHARP has bright-blue flowers with a yellow eye, larger than Jersey Gem and produced with prodigality.

FLORAIRE has lavender-blue flowers produced from March to December.

JERSEY GEM has violet flowers in the style of V. cornuta, and often figures as the Violet of the buttonhole.

*½-ft. May–September. 1-ft. Sq. E. Sd9. N.*

V. ELATIOR (Lofty), Europe, is a tall-growing Viola with long leaves on long stems, and bearing upon long stalks large flowers of soft lavender with creamy eyes. It is unfortunately sometimes cleistogamous after the first few weeks of flowering, but this does not affect its usefulness in the border.

*1-ft. May–June. 1-ft. Sq. H. Sd9. N.*

V. GRACILIS (Slender), Asia Minor, is perhaps the most delightful of all the Violas, forming a close mat of deep-green leaves over which the orderly violet-purple flowers are borne in serried ranks. The individual flowers have the same grace of line as the flowers of V. cornuta, but they are a little wider and the colour a little deeper. It succeeds well in sun or shade in almost any kind of soil, many hybrids existing of which the following are the best:—

| | |
|---|---|
| alba | white |
| Black Knight | purple-black |
| Cornelia | bluish-mauve |
| lutea | golden-yellow |
| major | purple-blue |
| Moonlight | creamy-yellow |

*⅓-ft. May–September. E. 1½-ft. Sq. Cg9. AN.*

V. ODORATA (Sweet-smelling), Europe, is the Sweet-scented Violet, which form tufts of leaves of kidney shape and bears flowers of variable colour, the type having deep-violet flowers. A large number of variations exist both in size, colour, and shape. *V. odorata Cœur d'Alsace* is probably the most fascinating of all Violets, having sweetly scented flowers of deep-pink, borne in the utmost profusion. *V. odorata sulphurea* has flowers of soft yellow, and its variety *Irish Elegance* adds to this beauty by producing a deep-apricot heart. All the varieties increase rapidly by means of runners, and are undeniably worthy of a place even in the smallest of gardens.

*⅓-ft. April–May. E. 1-ft. Sq. D9. N.*

V. ODORATA has given rise to the Sweet-scented garden Violets, of which the following are exceptionally fine examples:—

| | |
|---|---|
| Admiral Avelon | rose |
| Askania | deep violet |
| La France | violet-blue |
| Princess of Wales | large violet-blue |
| White Tsar | white |

Double-flowered varieties:

| | |
|---|---|
| Comte de Brazza | white |
| de Parme | lavender-blue |
| Marie Louise | mauve-blue |

They should be grown in a partly shaded position in the garden, generally facing west. The soil should be deeply dug and enriched with well-rotted manure, and should not be, under any circumstances, allowed to dry out quickly. The Viola bed should be remade each year when flowering is over, generally in May. The older plants should be lifted, broken up into pieces with roots, and replanted. They should be set about a foot apart generally, with roughly the same distance between the ranks. Under these circumstances the Violets will be a continual source of beauty.

V. STRIATA (Striped), N. America, is one of the most attractive large-flowered Violas, and has thick fleshy roots, large rounded leaves, and innumerable flowers like big white Violets heavily pencilled with blue lines. It should be grown in a position of some shade.
*½-ft. April–June. H. 1½-ft. Sq. D9. N.*

**ZAUSCHNERIA** (Onagraceae), named after N. Zauschner, a German botanist.

The genus comprises two plants of shrubby growth, very useful for late colour in the front of the herbaceous border, and which thrive in any good garden soil in a comparatively sunny place.

Z. CALIFORNICA (Californian), California, forms a rounded tuft of grey-green leaves, bearing in loose sprays bright tubular flowers of orange-scarlet in late summer.
*1-ft. September–October. H. 1½-ft. Sq. Cg6. D3. N.* 19/1.

Z. MICROPHYLLA (Small-leaved), S. California, is much woodier, with very narrow, small, ash-grey leaves and longer and more brilliant sprays of flowers of brighter colour. Is quite hardy and soon forms a large and impressive plant.
*1½-ft. September–October. H. 1½-ft. Sq. Cg6. D3. N.* 17/1.

# AN INDEX OF COMMON NAMES
## WITH THEIR BOTANICAL EQUIVALENTS

Aaron's Rod. *Verbascum*
Aconite. *Aconitum*
African Lily. *Agapanthus*
Agrimony, Hemp. *Eupatorium*
Alkanet. *Anchusa*
All-heal. *Prunella officinalis*
Alum Root. *Heuchera*
American Cowslip. *Dodecatheon*
— Wood-Lily. *Trillium*
— Swamp-Lily. *Lilium superbum*
Anemone, St. Brigid. *Anemone coronaria*
—, Snowdrop. *Anemone sylvestris*
—, Wood. *Anemone nemorosa*
Angel's Tears. *Narcissus triandrus*
Architect's Plant. *Acanthus*
Artichoke, Jerusalem. *Helianthus tuberosus*
Asphodel, Giant. *Eremurus*
—, Leafless. *Asphodeline lutea*
— Lily. *Crinum*
—, Yellow. *Asphodeline lutea*
Aster, New Zealand. *Celmisia*
—, Stokes's. *Stokesia Cyanea*
Auricula. *Primula auricula, P. pubescens*
Autumn Crocus. *Colchicum autumnale*
Avens. *Geum*

Baby's Breath. *Gypsophila paniculata*
Bachelor's Button, White. *Ranunculus aconitifolius fl. pl.*
—, Yellow. *Ranunculus acris fl. pl.*
Balloon-flower. *Platycodon*
Balm, Bastard. *Melittis*
—, Bee. *Monarda didyma*
—, Honey. *Melittis Melissophyllum*
Baneberry. *Actaea spicata*
Barberton Daisy. *Gerbera*
Barrenwort. *Epimedium*
Basket of Gold. *Alyssum saxatile*
Bastard Balm. *Melittis*
Baton Rod. *Asphodelus*
Beach Wormwood. *Artemisia Stelleriana*
Beard Tongue. *Pentstemon*
Bear's Breeches. *Acanthus*
Bear's Ear. *Primula Auricula*
Bearsfoot. *Helleborus*
Bear's-tail Mullein. *Celsia Arcturus*
Bee Balm. *Monarda didyma*
Bell, Canterbury. *Campanula medium*
Bell, Spring. *Sisyrinchium*
Belladonna Lily. *Amaryllis*
Bell-flower, Chinese. *Platycodon*
—, Gland. *Adenophora*
—, Nettle-leaved. *Campanula urticaefolia*
—, Persian. *Michauxia*
Bellwort. *Uvularia*
Bennet, Herb. *Geum*
Bergamot. *Monarda*
—, Wild. *Monarda fistulosa*
Bethlehem Sage. *Pulmonaria officinalis*
Betony. *Stachys*
Bird's-eye. *Adonis*
Bitter Cress. *Cardamine*
Bittersweet. *Spiraea Ulmaria*
Bitterwort. *Gentiana lutea*
Black Blood. *Lythrum*
— Snake-root. *Cimicifuga*
Bladder Herb. *Physalis Alkekengi*
Blanket Flower. *Gaillardia*
Blazing Star. *Liatris scariosa*
Bleeding Heart. *Dicentra eximia*
Blood-flower. *Asclepias curassavica*
Blue African Lily. *Agapanthus umbellatus*
— Alkanet. *Anchusa*
Bluebell, English. *Scilla nonscripta*
Blue-bells. *Mertensia*
Blue-bonnet. *Scabiosa*
Bluebottle. *Centaurea*
Blue Cupidone. *Catananche caerulea*
Blue-eyed Grass. *Sisyrinchium*
— Mary. *Omphalodes verna*
Blue Poppy. *Meconopsis betonicaefolia*
Bolts. *Trollius*
Boneset. *Eupatorium*
Borage. *Borago officinalis*
Bottlebrush, Japanese. *Poterium*
Bouncing Bet. *Saponaria officinalis*
Bourbon Lily. *Lilium candidum*
Breeches-flower. *Dicentra Cucullaria*
Bride-wort. *Spiraea Ulmaria*
Bronze-leaf. *Rodgersia*
Bugbane. *Cimicifuga*
Bugloss. *Anchusa*
Bugwort. *Cimicifuga*
Burnet. *Poterium*
Butter Burr. *Petasites*
Buttercup. *Ranunculus*

Butterfly Weed. *Asclepias tuberosa*
Button Snake-root. *Liatris*

Californian Fuchsia. *Zauschneria*
Camomile. *Anthemis*
Campion. *Lychnis; Silene*
—, Crowned. *Lychnis coronaria*
—, Rose. *Lychnis coronaria*
Candlestick Lily. *Lilium dauricum*
Canterbury Bell. *Campanula Medium*
Cape Gooseberry. *Physalis Alkekengi*
— Lily. *Crinum longifolium*
Carline Thistle. *Carlina*
Carnation. *Dianthus caryophyllus*
Catchfly. *Silene*
—, German. *Lychnis Viscaria*
Cat-mint. *Nepeta*
Celandine, Greater. *Chelidonium majus*
—, Lesser. *Ranunculus Ficaria*
— Poppy. *Stylophorum diphyllum*
—, Tree. *Bocconia*
Chalk Plant. *Gypsophila*
Chamomile. *Anthemis*
—, Dyer's. *Anthemis tinctoria*
Chatham Island Forget-me-not. *Myosotidium*
Cheddar Pink. *Dianthus caesius*
Cherry, Winter. *Physalis*
Chickweed, Mouse-ear. *Cerastium*
Chilean Rhubarb. *Gunnera*
China Poppywort. *Eomecon chionantha*
Chinese Bellflower. *Platycodon*
— Lantern. *Physalis Alkekengi*
Chinese Poppy, Yellow. *Meconopsis integrifolia*
Christmas Rose. *Helleborus niger*
Christopher, Herb. *Actaea*
Cinquefoil. *Potentilla*
Clary. *Salvia Sclarea*
Clove Pink. *Dianthus caryophyllus*
Colewort. *Crambe*
Coltsfoot, Sweet. *Petasites fragrans*
Columbine. *Aquilegia*
Coneflower. *Rudbeckia*
—, Hedgehog. *Echinacea*
—, Purple. *Echinacea*
Coral-bells. *Heuchera sanguinea*
Corfu Lily. *Funkia*
Corn Flag. *Gladiolus*
Cornflower. *Centaurea*
Corn Lily, African. *Ixia*
Cotton-plant, New Zealand. *Celmisia coriacea*
Cowslip, American. *Dodecatheon*
—, Virginian. *Mertensia*
Crane's-bill. *Geranium*
Creeping Forget-me-not. *Omphalodes verna*
Cress, Bitter. *Cardamine*
—, Indian. *Tropaeolum*
—, Rock. *Arabis*
Crimson Flag. *Schizostylis*
Crocus, Autumn. *Colchicum autumnale*
—, Saffron. *Crocus sativus*
—, Scotch. *Crocus biflorus*
Cross of Jerusalem. *Lychnis chalcedonica*
Crowfoot. *Ranunculus*
Crown Imperial. *Fritillaria imperialis*
Cuckoo-flower. *Cardamine; Lychnis flos-cuculi*
Cudweed Wormwood. *Artemisia Ludoviciana*
Cupidone, Blue. *Catananche caerulea*
Cupid's Dart. *Catananche*
Cypress Spurge. *Euphorbia Cyparissias*

Daffodil. *Narcissus*
—, Winter. *Sternbergia lutea*
Daisy. *Bellis*
—, Barbeton. *Gerbera*
—, Michaelmas. See *Aster Novi-Belgii*
—, Orange. *Erigeron aurantiacus*
—, Ox-eye. *Chrysanthemum maximum*
—, Shasta. *Chrysanthemum maximum*
—, Transvaal. *Gerbera*
Dame's Violet. *Hesperis*
David's Harp. *Polygonatum multiflorum*
Dawn Poppy. *Eomecon*
Day-flower. *Commelina*
Day-lily. *Hemerocallis*
Deptford Pink. *Dianthus Armeria*
Desert Candle. *Eremurus*
Dog's-tongue. *Cynoglossum*
Dog's-tooth Violet. *Erythronium Dens-canis*
Dragon-fly. *Lobelia*
Dragon's-head. *Dracocephalum*
—, False. *Physostegia*
Drop-wort. *Spiraea Filipendula*
Dusty Miller. *Artemisia Stelleriana; Centaurea gymnocarpa; Lychnis; Primula Auricula*
Dutchman's Breeches. *Dicentra cucullaria*
Dwarf Iris. *Iris pumila*
Dyer's Chamomile. *Anthemis tinctoria*

Elecampane. *Inula Helenium*
English Iris. *Iris xiphioides*
Evening Primrose. *Oenothera*

Fair Maids of February. *Galanthus nivalis*
Fair Maids of France. *Ranunculus aconitifolius*
False Dragon's-head. *Physostegia*
— Goat's-beard. *Astilbe*
— Mallow *Malvastrum*
— Mitrewort. *Tiarella*
— Starwort. *Boltonia asteroides*
— Wall-Cress. *Aubrieta*
Feather Hyacinth. *Muscari plumosum*
—, Kansas. *Liatris*
Fernleaf Yarrow. *Achillea filipendulina*
Feverfew. *Pyrethrum*
Figwort. *Ranunculus Ficaria*
Flag. *Iris*
—, Corn. *Gladiolus*
—, Crimson. *Schizostylis*
—, Water. *Iris Pseudacorus*
Flame-flower. *Phlox*
Flax. *Linum*
—, New Zealand. *Phormium tenax*
—, Perennial. *Linum perenne*
Fleabane. *Inula; Erigeron*
Fleece-flower. *Polygonum*
Flower of a Day. *Tradescantia virginiana*
— of Adonis. *Adonis*
Foam-flower. *Tiarella*
Forget-me-not. *Myosotis*
—, Chatham Island. *Myosotidium*
—, Creeping. *Omphalodes verna*
—, Japanese. *Cynoglossum*
Foxglove. *Digitalis*
—, Ladies'. *Verbascum Thapsus*
Foxtail Lily. *Eremurus*
Fritillary. *Fritillaria*
—, Snake's-head. *Fritillaria Meleagris*
Frog's-mouth. *Linaria*
Fuchsia, Californian. *Zauschneria*
Fumitory. *Corydalis*
—, Yellow. *Corydalis lutea*

Garlic. *Allium*
—, Golden. *Allium Moly*
Gauze-flower. *Gypsophila*
Gay-feather. *Liatris pycnostachya*
—, Kansas. *Liatris*
Gentian. *Gentiana*
Gentianella. *Gentiana acaulis*
German Catchfly. *Lychnis Viscaria*
Giant Asphodel. *Eremurus*
— Rhubarb. *Gunnera*
— Scabious. *Cephalaria*
Gilliflower. *Cheiranthus*
Gladwyn, Stinking. *Iris foetidissima*
Gland Bellflower. *Adenophora*
Globe Flower. *Trollius*
— Thistle. *Echinops*
Glory-Flower. *Eccremocarpus scaber*
Glory of the Snow. *Chionodoxa*
Goat's-beard. *Spiraea Aruncus; Astilbe rivularis*
—, False. *Astilbe*
Goat's-Rue. *Galega*
Gold-dust. *Alyssum saxatile*
Golden Garlic. *Allium Moly*
Golden Knee. *Chrysogonum*
Goldenrod. *Solidago*
Golden-star. *Chrysogonum virginianum*
Golden-tuft. *Alyssum saxatile*
Goldilocks. *Aster Linosyris*
Gooseberry, Cape. *Physalis Alkekengi*
Gowan, Locker. *Trollius*
Grape Hyacinth. *Muscari*
Grass, Blue-eyed. *Sisyrinchium*
Greater Celandine. *Chelidonium majus*
Greek Valerian. *Polemonium caeruleum*
Groundsel. *Senecio*
Guernsey Lily. *Nerine*

Harebell, Hensol. *Aquilegia alpina*
Hebe. *Veronica*
Hedgehog Coneflower. *Echinacea*
Hedge-nettle. *Stachys*
Heliotrope, Winter. *Petasites fragrans*
Hellebore. *Helleborus*
Helmet Flower. *Tropaeolum; Aconitum; Scutellaria*
Hemp Agrimony. *Eupatorium*
Hensol Harebell. *Aquilegia alpina*
Herb Bennet. *Geum*
— Christopher. *Actaea*
— Lily. *Alstroemeria*
Holly, Sea. *Eryngium*
Hollyhock. *Althaea rosea*
Honey Balm. *Melittis Melissophyllum*
Horned Rampion. *Phyteuma*
— Violet. *Viola cornuta*
Horsemint. *Monarda*
Hound's-tongue. *Cynoglossum*
Hyacinth, Feather. *Muscari plumosum*
—, Grape. *Muscari*
—, Musk. *Muscari*

Indian Cress. *Tropaeolum*
Iris, Dwarf. *Iris pumila*
—, English. *Iris xiphioides*
—, Mourning. *Iris susiana*
—, Scorpion. *Iris alata*
Ivory Thistle. *Eryngium*

Ivy, Kenilworth. *Linaria*
Ixia Lily. *Ixiolirion*

Jacob's Ladder. *Polemonium caeruleum*
— Staff. *Verbascum*
Japanese Anemone. *Anemone japonica*
— Bottlebrush. *Poterium*
— Forget-me-not. *Cynoglossum*
— Roof-Iris. *Iris tectorum*
— Windflower. *Anemone japonica*
Jerusalem Artichoke. *Helianthus tuberosus*
— Cross. *Lychnis chalcedonica*
Joe-Pye-weed. *Eupatorium*
Jupiter's Beard. *Centranthus ruber*

Kaffir Lily. *Schizostylis*
Kale, Sea-. *Crambe*
Kansas Feather. *Liatris*
— Gay-feather. *Liatris*
Kenilworth Ivy. *Linaria*
King's Spear. *Eremurus*
Knapweed. *Centaurea*
Knotgrass. *Polygonum*
Knotweed. *Polygonum*

Ladies' Foxglove. *Verbascum Thapsus*
Lady-Bell. *Adenophora*
Lady's Seal. *Polygonatum*
— Slipper. *Cypripedium*
— Smock. *Cardamine pratensis*
Lady-Tulip. *Tulipa Clusiana*
Lamb's Ear. *Stachys lanata*
— Tongue. *Stachys lanata*
Lamp-shade Poppy. *Meconopsis integrifolia*
Larkspur. *Delphinium*
Lavender, Sea. *Statice*
Leafless Asphodel. *Asphodeline lutea*
Leather-plant, New Zealand. *Celmisia coriacea*
Lenten Rose. *Helleborus orientalis*
Leopard Flower. *Belamcanda chinensis*
— Lily. *Lilium pardalinum*
Leopard's-bane. *Doronicum*
Lesser Celandine. *Ranunculus Ficaria*
Lily. *Lilium*
—, African. *Agapanthus*
—, American Wood-. *Trillium*
—, Asphodel. *Crinum*
—, Belladonna. *Amaryllis*
—, Blue African. *Agapanthus umbellatus*
—, Bourbon. *Lilium candidum*
—, Candlestick. *Lilium dauricum*
—, Cape. *Crinum*
—, Corfu. *Funkia*
Lily, Corn. *Ixia*
—, Day-. *Hemerocallis*
—, Foxtail. *Eremurus*
—, Guernsey. *Nerine*
—, Herb. *Alstroemeria*
—, Ixia. *Ixiolirion*
—, Kaffir. *Schizostylis*
—, Leopard. *Lilium pardalinum*
—, Madonna. *Lilium candidum*
—, May. *Convallaria*
—, Meadow. *Lilium carolinianum*
— of the Nile. *Agapanthus*
— of the Valley. *Convallaria majalis*
—, Orange. *Lilium croceum*
—, Orange-cup. *Lilium philadelphicum*
—, Panther. *Lilium pardalinum*
—, Parrot. *Alstroemeria psittacina*
—, Peruvian. *Alstroemeria*
—, Pink. *Aphyllanthes*
—, Plantain. *Funkia*
—, Rush. *Sisyrinchium*
—, St. Bernard's. *Anthericum Liliago*
—, Scarlet Turk's-cap. *Lilium chalcedonicum*
—, Silvery. *Anthericum Liliago*
—, Snake's-head. *Fritillaria*
—, Swamp. *Lilium superbum*
—, Sword-. *Gladiolus*
—, Thimble. *Lilium Bolanderi*
—, Tiger. *Lilium tigrinum*
—, Torch. *Kniphofia*
—, Trumpet. *Lilium longiflorum*
—, Turk's-cap. *Lilium Martagon*
—, Wheel-. *Lilium medeoloides*
—, White. *Diplarrhena Moraea*
—, Wood. *Trillium*
—, Yellow Turk's-cap. *Lilium pyrenaicum*
Lily-wort. *Anthericum*
Liver-leaf. *Anemone Hepatica*
Locker Gowan. *Trollius*
Loosestrife. *Lysimachia*
—, Purple. *Lythrum*
Love-in-Idleness. *Viola*
Lungwort. *Pulmonaria*
—, Smooth. *Mertensia*
Lupin. *Lupinus*
—, Sham. *Thermopsis*
Lyre Flower. *Dicentra*

Madonna Lily. *Lilium candidum*
Madwort. *Alyssum*
Maid-of-the-Mist. *Gladiolus hybridus primulinus*
Mallow. *Malva; Sidalcea*

Pretty Betsy. *Centranthus ruber*
Prickly Rhubarb. *Gunnera*
Primrose. *Primula*
—, Evening. *Oenothera*
Purple Coneflower. *Echinacea*
— Loosestrife. *Lythrum*
Purslane, Winter. *Claytonia*

Quamash. *Camassia esculenta*
Queen of the Meadow. *Spiraea Ulmaria*
— of the Prairie. *Spiraea lobata*

Ragged Robin. *Lychnis Flos-cuculi*
Ragwort. *Senecio*
Rainbow Flower. *Iris*
Rampion. *Campanula Rapunculus*
—, Horned. *Phyteuma*
Ranunculus, Turban or Persian. *Ranunculus asiaticus*
Red-hot Poker. *Kniphofia*
Red-Ink Plant. *Phytolacca*
Red Valerian. *Centranthus ruber*
Rhubarb, Chilean. *Gunnera*
—, Giant. *Gunnera*
—, Prickly. *Gunnera*
—, Wild. *Rheum*
Rock Cress. *Arabis*
Rocket, Sweet. *Hesperis matronalis*
Rose-Campion. *Lychnis coronaria*
Rose, Christmas. *Helleborus*
—, Lenten. *Helleborus orientalis*
— Mallow. *Lavatera*
Round Heads. *Cephalaria*
Rue, Goat's. *Galega*
—, Meadow. *Thalictrum*
Rush Lily. *Sisyrinchium*
Russian Sage. *Perowskia*

Saffron Crocus. *Crocus sativus*
—, Meadow. *Colchicum*
Sage. *Salvia*
—, Bethlehem. *Pulmonaria saccharata*
—, Meadow. *Salvia pratensis*
—, Russian. *Perowskia*
—, Violet. *Salvia nemorosa*
St. Bernard's Lily. *Anthericum Liliago*
St. Brigid Anemone. *Anemone coronaria*
St. George's Herb. *Valeriana officinalis*
Sand Verbena. *Abronia*
Satin-flower. *Sisyrinchium*
—, New Zealand. *Libertia grandiflora*
Satin-leaf. *Heuchera*
Satin Poppywort. *Meconopsis Wallichii*
Scabious. *Scabiosa*
Scabious, Giant. *Cephalaria*
Scarlet Pompone. *Lilium pomponium*
— Turk's-cap Lily. *Lilium chalcedonicum*
Scorpion Grass. *Myosotis*
— Iris. *Iris alata*
Scotch Crocus. *Crocus biflorus*
Sea Holly. *Eryngium*
— -kale. *Crambe*
— Pink. *Armeria; Statice*
Self-heal. *Prunella*
Sham Lupin. *Thermopsis*
Shasta Daisy. *Chrysanthemum maximum*
Shepherd's Club. *Verbascum*
Shooting Stars. *Dodecatheon Meadia*
Silken Cissy. *Asclepias*
Silkweed. *Asclepias*
Silver Rod. *Asphodelus*
Silvery Lily. *Anthericum Liliago*
Skull-cap. *Scutellaria*
Smooth Lungwort. *Mertensia*
Snake-root, Black. *Cimicifuga*
—, Button. *Liatris*
Snake's-head Fritillary. *Fritillaria Meleagris*
— Lily. *Fritillaria*
Snake-weed. *Polygonum*
Sneezeweed. *Helenium*
Sneezewort. *Achillea Ptarmica*
Snow Poppy. *Eomecon*
Snowdrop. *Galanthus*
— Anemone. *Anemone sylvestris*
Snow-in-Summer. *Cerastium tomentosum*
Snow-on-the-Mountain. *Arabis*
Soapwort. *Saponaria*
Solomon's Seal. *Polygonatum*
Sorrel, Wood-. *Oxalis*
Southernwood. *Artemisia*
Sowbread. *Cyclamen*
Spanish Squill. *Scilla hispanica*
Speedwell. *Veronica*
Spiderwort. *Tradescantia*
Spring Beauty. *Claytonia virginica*
— Bell. *Sisyrinchium*
Spurge. *Euphorbia*
—, Cypress. *Euphorbia Cyparissias*
Spur Valerian. *Centranthus*
Squaw-root. *Cimicifuga*
Squill. *Scilla*
—, Spanish. *Scilla hispanica*
Star-of-the-Veldt. *Dimorphotheca*
Starwort. *Aster*
—, False. *Boltonia asteroides*
—, Summer. *Erigeron*
Stinking Gladwyn. *Iris foetidissima*

Stokes's Aster. *Stokesia cyanea*
Stonecrop. *Sedum*
Summer Starwort. *Erigeron*
Sun-drops. *Oenothera fruticosa*
Sunflower. *Helianthus*
—, Orange. *Heliopsis*
Swallow-wort. *Asclepias*
Swamp-lily, American. *Lilium superbum*
Swamp Milk. *Asclepias*
Sweet Coltsfoot. *Petasites fragrans*
— Rocket. *Hesperis matronalis*
— Sultan. *Centaurea*
— Violet. *Viola odorata*
— William. *Dianthus barbatus*
Sword-lily. *Gladiolus*

Tea, Oswego. *Monarda didyma*
Thimble Lily. *Lilium Bolanderi*
Thistle, *Carduus*
—, Carline. *Carlina*
—, Globe. *Echinops*
—, Ivory. *Eryngium*
—, Melancholy. *Carduus heterophyllus*
Thrift. *Armeria*
Throatwort. *Uvularia*
Tickseed. *Coreopsis*
Tiger Lily. *Lilium tigrinum*
Toad-flax. *Linaria*
Torch Lily. *Kniphofia*
Transvaal Daisy. *Gerbera*
Traveller's Joy. *Clematis*
Treasure Flower. *Gazania*
Tree Celandine. *Bocconia*
— Lupin. *Lupinus*
Tree Mallow. *Lavatera*
Trinity Flower. *Tradescantia virginiana*
Trumpet Flower. *Incarvillea*
— Lily. *Lilium longiflorum*
Trumpet-weed. *Eupatorium purpureum*
Tulip. *Tulipa*
—, Lady-. *Tulipa Clusiana*
Turban Ranunculus. *Ranunculus asiaticus*
Turk's-cap Lily. *Lilium Martagon*
— —, Scarlet. *Lilium chalcedonicum*
— —, Yellow. *Lilium pyrenaicum*
Twin-spur. *Diascia*

Valerian. *Valeriana*
—, Greek. *Polemonium caeruleum*
—, Red. *Centranthus ruber*
—, Spur. *Centranthus*
Venus's Navelwort. *Omphalodes*
Verbena, Sand. *Abronia*
Vervain. *Verbena*
— Mallow. *Malva Alcea*
Violet. *Viola*
—, Dame's. *Hesperis*
—, Dog's-tooth. *Erythronium Dens-canis*
—, Horned. *Viola cornuta*
— Sage. *Salvia nemorosa*
—, Sweet. *Viola odorata*
Virginian Cowslip. *Mertensia*
— Pokeweed. *Phytolacca americana*

Wake-Robin. *Trillium*
Wall-Cress. *Arabis*
—, False. *Aubrieta*
Wallflower. *Cheiranthus*
Wand-flower. *Dierama*
Water Flag. *Iris Pseudacorus*
Welsh Poppy. *Meconopsis cambrica*
Wheel Lily. *Lilium medeoloides*
White Bachelor's Button. *Ranunculus aconitifolius fl. pl.*
— Lily. *Diplarrhena Moraea*
— Mugwort. *Artemisia lactiflora*
Whitwort. *Pyrethrum*
Whorl-flower. *Morina*
Wild Bergamot. *Monarda fistulosa*
— Rhubarb. *Rheum*
Willow Gentian. *Gentiana asclepiadea*
Windflower. *Anemone*
Winter Cherry. *Physalis*
— Daffodil. *Sternbergia lutea*
— Heliotrope. *Petasites fragrans*
— Purslane. *Claytonia*
Woad. *Isatis*
Wolf's-bane. *Aconitum Lycoctonum*
Wolf's-milk. *Euphorbia*
Wood Anemone. *Anemone nemorosa*
— Aster. *Aster cordifolius*
— Lily. *Trillium*
Wood-sorrel. *Oxalis*
Wormwood. *Artemisia*
—, Beach. *Artemisia Stelleriana*
—, Cudweed. *Artemisia Ludoviciana*
Woundwort. *Stachys*

Yarrow. *Achillea*
—, Fernleaf. *Achillea filipendulina*
Yellow Asphodel. *Asphodeline lutea*
— Bachelor's Button. *Ranunculus acris fl. pl.*
— Chinese Poppy. *Meconopsis integrifolia*
— Fumitory. *Corydalis lutea*
— Turk's-cap Lily. *Lilium pyrenaicum*

| | | | |
|---|---|---|---|
| A | B | C | D |
| E | F | G | H |
| J | K | L | M |
| N | O | P | Q |
| R | S | T | U |

## IDENTIFICATION

To use the template, place it over the plate with the top white line coincident with the top edge of the picture. Each species named below will then be found to lie within the squares indicated by the letters following the name. Thus in Plate I for example:

> Anthemis tinctoria Buxton's variety falls in the squares ABCDEFGHJ.
> Phlox decussata Mia Ruys falls in the squares KLOPQRSU.
> Anthemis Sancti-Johannis falls in the squares MQT.

TELEPHONE
BRIDGE OF EARN
389

LILYBROOK
HEUGHFIELD
BRIDGE OF EARN
PERTHSHIRE

TELEPHONE
BRIDGE OF EARN
389

LILYBROOK
HEUGHFIELD
BRIDGE OF EARN
PERTHSHIRE